Economic Issues, Problems and Perspectives

Social Welfare Policies and Programs – Patterns, Implications and Prospects

nova
science publishers
www.novapublishers.com

Economic Issues, Problems and Perspectives

Global Challenges of Digital Transformation of Markets Volume II
Elena de la Poza, PhD, Sergey E. Barykin, PhD
2022. ISBN: 978-1-68507-989-5 (eBook)

Dynamics of International Finance
Ruchi Mehrotra Joshi, PhD
2022. ISBN: 978-1-68507-838-6 (Hardcover)
2022. ISBN: 979-8-88697-011-1 (eBook)

Economic and Legal Foundations of Innovative Development in the Digital Age
Gabibulla Khasaev (Editor)
Victoria Bolgova (Editor)
Sergey Bortnikov (Editor)
Yurii Shul'zenko (Editor)
Evgenia Medentseva (Editor)
2022. ISBN: 978-1-68507-730-3 (Hardcover)
2022. ISBN: 978-1-68507-946-8 (eBook)

Economic Crises: A Review and Directions for Research
Budi Santosa, PhD, Tulus T.H. Tambunan, PhD
2022. ISBN: 978-1-68507-613-9 (Hardcover)
2022. ISBN: 978-1-68507-692-4 (eBook)

More information about this series can be found at
https://novapublishers.com/product-category/series/economic-issues-problems-and-perspectives/

Lidiya V. Zhukovskaya

Balancing Economic, Legal, and Social Macrosystems Based on Modelling Decision Processes

nova
science publishers
www.novapublishers.com

DOI: https://doi.org/10.52305/IFWN9299

NOTICE TO THE READER

Library of Congress Cataloging-in-Publication Data

ISBN: 979-8-88697-093-7

Published by Nova Science Publishers, Inc. † New York

Dedicated to my dear father,
Dr. Sci. (Phys.-Math.), Prof. Vladislav I. Zhukovskiy

Contents

Preface ix

Acknowledgments xi

Basic Notations and Abbreviations xiii

Introduction xv

Chapter 1 **Features of Strategic Decision-Making in Stationary and Nonstationary Macrosystems** 1

Chapter 2 **Equilibrium Models of the Complex National Metasystem** 21

Chapter 3 **Modelling Decision Processes in the Social Sphere at the Macrolevel** 53

Chapter 4 **Guaranteed Solutions and Risks in Multicriteria Choice and Conflict Systems under Uncertainty** 89

Chapter 5 **The Guaranteed Berge Equilibrium in Payoffs and Risks for a Noncooperative N-Player Game under Uncertainty** 115

Chapter 6 **The Concept of Equilibrium in Sanctions and Countersanctions in a Differential Game of $N \geq 2$ Players** 131

Chapter 7 **Structural Analysis of Intelligent Decision Support Systems under Uncertainty** 167

Chapter 8 **A Mechanism for Implementing Berge Equilibrium of the Complex Metasystem Based on Modelling Decision Processes** 173

Conclusion 181

References 187

About the Author...203

Index 205

Preface

The author considers the interaction of three national macrosystems (economic, legal, and social) within a national public metasystem, justifying and solving the problem of their balancedness using the concept of Berge equilibrium. This equilibrium mathematically expresses the Golden Rule of ethics (GR), one of the most ancient, specific, and widespread moral generalizations that appear in Christianity, Islam, Judaism, Buddhism, and Confucianism. It instructs: "Do to others as you would like them to do to you." The author studies the influence of morality (in the sense of Kant's imperative or the GR) on strategic decision-making in the national public metasystem. The Nash equilibrium of the three macrosystems reflects the neoliberal economic doctrine widespread currently. An alternative moral-philosophical economic doctrine based on the GR is substantiated using systems theory and game theory.

The author develops a metasystem equilibrium model for the national public metasystem based on the GR to determine effective strategic decisions under uncertainty in the social sphere, implementing the social state idea.

The research presented in the book is interdisciplinary. It involves scientific approaches of systems analysis, philosophical ethics, economics, law, sociology, game theory, and management.

Acknowledgments

This book is based on the author's many years of research performed at Central Economics and Mathematics Institute, Russian Academy of Sciences, Moscow, Russia. The author expresses sincere gratitude to her scientific consultant, Corresponding Member of the Russian Academy of Sciences, Dr. Sci. (Econ.), Prof. Georgy B. Kleiner and Dr. Sci. (Econ.), Prof. Veniamin N. Livshits. With their permanent support, the main idea outlined in the title has been successfully implemented, and new scientific results have been obtained. Finally, the author thanks Alexander Yu. Mazurov, Cand. Sci. (Phys.–Math.), for his careful translation of the Russian text, permanent feedback and negotiations with the publisher, and valuable contribution to the English version of the book.

Basic Notations and Abbreviations

$\mathbb{R}^k$—the k-dimensional Euclidean space with the Euclidean norm $\|\cdot\|$;

$\mathbb{N}$—the set of players;

X_i—the set of strategies x_i of player $i \in \mathbb{N}$ (the set of alternatives in multicriteria choice problems);

Y—the set of uncertainties y;

$\{\mu_i\}$—the set of mixed strategies $\mu_i(\cdot)$ of player $i \in \mathbb{N}$;

$\{\mu\}$—the set of mixed strategy profiles $\mu(\cdot)$;

$\{\eta_i\}$—the set of mixed strategies $\eta_i(\cdot)$ of player $i \in \mathbb{N}$;

$\{\eta\}$—the set of mixed strategy profiles $\eta(\cdot)$;

X^e—the set of Nash equilibria x^e;

X^B—the set of Berge equilibria x^B;

$\mu^{P_e}(\cdot) \in \{\mu\}$—a Pareto-maximal Nash equilibrium in mixed strategies;

$\mu^{P_B}(\cdot) \in \{\mu\}$—a Pareto-maximal Berge equilibrium in mixed strategies;

$f_i(x, y)$—the payoff function of player $i \in \mathbb{N}$;

$f_i(x, y) = (f_1(x, y), \dots, f_N(x, y))$—the row vector composed of the payoff functions of players $1, \dots, N$;

$F_i(x, y)$—the risk function of player $i \in \mathbb{N}$;

$F_i(x, y) = (F_1(x, y), \dots, F_N(x, y))$—the row vector composed of the risk functions of players $1, \dots, N$;

$\mathrm{X} = \prod_{i \in \mathbb{N}} \mathrm{X}_i \subseteq \mathbb{R}^n$—the set of strategy profiles $x = (x_1, \dots, x_N) \in \mathrm{X}$;

X^Y—the set of functions $x(y)$ with a domain of definition Y and a codomain X;

$[x\|z_i]=[x_1,\ldots,x_{i-1},z,x_{i+1},\ldots,x_N]$;

$comp\square^{k}$—the set of all compact sets in $\square^{k}$;

$k=S,P$—Slater optimality and Pareto optimality, respectively.

Introduction

In 2010, J. Stiglitz, A. Sen, and J.-P. Fitoussi published their famous report [199], explaining the gap between statistical measurements of socio-economic phenomena (particularly the real significance of GDP) and perceptions of these phenomena by common people. Why does this gap exist in national public metasystems? Does the current economic doctrine contribute to the development of social sectors (science, education, health care, and others)? In this book, we endeavor to answer both questions.

This book considers a public metasystem: a complex public formation with a functional mutual influence of its main structural components (economic, legal, and social macrosystems), each performing a definite function and contributing to the metasystem performance in the course of interaction.

The interaction model of the three macrosystems is as follows. On the one hand, the economic macrosystem is an integral part of the public metasystem; on the other, one of the foundations of its development [225]. The economy as a macrosystem has several features. For example, its state and operation are determined, among other things, by both objective and subjective factors. One of the main instruments is government regulation (public administration) through national legislation: a certain order of economic and entrepreneurial activity is established, and various economic criteria and indicators are adopted (e.g., tax rates, fees, tariffs, duties, prices for certain categories of goods, etc.).

On the other hand, the law as a macrosystem fixes the current economic relations and is determined by the existing economic model (i.e., by the structure of the national economic macrosystem).

Economic relations are reflected in legal relations and fill them with economic content. The income generated in the economy, including tax law instruments, is redistributed into the social sphere, formed using social legislation. The population is the "common denominator" uniting the three macrosystems under consideration.

In the economic macrosystem, a model oriented towards the market and maximum profit matches the interests of economic agents. The transfer of the existing market model to the social sphere causes several integral problems.

In this book, we study the interaction of three national macrosystems (economic, legal, and social) within a national public metasystem and the mechanism of strategic decision-making in the social sphere, on an example of Russia.

The ultimate goals of the research are to develop a theoretical approach to modelling decision processes in the social sphere at the macrolevel, suggest a concept, and construct models of the metasystem equilibrium of the economic, legal, and social macrosystems for efficient strategic decision-making under uncertainty.

The approach below proceeds from the assumption that all participants in economic, legal, and social relations incline to some equilibria. Equilibrium means that the interests, opportunities, and actions of the three macrosystems are coordinated or balanced.

Nash equilibrium is considered a formal reflection of the neoliberal economic doctrine. It is often called "selfish equilibrium": each control system in the three macrosystems pursues its interests, separately achieving its goals by solving individual problems (implements its strategies to improve its performance only).

In an equilibrium, each macrosystem cannot improve its performance by individually changing its strategy if the other participants do not change their strategies.

As is well known, the set of Nash equilibria has internal instability. This mathematical property leads to the problem of unbalanced macrosystems. For example, suppose that the legal macrosystem implements its goal and strategies, neglecting the performance of the other two macrosystems. In this case, the metasystem imbalance may be due to the following factors:

- In the economic macrosystem: the increased density of law around the economic agents overregulates their activities, negatively affecting their income and, accordingly, the state of the social sphere (the income generated in the economy is redistributed through legal instruments and mechanisms into the social sphere).
- In the social sphere: the increased density of law makes the social services of the required quality (health care, education, culture, and sports) unavailable for certain categories of the population.

The adjuster responds, e.g., by applying the "legal guillotine" to balance the operation of these macrosystems. Formal modeling yields a new equilibrium, which may or may not be better than the previous one.

We highlight the second, no less important problem: the destruction of social sectors due to changes in the economic and legal macrosystems. This problem directly relates to strategic decision-making based on the neoliberal economic model.

The third problem is a consequence of the first two ones: poverty of the population in all forms (poverty zones, persistent poverty, and poverty of the economically active and able-bodied population).

Thus, an objective need is to develop a theoretical approach to modelling strategic decision processes at the macrolevel by creating a mechanism for balancing the economic, social, and legal macrosystems. These macrosystems can be balanced using economic modeling jointly with methods of systems analysis, economics, law, sociology, game theory, management, and performance measurement.

A new strategic decision methodology for managing the socio-economic sphere is developed by constructing and justifying a hierarchical management model for the social sphere under uncertainty. This model consists of several models:

a) a dynamic model for managing complex socio-economic systems,
b) game-theoretic models of decision-making under uncertainty based on the formal concept of a guaranteed solution and risk using a modification of Savage's principle of minimax regret.

A new mechanism for balancing the economic, social, and legal macrosystems proposed below involves an original equilibrium model with the social state idea underlying their mutual influence and interaction. The new mechanism is based on the concept of Berge equilibrium, which reveals the meaning of the Golden Rule of ethics (GR) [68] ("Do to others as you would like them to do to you") and the concept of Nash equilibrium [153-156] (individual rationality) for each macrosystem of the complex metasystem. Note that the systems analysis methodology used below reveals the mutual influence mechanisms of the structural components of the complex metasystem.

Berge equilibrium is a relatively new area of research in game theory and decision-making. The well-known Nash equilibrium, expressing the principle of individual rationality of players in the extreme (selfish) form, is widely used in applications. On the one hand, Berge equilibrium does not exclude this principle. On the other, it supposes that each player acts in the interests of all other players, not ignoring his (its) interests. This supposition is based on the definition of economic relations as relations developing between agents regarding the production, distribution, consumption, and exchange of goods, products of labor, and services. Economic relations have the motive of benefit (any, financial or nonfinancial). The principle of individual rationality is inherent in almost all economic relations. (Otherwise, the issue of their reasonability arises).

The recent books [269] and [270] were devoted to Berge equilibrium in static and dynamic games, respectively. The authors studied the properties of Berge equilibria, established sufficient conditions for existence, and considered some applications to the problems of competitive economics. This monograth continues that research.

Synthesizing the methodology of systems analysis with the game-theoretic approach, we reveal the definition of Berge equilibrium at the conceptual level. It means a strategy profile a unilateral deviation from will contradict the GR determining the behavior and relationships of the three macrosystems.

In other words, the activity of each macrosystem is aimed at improving the performance of the other two, and any deviation from the equilibrium is impossible due to philosophical and moral principles (the GR). Ethics and humanity therefore underlie the culture of strategic decision-making: this principle is the main prerequisite and ultimate goal when developing the three national macrosystems.

The new Berge equilibrium models focus on implementing the social state idea, contributing in the long run to the development of science, education, population's social security and support, and other sectors of the social sphere.

In this case, *the interaction model of the three macrosystems is based on the philosophical and moral concept of the GR.*

The national legal macrosystem still affects the economy through establishing a certain order of economic relations and using various economic criteria and indicators.

As a macrosystem, the national law fixes the existing economic relations and is driven by a new (moral) economic model towards the population's welfare. Moreover, the legal macrosystem is determined by the structure of the economic macrosystem. Economic relations are also reflected in legal relations, filling them with real economic content. The income generated in the economy is redistributed into the social sphere, which can be formed using the new social legislation.

In addition, the social sphere infrastructure envisages no privatization processes, and the price of social products and services is set the philosophical and moral concept instead of market laws.

Thus, *the correlation between the economic, legal, and social macrosystems is manifested in their interaction: the legal order of economic and social relations corresponds to the patterns and trends in the development of the national metasystem.*

The new models of decision-making and the altruistic Berge equilibrium in modern management practice solve the integral problems mentioned. They may become a mathematical justification for designing national social and economic policy within a new economic paradigm based on the GR.

Note that hybrid approaches can also be used in a real public metasystem: the selfish Nash equilibrium in the economic macrosystem and the altruistic Berge equilibrium in the social macrosystem.

Nowadays, no generally accepted theoretical and methodological approaches reflect the moral and humanistic essence and specifics of strategic decision-making in complex macrosystems using the synthesis of game theory, management, economics, law and sociology, the social state mechanism, and the decision methodology in the social sphere. These factors indicate the interdisciplinary character of the research presented below, determining its relevance.

Note that the general methodological foundations of the systems analysis of transformation processes and management of socio-economic development were described in a vast literature. For example, these issues were studied by the following (Russian and foreign) researchers: J. Stiglitz [198], J. Stiglitz, A. Sen and J. Fitoussi [199], R. Ackoff [1], L. von Bertalanffy [225, 226], J. Kornai [101], V.A. Lefebvre [112, 113], M. Mesarovic and Y. Takahara [142], A. Rapoport [172], D.S. L'vov [127-133], V.L. Makarov [134, 135], S.A. Aivazyan [2-4], V.M. Polterovich [166, 165], G.B. Kleiner [49, 95, 96], N.M. Rimashevskaya [175, 176], I.V. Prangishvili [170], M. Intriligator [84], V.A. Volkonskii [224], V.N. Kostyuk [102, 103], V.N. Livshits [115-123], and others.

Game theory and decision-making, particularly with application to economic research, were considered by A. Wald [234-236], E.J. Vilkas [220-222], J.D. Williams [237], R.D. Luce and H. Raiffa [126], J. von Neumann and O. Morgenstern [227-229], R. Bellman [14], L. Zadeh [239, 240], H. Moulin [149], J. Harshanyi [72-75], R.L. Keeney [92], K. Lancaster [107],

N.N. Vorob'ev [230, 231], Yu.B. Germeier [63, 64], L.V. Kantorovich [89], V.V. Podinovskii and V.D. Noghin [164], S. Karlin [91], V.I. Zhukovskii [263-281], A.A. Chikrii [39], M.E. Salukvadze [267, 270], L.A. Petrosyan [163], and others.

In the area of performance measurement, note A. Damodaran [46], V.N. Livshits [115-123], P.L. Vilenskii [214-218], and others.

The problems of improving management systems by applying risk theory were examined by P. Bernstein [17], A. Wald [234-236], L. Savage [181, 182], F.H. Knight [99], H. Raiffa [171], P.C. Fishburn [57], R.M. Kachalov [87], E.D. Solozhentsev [195], and others.

According to the literature on economic-mathematical modeling of complex systems and risk management, underinvestigated issues include the methodological support of game-theoretic modeling of decision processes under uncertainty and risk, the determination of guaranteed solutions in complex systems, and the use of different concepts of equilibrium. In particular, the decision methodology in the social sphere is not developed in proper detail: no definition of social guarantees through the concept of guaranteed solutions, and no adequate methods for considering conflict, uncertainty, and multiple criteria of the decision processes and associated risks. Meanwhile, the possibilities of applying the concepts of equilibrium, including Berge equilibrium, are much wider than the current research on game-theoretic modeling [250].

This book suggests a theoretical approach to modelling decision processes at the macrolevel in the social sphere, conceptualizes metasystem equilibrium, and constructs corresponding models of the economic, legal and, social macrosystems for effective strategic decision-making under uncertainty. The research results presented below contribute to solving the integral problems mentioned above.

The balancedness of the complex metasystem, an original concept put forward in the book, differs from other well-known approaches [260]:

- This concept models strategic decision-making with adequate consideration of uncertainty (incomplete information), conflict, and risks in the social sphere as a complex controlled macrosystem.
- Previously, the balancedness of the economic, legal, and social macrosystems has not been examined within a game-theoretic approach based on Berge equilibrium.

The results obtained in the book are novel. A new concept of balanced Berge equilibrium has been formalized, justified, and developed for the economic, legal, and social macrosystems of the complex metasystem. Moreover, a new theoretical approach has been elaborated to improving guaranteed decision-making in the social sphere at the macrolevel under uncertainty. The new approach to balancing the economic, legal, and social macrosystems is considered for Russia's public metasystem as an example. However, it is rather general and therefore applicable to public metasystems of Western countries with minor modifications.

1. Involving the ideas of the moral economy of Academician D.S. Lvov [130], the problem of balancing the complex metasystem has been formulated for the first time at the macrolevel. A methodology for designing a metasystem equilibrium of the economic, legal, and social macrosystems has been developed using the GR, expressed by Berge equilibrium [269, 270].

1.1) The interaction and mutual influence of the economic, legal, and social macrosystems as stationary and (or) non-stationary objects have been structurally analyzed within the social state idea declared in Russia.

1.2) For the first time in the literature, the interaction of these systems has been modeled at the macrolevel. In addition, their Berge and Nash equilibria have been formalized and justified.

1.3) As an example of such interaction, the dynamics of marriage structures and internal relations in nuclear and traditional families have been studied. For the first time in the literature, mathematical models of family relations have been formalized using the concepts of Berge and Nash equilibria for a three-person family.

1.4) The national social legislation since 1991 has been examined, and the transformation of the social sphere from the universal social security system to the targeted (currently existing) one has been shown.

2. For improving decision processes in the social sphere at the macrolevel, a new hierarchical model for managing the dynamics of the social sphere and decision-making at each level of the hierarchy has been developed and justified. This model rests on the ideas of designing hierarchical management systems of Academician N.N. Moiseev.

2.1) A multilevel mathematical model for managing the dynamics of the population's social security and support system has been constructed.

2.2) For the first time in the literature, guaranteed solutions have been formalized for multicriteria management problems in complex socio-economic systems under interval uncertainty with given limits.

2.3) For the first time in the literature, the concept of a guaranteed solution has been formalized by modifying Savage's principle of minimax regret. To this end, the following pair has been considered: the set of social state guarantees for the population and life risks in case of which definite categories of the population exercise their constitutional right to obtain appropriate social guarantees. An existence theorem for the guaranteed solution has been proved under standard assumptions of multicriteria choice problems, and a method to find this solution has been proposed.

3. The theory and methodology of economic-mathematical modeling have been further developed: new game-theoretic approaches have been introduced to model decision-making, increasing the outcomes and simultaneously reducing the associated Savage risk.

4. The theoretical approach to improving decision processes at the macrolevel has been justified: a methodology has been proposed to design guaranteed solutions and risks and study the corresponding Berge equilibrium. Important properties of this equilibrium (particularly stability and unimprovability) have been revealed by formalizing an original solution—the so-called guaranteed solution in payoffs and risks (guarantee)—in a noncooperative N-player game. The guaranteed solution is efficient (represents a Pareto-maximal Berge equilibrium). Its existence in mixed strategies has been proved, and some properties have been established.

5. The concept of equilibrium in sanctions and countersanctions has been developed for a separate class of problems. Coefficient criteria have been derived under which the game has an equilibrium in sanctions and countersanctions and, at the same time, no Nash equilibrium. The economic and legal model of active equilibrium has been considered through the legal concept of sanctions, which enlarges the practical application of this class of problems.

Distinctive features of the constructed macromodels are, first, using the GR (expressed by Berge equilibrium) as an economic doctrine for strategic decision-making under uncertainty and, second, the Pareto-maximal (efficient) guaranteed solutions based on the "social guarantee–life risk" pair. If one of the macrosystems (economic or social) generates uncertainty in real conditions, the guaranteed solution is also formalized, but it satisfies Slater optimality (weak efficiency). In contrast to this book, traditional economic modeling involves equilibrium models based on Nash equilibrium (individual rationality) as the neoliberal economic concept for decision-making.

Theoretically and methodologically, this research is based on systems analysis, economics, the theory of state and law, sociology, economic-mathematical modeling, game theory, management, and decision-making in complex systems under uncertainty.

The book consists of the Introduction, 8 Chapters, Conclusions, and the Appendix. The list of references includes 283 titles.

In the Introduction, we justify the relevance of this research and estimate the degree of elaboration of the problems. Also, we formulate the goal and tasks of the research and argue the novelty of the results.

Chapter 1 is devoted to the systems analysis of the interaction and mutual influence of the economic, legal, and social macrosystems as a stationary and (or) nonstationary complex metasystem within Russia's constitutional social state doctrine. Note that the peculiarities of strategic decision-making under uncertainty are taken into account. In addition, Chapter 1 considers the features of the interaction and mutual influence of the economic, legal, and social macrosystems (as the basic structural elements of the complex metasystem) and substantiates the problem of their balancedness, formalized and solved in the subsequent chapters.

Chapter 2 proposes a new concept of equilibrium for the economic, legal, and social macrosystems based on Slater-guaranteed balanced Berge equilibrium. This type of equilibrium is designed and justified. The equilibrium model considers the effect of uncertain factors: the modern economic system has such intrinsic properties as uncertainty, inconsistency, multiple criteria, and incomplete information. Thus, Chapter 2 describes a new approach to strategic decision-making to solve the integral problem of balancing the three macrosystems mentioned by constructing and justifying Slater-guaranteed balanced Berge equilibrium. This approach contributes to eliminating the problem of population poverty. Opposing to the neoliberal economic doctrine and supplementing the individual rationality-based Nash equilibrium, Berge equilibrium suggests a way of balancing based on philosophical and moral principles. Some positive and negative properties of Berge equilibrium are discussed (particularly internal instability). As an application of the Berge equilibrium model, Chapter 2 considers the dynamics of family structures and relations affecting the population's life system as well as the current state, prospects, and capabilities of government regulation (public administration) of sociodemographic processes in Russia. Mathematical models of family relations are based on the concepts of Berge and Nash equilibria in a three-person family.

Chapter 3 justifies a new theoretical approach to improving decision processes in the social sphere at the macrolevel. More specifically:

- We construct a new multilevel mathematical model for managing the dynamics of complex socio-economic systems under uncertainty and suggest a scientifically grounded approach to posing and solving this management problem on an example of the population's social security and support system.
- We propose a method for formalizing guaranteed solutions in multicriteria problems of managing complex socio-economic systems under interval uncertainty with given limits.
- We formalize a guaranteed solution by modifying Savage's principle of minimax regret. Also, we prove an existence theorem for this solution under standard assumptions of multicriteria choice problems and develop a method to find it.

In the social state, strategic decision-making at the macrolevel secures the population against guaranteed (life) risks, such as old age, illness, unemployment, accidents, etc. Chapter 4 presents in detail the mathematical apparatus used in Chapter 3. We suggest new game-theoretic approaches to modelling decision processes, increasing the outcomes and simultaneously reducing the associated Savage risk. We construct the guaranteed solutions and risks and explore the features of Nash equilibrium.

The new methodology, proposed in Chapter 5 and proved in Chapter 4, involves the GR to design the guaranteed solutions considering the associated risks and study the features of Berge equilibrium. To identify the features (stability and unimprovability), we formalize the Pareto-guaranteed Berge equilibrium, establish its existence in mixed strategies, and examine its properties. The mathematical framework of Chapter 5 justifies the studies carried out in Chapter 2, that is, the model of balanced equilibrium of the complex national metasystem.

Chapter 6 introduces a new concept of sanctions and countersanctions and develops the economic and legal model of active equilibrium through the legal concept of sanctions, contributing to the balancedness of systems and forming a new mechanism for the stability of equilibria. The concept aims to develop an applied analysis of economic models of the national economy and its sectors.

Chapter 7 identifies and discusses new approaches to modelling decision processes in complex socio-economic systems under uncertainty to increase their validity and support in the social sphere. They can be used when designing intelligent decision support systems, where formal mathematical models are adopted at the modeling stage.

Chapter 8 proposes and justifies a mechanism for implementing the Berge equilibrium of the complex metasystem based on modelling decision processes with the social state paradigm.

As emphasized above, the new approach to balancing the economic, legal, and social macrosystems is considered for Russia's public metasystem as an example. However, it is rather general and therefore applicable to public metasystems of Western countries with minor modifications.

This book is based on the author's many-years research performed at Central Economics and Mathematics Institute, Russian Academy of Sciences, Moscow, Russia. The author expresses sincere gratitude to her scientific consultant, Corresponding Member of the Russian Academy of Sciences, Dr. Sci. (Econ.), Prof. Georgy B. Kleiner and Dr. Sci. (Econ.), Prof. Veniamin N. Livshits. With their permanent support, the main idea outlined in the title has been successfully implemented, and new scientific results have been obtained. Finally, the author thanks Alexander Yu. Mazurov, Cand. Sci. (Phys.–Math.), for his careful translation of the Russian text, permanent feedback and negotiations with the publisher, and valuable contribution to the English version of the book.

Chapter 1

Features of Strategic Decision-Making in Stationary and Nonstationary Macrosystems

Introduction

At the present stage, strategic decision-making in stationary and nonstationary economic macrosystems is studied using economic-mathematical modeling, including game theory. An economic macrosystem is generally defined as the set of all economic phenomena, processes, and relations that develop in a particular society based on a corresponding economic mechanism [101, 172, 225]. A legal system fixes the existing economic mechanisms and regulates relations within a particular society using interconnected, coordinated, and interacting legislation and legal norms. By improving legal tools, new economic and social macrosystems are being constructed, where a social system can be defined as a set of subsystems and their relations formed and manifested in a particular society.

Thus, a triad of interdependent and interacting systems—a complex metasystem consisting of economic, legal, and social macrosystems—arises naturally. Several factors determine the behavior of each macrosystem in this triad. For example, the functions of the complex metasystem are often substituted during operation through social design methods: the subjects of economic, legal, and social relations (agents) start executing unusual actions. As a result, the balance of the metasystem's structural and personal elements is disrupted. Its behavior turns out dysfunctional and difficult to predict, and the system itself becomes nonstationary.

The concepts of stationarity and nonstationarity are rather general. A stationary complex metasystem will be understood below as a complex structure with monotonically varying macroindicators within given limits whose dynamics are well predictable for short and medium-term periods [103, 120]. In the economic literature, system's stationarity is often defined through equilibrium. Such an approach does not contradict the concepts described above but only indicates an additional feature of these systems.

In this book, a nonstationary system will be interpreted as a complex system with jumping and difficult-to-predict dynamics of performance indicators [116-121]. Nonstationarity concerning controlled systems is often used with the concepts of conflict, uncertainty, risk, and dysfunction.

Traditionally, game theory is treated as a theory of conflicts [112] and applied jointly with decision-making to analyze and solve control and management problems under uncertainty and risk in static and dynamic conditions. Nonstationary macrosystems can be in system equilibrium (balanced equilibrium). This feature does not contradict the concept described above but only highlights the class of decision problems under uncertainty and risk.

The equilibrium of a complex metasystem will be interpreted below as a certain state of the metasystem that none of the three interacting and interconnected macrosystems (economic, legal, and social) is interested to change.

System equilibrium will be understood as the balanced equilibrium of the systems formalized by V.I. Zhukovsky and M.E. Salukvadze [268]; also, see its justification in Section 2.4 of the book. The reasons for the disinterest will be considered for each equilibrium state of the macrosystems separately.

Chapter 1 is devoted to the systems analysis of the interaction and mutual influence of the economic, legal, and social macrosystems as a stationary and (or) nonstationary complex metasystem within Russia's constitutional social state doctrine. Note that the peculiarities of strategic decision-making under uncertainty are taken into account.

1.1. Systems Analysis of Interaction and Mutual Influence of National Economic, Legal, and Social Macrosystems

As already noted, the legal system fixes the existing socio-economic relations. The economic and legal spheres have complex interactions because the economic system is determined by the volume and nature of the rights of economic agents. Economic patterns are mediated by legal and social factors affecting the individual's behavior in society. The transformation processes in the economic and social macrosystems are mostly concentrated in the structure of individual relations and property relations. According to the neoliberal economic doctrine, property relations evolve along an individual private path [98, 115-119, 122, 129]. This evolution associates the economic status of an individual with that of the owner of production means [127-130].

However, note that there are other ways to ensure this status, e.g., strengthening the legal status of the population and improving the relevant legal institutions. Presently, the legal institutions guaranteeing the population's quality of life need filling with real economic and social content. The complex of rights defining the citizen as a participant of social production should be improved as well: the subjective right to work should be legally diversified considering socio-economic factors. Under the inevitable transformation of society (e.g., due to the introduction of new technologies in the economy and, consequently, the release of workers from technologically outdated industries), the law should synthesize economic efficiency and social security of the population. It is also necessary to develop and augment legal means of adapting the population to the negative effects of the economic macrosystem. National social programs should not hinder economic incentives for the population to work. The existing system of state guarantees should be economically and socially filled and flexible, covering all life risks.

The use of economic and legal mechanisms in strategic decision-making on the quality and structure of the national social macrosystem cannot deprive the population of its social rights. The current legal regulation of the social sphere aims to denationalize its sectors through developing privatization processes in the infrastructure of the social macrosystem. This reason explains the expanding poverty zone and the thesis about the population's social insecurity. Thus, the following doctrinal claims included in the Constitution of the Russian Federation are violated: Russia is "a social state, the policy of which is aimed at creating conditions for a decent life and free human development" [124]. Decision-making on the population's social and legal security is mechanical: the sphere and density of the action of law are enlarged around the individual during the operation of society [192]. Meanwhile, legal security should have a social aspect with appropriate economic content, patterns, and restrictions.

Under the growing nonstationarity of the economic macrosystem, it is necessary to increase the population's legal and social security means and strengthen the individual's status in the sphere of social rights of citizens with the corresponding economic content. At the same time, the population's social security should not cause the unjustified extension of the legal infrastructure that hinders the country's economic development. Some public trends that are currently taking shape, on the one hand, stimulate the growing economic and social infantilism of certain population groups (e.g., through manual control and the "ideal adjuster" image); on the other hand, they increase social tension, thereby contributing to the dysfunctionality and nonstationarity of the economic and social macrosystems.

These facts call for transforming the existing approaches to the public administration of socio-economic systems, which can become prerequisites for designing a mechanism of the national legal system focused on the population's interests and the real implementation of the social state idea. This problem can be solved by strategic decision-making on a new structure of the national legal system that adjusts the economic and social macrosystems and provides the economic and socio-legal security of the population: from revising the existing norms defining the list and minimum amount of social guarantees to designing a new, meaningful, and multifunctional organizational infrastructure of universal social security.

This book generally shows the interaction and mutual influence of the three macrosystems: economic, legal, and social. Each sphere mentioned is governed by a control system acting based on appropriate strategic and operational decisions. In reality, decision-making is carried out under uncertainty.

1.2. Uncertainty and Risk as Characteristics of Strategic Decision-Making in Nonstationary Economic, Legal, and Social Macrosystems

Game theory is a set of mathematical models and tools for analyzing and designing short- and long-term strategies (the behavioral rules of systems) and making optimal managerial decisions under a conflict of interests and uncertainty. Generally speaking, there are two classes of uncertainty: fundamental uncertainty (also called the uncertainty of the future) and uncertainty due to the unknown values of the current characteristics of processes and phenomena.

In decision-making, several types of uncertainty are distinguished: strategic uncertainty, the uncertainty of goals and other interacting participants in the system [219], and exogenous and endogenous uncertainty. Exogenous uncertainty affects the evolution of a complex system from the outside, causing its destabilization or even degradation. Endogenous uncertainty is associated with unforeseen factors within the macrosystem. Among other sources of this uncertainty, we mention the so-called behavioral factor, which is generally determined by sociodemographic and socio-economic processes in society.

The uncertainty generated by external and internal factors often manifests itself in incomplete or inaccurate information about the operating conditions of the macrosystem, the connections between its systems, their parameters, and their conflict.

Uncertainty occurs due to different reasons, e.g., from the difficult-to-predict scientific and technological progress and forecasting errors to dynamic changes in the internal and external conditions for the stable development of macrosystems; from a qualitative change in the population's intellectual, educational, labor, and cultural potential, and the state of health to the probabilistic forecasting errors of the macroparameters, etc.

For this research, *uncertainty can be characterized as unreliable, insufficient, or even absent information for decision-making* in complex macrosystems [273-275]. The more complex the system is, the greater role the uncertainty factor will play in its behavior.

Uncertainty causes risk. Both theorists and practitioners study the concept and phenomenon of risk within various economic schools and lines. According to German sociologist and political philosopher U. Beck, humanity is drawn into the so-called risk society because it does not reflect the situation properly and, consequently, generates new sources of risk or enhances the negative impact of the known and previously encountered sources of risk [87].

Many authors studied the etymology and history of the word "risk." In N. Luhmann's *Risk: A Sociological Theory*, the Arabic origin of this word was considered. In Europe, the word "risk" was mentioned in medieval sources and spread in Spain and Italy with book-printing. It indicates a problem situation difficult to express in existing words; according to Luhmann, the history of the term "risk" shows the ways of decisions linking the times, although the future cannot be sufficiently known, even when it is created by decisions of the people [194].

The etymology of this concept implies that risk is due to uncertainty and the multialternative choice of behavioral strategies. Webster's Dictionary defines risk as "possibility of loss or injury; someone or something that creates or suggests a hazard." The word "risk" in the English language is borrowed from French *risque* and Italian *risco*, both meaning "danger." They go back to Greek *rizikon*, literally meaning "root" but later on used in Latin for "cliff." That is, "to take the risk" is "to go around the cliff."

Risk is also defined as a possible deviation between the factual and planned values and (or) a possible non-occurrence of anticipated events. In decision-making, risk means the ability to choose between accepting or not the responsibility for the results of a decision made under uncertainty and implemented at the level of an individual, an economic entity, and society. In his unique study devoted to the social role of risk, P. Bernstein showed that adopting an appropriate methodology for measuring, assessing, and managing risk is a catalyst for the development of society [17].

Note that game theory suggests formalized rules for the analysis and choice of decisions under uncertainty. New game-theoretic approaches yield the least risky and, at the same time, guaranteed solutions, which stabilize complex macrosystems in particular and complex metasystems in general under uncertainty.

1.2.1. Classification of Uncontrolled Factors in Game Theory

In game-theoretic models, the players' strategies are factors that they control. In addition, there exist uncontrolled factors affecting the outcome, e.g., economic and social shocks. When making decisions, players need complete information about the significance of such factors. Operations research [64] distinguishes three groups of uncontrolled factors depending on the awareness of the decision-maker (DM): fixed, random, and uncertain.

Fixed factors are the ones with determinate values. Random factors are random variables with given distributions. Uncertain factors (further referred to as uncertainties) are deterministic variables taking arbitrary values from given sets (particularly intervals) or random variables with an arbitrary distribution from a given class [275].

In this book, random factors and uncertainties will be considered. Fixed factors are no different from other mathematical model parameters: by definition, their values are known in advance and cannot be changed by the players. Random factors and uncertainties cannot be changed by the players as well but take unknown values. Concerning the former, a probability distribution is usually given. For example, a discrete random factor takes on a finite set of values $y_1,\ldots,y_m$ with probabilities $p_1,\ldots,p_m$. If the random factor is a continuous random variable, then its probability density $p(x)$ is usually given. In both cases mentioned, the criteria are replaced by their mathematical expectations.

If the uncertainty is a deterministic variable, then the set of its possible values Y is given. In other words, only the inclusion $y \in \mathrm{Y}$ is taken into account. If the uncertainty is a random variable, then the class of admissible probability densities is given. Note that uncertainties in a complex metasystem are often caused by a nonstationary economic macrosystem [122]: its transformation processes generate uncontrolled factors affecting the entire metasystem.

1.2.2. Classification of Uncertainties

The uncertainties in strategic decision-making can be divided into the following groups [273-275]:

1. Uncertainties due to the actions of third parties with individual goals (non-DMs) [275].

As a rule, real control and controlled systems operate under conflict. In such conditions, uncertainty is associated with the actions of parties to the conflict, who have their strategic goals. Uncertainties of this type are commonly referred to as strategic uncertainties. They are caused by the persons participating in the conflict but not representing decision-makers. For example, the results of a strategic decision in a real economic macrosystem are affected by the operation and transformation of legal and social macrosystems directly interconnected with the former macrosystem. These interconnections are incorporated into the mathematical model through several parameters with given limits. The particular values of the parameters are determined by the actions of the two other macrosystems (legal and social), and these parameters are uncertainties. Strategic uncertainties also include endogenous uncertainties (e.g., the dysfunctionality of social processes and the reverse impact of countersanctions on the economic macrosystem) and exogenous uncertainties (e.g., sanctions).

A complex metasystem undergoes internal perturbations since each macrosystem of this metasystem has conflicts: economic, legal, social, etc. Let us consider only the conflicts occurring in a complex metasystem and causing uncertainty due to the actions of other subjects with their goals and interests (non-DMs). Several conflicts can be separated out from the viewpoint of balancing the economic, social, and legal macrosystems; see below.

Economic conflicts can be represented as a clash of interests for at least two economic agents. These contradictions are reflected in society by the population's dissatisfaction, primarily with the quality of life, subjectively considered either as deterioration compared to the usual one (a real conflict of needs) or an inferior position compared to other social groups (a conflict of interests). In the second case, a conflict may arise even under some improvement in the quality of life psychologically perceived as insufficient or inadequate. Here, economic conflicts are conflicts over the economic means of the population's life support, wages, prices for goods and services, the use of professional and intellectual potential, and access to the distribution of material and spiritual benefits.

Legal collisions in the social sphere occur because the population's social security system is based on federal frame laws and normative legal acts without appropriate economic content that regulate only some forms and types of social interaction between the adjuster and the population. Thus, specifying the Constitutional claims on the social state, national legislation does not implement this idea equally and fully. Most of the normative legal acts in the social sphere have little to do with real financing, are declarative, and require a gradual reduction of budgetary allocations to social state programs. Normative contradictions still exist: for example, no strict delineation of power between different authorities engaged in the population's social security.

The current negative trend of expanding the poverty zone testifies to the contradictory and often unsystematic rule-making in the social sphere, which agrees neither with the economic situation nor the individual needs of citizens in social services and the needs of society. Moreover, rule-making in the social sphere conflicts with other legal norms.

Social conflict is a clash of two or more subjects of social interaction (agents) due to incompatible needs, interests, and values. The subjects of social interaction have clear and definite individual goals, and they are not decision-makers. Uncertainty in social conflicts is associated with the following. First, social agents can have both positive and negative impacts on the development of society. Second, social conflicts can be a source of economic changes preventing stagnation of macrosystems and motivating the modification of socio-economic relations and structures. In this sense, conflicts can be a form of regulation of the conflicting interests of various social groups and reduce tension in their relations. On the other hand, social conflicts threaten to destabilize the economic macrosystem and the entire society and can lead to catastrophic consequences.

We emphasize again that in the above situations, uncertainty is due to the actions of the conflicting parties with individual goals (non-DMs).

2. Uncertainties reflecting the incorrect goals of DMs [275].

Let us highlight the uncertainty in the understanding of DMs and their goals. Strictly speaking, this uncertainty is a controllable factor since choosing appropriate goals is at the DM's disposal. However, if the DM cannot make his (its) choice or doubts for some reason, the situation resembles uncontrolled factors.

On the one hand, any economic system embodies a strategy for producing public goods at the micro and macrolevels. On the other, it is under constant pressure from society, which seeks to maintain or improve the quality of life. The key problem is that the goals of an individual, a group of people, or society do not necessarily coincide with those of strategic decision-makers, or there is no clear idea of a common criterion (a single indicator) to assess strategic decision-making.

When the balance of economic, legal, and social macrosystems is considered, strategic decisions are understood as mechanisms for transforming public requirements into compulsory public rules of law that regulate relations and determine the distribution of resources to solve socially significant problems.

This definition can be associated with a set of indicators $f_1(x),\ldots,f_N(x)$, each optimized by the DM without a clear idea of a common criterion (a single indicator). Here, $\square = \{1,\ldots,N\}$ denotes the set of players. Therefore, the DM is in the same position as in the presence of uncontrolled factors. These cases are common: each value of an uncontrolled factor has its outcome for the DM, which depends only on the current situation x. Hence, the model with uncontrolled factors and a single indicator contains as many criterion values as these factors take. Each situation yields many values of a single criterion.

The uncertainty factor characterizes the macrosystem's state, and uncertainty consists in incomplete information of the control system about the problems of the controlled one, e.g., the individual problems of the population. Due to this feature, the results of decisions cannot be predicted accurately. The existing uncertainty leads to inaccurate, inconsistent, or ambiguous goals. As a result, the expected losses of all participants in the socio-economic process cannot be thoroughly considered even under a finite set of alternatives. Moreover, the existing uncertainty leads to unexpected decisions and (or) undesirable consequences. For example, consider the purchases of vital medicines in the modern healthcare system. When planning the purchases, the problems associated with replacing original medicines with generics are neglected: DMs have incomplete information about the individual needs of certain population categories and the consequences of using substitutes for original medicines. Unfortunately, this uncertainty contributes to the growth of diseases and even deaths.

Let the DM's criterion depend on uncertainty with a finite set of values. After substituting these values, the criterion becomes a vector one with each component corresponding to a particular value of the uncertainty.

Then a topical problem is to construct a single scalar criterion considering the "desires" of all components of the vector criterion (the convolution of criteria). There are two widespread methods to convolute criteria $f_1(x),\dots,f_N(x)$: weighted summation $\sum_{i=1}^{N}\alpha_i f_i(x)$ and weighted minimization $\min_{1\le i\le N}\alpha_i f_i(x)$. The weight coefficients usually satisfy the normalization conditions $\alpha_i > 0$ and $\sum_{i=1}^{N}\alpha_i = 1$ $(i=1,\dots,N)$. These coefficients can be conversion factors into a single measurement system. The inaccurate goal is reflected by the uncertain values $\alpha_i (i=1,\dots,N)$ that satisfy only the normalization conditions [244].

However, such an approach suffers from obvious drawbacks. First, it does not eliminate the uncertainties: α appears instead of *y*. Second, it applies only to the uncertainty with a finite set of values. If there are infinitely many values (or even a continuum of values), the approach becomes fruitless. The criterion values may depend on uncertainty due to different reasons, e.g., the exogenous and endogenous factors mentioned above.

3. Uncertainties due to insufficient knowledge of socio-economic processes

The increasing volumes of information cause uncertainty due to the underinvestigated socio-economic, political, and other processes. Information flows primarily affect the individual's consciousness. In addition to negative emotions, information can concentrate, e.g., significant forces destroying rational arguments and material obstacles. Insufficient understanding, incomplete information, and unawareness of the social reality often incur economic (and other) losses, exceeding manifold the positive potential of information. All these factors explain, e.g., difficulties in predicting the population's social well-being under economic instability.

The low-efficiency forecasting of the population's socio-economic discomfort originates from the insufficient knowledge of its behavior under uncertainty. Managerial decisions incorrect by the degree of data elaboration and completeness cannot balance the population's conflicting interests and attitudes concerning certain events. Some examples are the following: the concentration of conflict situations in some public spheres and a relative indifference of the population in others; the calming effect of measures on the stabilization of the national economic system, which is purely symbolic (the increased anxiety and growing distrust of the population concerning the pension and healthcare reforms). The increasing uncertainties also reflect scientific and technological progress: when developing any branch of knowledge, the number of unsolved fundamental and applied problems grows faster than the number of solved ones.

In game theory, decision-making based on incomplete data is understood as "the conflict with nature" [275]. This uncertainty factor is subjective and can be partially compensated by expert assessments: it depends on the accumulated experience, the completeness of modern scientific knowledge, and access to new information.

4. Uncertainties in collecting, processing, and transmitting information

The control and controlled systems cannot interact without communication and information exchange. It is important to organize proper information support for control and management in modern conditions: collect and process information necessary for making and implementing justified decisions. The DM and (or) control systems have to acquire and process information as well as to generate and transmit new derivative information in the form of control actions executed strategically and operationally.

In applications, we deal with approximate solutions containing uncertainty elements. Approximate information appears for several reasons:

- elementary computational errors;
- data transmission errors, especially under growing information volumes;
- the limited accuracy of data representation and processing;
- restrictions on the accuracy of measurements and other numerical solutions, which are also approximate.

Errors in approximate solutions occur due to the following factors:

- The mathematical model is inadequate to the real object under study.
- Initial data are incomplete.
- The numerical method selected has computational features affecting its accuracy.
- The values of model parameters are rounded.

The rounding problem can be resolved by determining admissible domains (intervals). Withing this approach, each parameter is assigned limits (the maximum and minimum values it can take). Each parameter is hence replaced by an interval covering its exact value. When performing calculations, a new interval is obtained from the given ones using an appropriate rounding procedure. Therefore, the correct result at each stage of calculations belongs to some interval. All these issues are considered in interval analysis. In recent years, interval analysis has been actively used to monitor demographic indicators (the dynamics of morbidity and mortality, e.g., for unestablished diagnoses).

Direct application of such methods allows enclosing the problem solutions and rounding and approximation errors in intervals. Algorithms with two-sided estimation are promising since the resulting errors are quantified. Interval calculus is used for two-sided estimation. Here, the main element is an interval $[a,b]$ (also called range) defined as a set of real numbers x such that $\{x \in \mathbb{R} \mid a \le x \le b\}$. An interval function containing the exact solution is obtained using an interval algorithm to solve some problem. In this case, we can a priori analyze the rounding errors, achieving the desired accuracy of the solution.

Almost any decisions require processing large data sets. The DM's competence depends not so much on his experience and skills but on sufficient information about situation dynamics and his ability to use this information. According to management practice, incorrect analysis yields useless information or even eliminates significant information for decision-making. (In other words, it causes uncertainty). On the other hand, redundant information imposes the risk of losing vital and relevant information. The process of using information is cyclical and consists of several stages: collecting (in the form of facts, figures, and data), storing, processing, converting into messages for the researcher and analyst, and reflecting in analytical documents for DMs and control systems at different hierarchy levels. Note that decision support systems have been actively used since the 1970s. Such systems provide assistance in decision processes in some economic sectors and partially replace DMs (e.g., heat, water, and electricity supply in the housing and communal services system).

Among other things, the use of information in decision-making is based on knowledge and experience. The information is updated, enriched, and concretized as new data arrive from research, experiments, and observations. Anticipatory information is of particular value: it predicts (to some extent) the course of events and allows setting goals and elaborating action plans, programs, and development strategies for future periods. This type of information has the greatest uncertainty factor.

Note that the constantly increasing amount of information objectively accompanies the complication of strategic decision-making. Despite some successes in the informatization and digitalization of society, there are serious problems: the informational overload of DMs and the redistribution of information flows between different hierarchy levels in control systems, causing information loss during transmission. An acute issue concerns the content and volume of managerial and special awareness, the professional training of managers, and an optimal balance of their functional duties. These problems are fundamentally solved by improving the scientific and methodological support of decision processes, and the approach proposed below is one of the possible recipes.

5. Special uncertainties arising in systems control and management

The design of different-purpose objects in controlled systems, direct control, and the complication of control goals pose various problems in the control and management of conflicting dynamic systems. A special role here is assigned to managing the evolution of complex systems and observation processes under incomplete information (uncertainty). These problems naturally generalize control problems under incomplete information and arise in numerous applications. Incomplete information in such problems is a consequence of several real-life factors. For example, underinvestigated exogenous disturbances affecting a dynamic controlled system cause uncertainty in the “forces” applied to it. The source of such disturbances can be associated, e.g., with some pressure. This type of uncertainty includes errors in implementing control algorithms described as perturbing forces added to the nominal ones. Incomplete information can be due to initial data errors, the scatter of controlled system’s parameters and characteristics, and other perturbations.

The list of uncertainties and their sources in real decision problems (see the classification above) does not claim to be exhaustive. However, it shows that uncertainties must be considered both in microeconomic problems and more complex conflict interactions with colliding interests of many parties (decision problems at the macrolevel). Thus, uncertainties are not negligible.

1.2.3. Considering Uncertainties When Making Decisions

The game-theoretic approach proposed below is based on formalizing three postulates: the features of the problems under study (conflicts); appropriate decisions, particularly those resolving the conflicts; the optimality of some decisions. In this subsection, we will consider conflicts where the parties seek to achieve the individual goals of the control system. This approach is well-justified: the corresponding model reflects real processes within the current economic doctrine. Such conflicts are explored using *noncooperative games.*

How can the uncertainties in decision-making (see above) be considered within noncooperative games? A possible approach, based on modifying the principle of guaranteed result [64], was developed for multicriteria choice problems [20, 253] and conflict systems [267, 273-275, 277, 278]. An alternative approach involves an appropriate modification of Savage's principle of minimax regret [273-275].

In the mathematical models of noncooperative games with uncertainty, the effect of several uncertain factors is assessed by specific values of scalar parameters $y_1,\dots,y_m$. We introduce a column vector of the form $y=(y_1,\dots,y_m)$, with the set of values denoted by $\mathrm{Y}\subset\mathbb{R}^m$ (a subset of the m-dimensional Euclidean space). Let the uncertainties y be not described by statistical methods. This situation occurs at least in two cases as follows:

- The probabilistic characteristics of *y* exist in principle, but statistical data are not available.
- The uncertainties *y* have no probability distribution.

Suppose that when making their decisions, the players know the entire set Y of the uncertainties *y* only: there are no probabilistic characteristics for *y*. Therefore, choosing their strategies, the players are expecting any realization of *y* from the set Y.

The following types of uncertainties are distinguished in the economic literature:

- interval uncertainties;
- random (or probabilistic) uncertainties with given characteristics of the distribution of y on the set Y;
- fuzzy uncertainties based on the concept of a fuzzy set [239].

Legislation is the mechanism and form to legitimize and implement strategic decisions in the public sphere [90].

1.3. Analysis of Strategic Decisions in the Social Sphere Considering Social Legislation Transformations in the Complex Metasystem

Strategic decision-making in the social sphere is a normative legal process that regulates social relations in the macrosystem under consideration. On the one hand, decisions at the macrolevel determine the behavioral rules of agents in economic and social macrosystems of a complex metasystem; on the other hand, they form a normative legal base for the operation of the macrosystems.

The current legal system in the social sphere is nonstationary and undergoes transformations based on the neoliberal economic doctrine principles. As a result, this system is a voluminous and constantly growing normative legal base [52, 124, 174]. In addition, public administration effects in the social macrosystem are often negative, causing several deformation processes: reducing consumer demand due to the population's lower incomes, decreasing the population's living standards, etc. The uncontrollable build-up of the contradictory normative legal base leads to inconsistency and disagreements over its implementation.

In particular, the social macrosystem was nonstationary due to changes within the neoliberal economic doctrine. Strategic decision-making was aimed to transfer the social macrosystem from the declared principles of universal social security to the European targeted social security model. (The main principle of this model is reducing public expenditures to support all categories of the country's population).

Note that by the mid-1990s, to save budgetary expenditures, the foundations were laid to administer modern socio-economic processes with the sequestering of state funding of the social sphere. At that stage of the social sphere transformation, *the possibilities to denationalize (privatize) organizations and institutions of different organizational and legal forms in the social sphere* were identified. When making such decisions, the differences in the levels of various forms of ownership (federal, regional, and municipal) were not considered properly. Thus, the decentralized management of the social macrosystem was gradually formed. Due to that policy, some sectors of the social sphere became degraded, were denationalized, and underfunded. In that period, the commercialization of social services and the provision of paid services to the population in the social sphere were initiated, a negative trend for the majority of the country's population.

Thus, the contours of the modern social macrosystem were regulatively determined in the mid-1990s. The strategic decisions taken led to an excessive financial load on the majority of the population and, in particular, the appearance of a new economic category—economic poverty—to describe part of the economically active and able-bodied population that cannot satisfy the minimum economic needs due to low incomes.

During that period of transformations in the national complex metasystem, each constituent of the Russian Federation independently developed a system of vital social indicators for the population using its methodological guidelines in the deteriorating economic conditions and reduced budgetary subsidies and subventions. The contours of the modern system of minimum social standards were formed, which also transformed the social sphere. The economic concept of living wage was fixed in the legal field at the federal and regional levels of public administration. Due to insufficient funding of regional and municipal budgets and low-quality lawmaking at the appropriate levels, the size and structure of living wage turned out to be significantly underestimated compared to the population's real needs in goods and services.

Against the background of general transformation processes of the late 1990s, regional budget deficits, and various levels of socio-economic development of regions, that dysfunctional processes occurring in the economic macrosystem were directly reflected in the transformed national legal and social macrosystems [165, 166] at all hierarchy levels.

In addition, in the late 1990s, civil law mechanisms for compensating the damage to the life and health of workers were abandoned, and the system of compulsory social insurance was modified. Since that period, the adjuster guarantees only minimum payments to compensate victims regardless of the employer's financial situation, thereby worsening their quality of life [124]. The strategic decisions in the social sphere mentioned above negatively affect the performance of the economic and social macrosystems by changing the economic and organizational foundations of the compulsory social insurance system as a structural component of the social sphere.

According to modern law and risk management, the following social guarantees are the types of population's compulsory social insurance against the life risks due to the individual's disability: pensions, various allowances and benefits, and insurance payments. Therefore, we will propose and justify the "life risk–social guarantee" pair as a key element of the new approach; see the subsequent chapters of this book.

Note that the social macrosystem in the 1990s still contained elements of the former (Soviet) social infrastructure. The new laws were implemented simultaneously with the existing social payments (allowances and pensions), social services in the population's social security and support system, and social benefits and compensations. For example, there were over 400 different social benefits, and they were provided to most of the population, in contrast to the present time [38]. Hence, the previous system of social benefits (e.g., payments for housing and communal services, free travel on transport, and free distribution of vital drugs) and the range of persons entitled to social benefits were much wider than nowadays [38].

Thus, since the mid-2000s, the adjuster has implemented strategic decisions on transforming the social sphere, developed and implemented legal mechanisms of social legislation on decentralizing and denationalizing the social macrosystem's infrastructure.

Up to the 1990s, there was a socially filled centralized system of population's social security, which operated in the post-Soviet period. Nowadays, we observe the multilevel and decentralized legal regulation of the social sphere in general and the population's social security in particular. Despite the actual strategic goal-setting towards improving the population's quality of life, the redistribution of powers between the federal, regional, and municipal authorities in the social sphere, carried out in the 20th century, has been neither funded adequately nor provided with a legal mechanism for protecting social rights so far. The still existing negative socio-economic consequences of strategic decision-making in the late 1990s conflict with the Basic Law on the Social State: the population cannot fully exercise the constitutional right to social security and the constitutional principle of equality [38, 124]. Strategic goals are not achieved, such as reducing social inequality, creating equal development opportunities, and providing an effective social support system. These factors unbalance the interactions of the economic, legal, and social macrosystems.

Thus, the current social security system, stemming from the transformations of the late 1990s, has a haphazard and contradictory legal support that does not correspond to the economic situation, the individual needs of the population in social services, and the needs of society. At the present stage, the national legal system in the social sphere is based on economically unsecured federal frame laws regulating separate forms and types of social security: compulsory social insurance, social services, social state assistance, labor pensions, etc. Refining the provisions of the Basic Law on the population's social security and support, *social legislation could not equally and fully reveal the meaning of the declared social state idea* [8, 38, 124, 192]. Among other reasons, this feature explains the unbalancedness of the economic, legal, and social macrosystems.

Conclusion

Chapter 1 has been devoted to the systems analysis of the interaction and mutual influence of the economic, legal, and social macrosystems as a stationary and (or) nonstationary complex metasystem within Russia's constitutional social state doctrine. Note that the peculiarities of strategic decision-making under uncertainty have been taken into account.

In addition, Chapter 1 has considered the features of the interaction and mutual influence of the economic, legal, and social macrosystems (as the basic structural elements of the complex metasystem) and substantiated the problem of their balancedness, formalized and solved in the subsequent chapters.

As shown by systems analysis, the operation of the economic macrosystem is determined by market laws and regulated by the national legislation (legal macrosystem) establishing the order of economic activity for economic agents. At the same time, the law as a macrosystem is determined by the economy, its structure, and economic relations, which are reflected in legal relations and fill them with economic content. The country's economic development determines the state of the social sphere, and economic patterns are mediated by legal and social factors affecting the behavior of economic agents.

The correlation between the economic, legal, and social macrosystems is manifested in their interaction: the legal order of economic and social relations corresponds to the patterns and trends in the country's socio-economic development.

Within the game-theoretic approach, the concept of Berge equilibrium is a strategy profile reflecting the Golden Rule of ethics (GR), a well-known philosophical and moral principle of behavior. The GR applies to the behavior and relations between the three macrosystems of the complex metastructure under consideration.

This book suggests the transition from the outdated neoliberal economic doctrine based on individual rationality (Nash equilibrium) to the philosophical and moral concept of the Golden Rule of ethics (Berge equilibrium). This transition will give a new interpretation of macrosystem equilibrium for further use in the economic-mathematical modeling of socio-economic processes.

Uncertainties and risks as characteristics of strategic decision-making in a nonstationary complex metasystem have been identified and classified in terms of game theory. As emphasized, when modelling socio-economic processes, it is necessary to consider uncertainty, randomness, incomplete information, conflict, and risk. On the one hand, these factors accompany the operation of macrosystems. On the other hand, they require improving the models and tools for strategic decision-making and developing new, particularly game-theoretic, decision methods under uncertainty and interaction models for macrosystems. According to E.I. Vilkas and E.Z. Maiminas, the factors that have to be considered when making each decision are becoming more and more numerous, diverse, and interrelated [219].

The analysis of the legitimized strategic decisions in the social sphere has showed that the existing social legislation does not fully and equally reveal the declared social state idea. Most of the regulatory legal acts in the social sphere are not properly funded, and the amount of budgetary allocations for implementing social state programs is being reduced. The laws covering the social sphere and the population's social security often operate generalized concepts, not regulating the types of social support. Moreover, the competence of different-level public authorities in social security, the volume of social services and social assistance, and the quality of social services are not clearly specified. Undoubtedly, these features affect the implementation of social guarantees for the population. Hence, the current social security system has a haphazard and contradictory legal support that does not correspond to the economic situation, the individual needs of the population in social services, and the needs of society.

Therefore, it is necessary to develop a new approach to improving decision processes in the social sphere at the macrolevel and design a mechanism for balancing the economic, legal, and social macrosystems.

The subsequent chapters will present a new mechanism for balancing the economic, legal, and social macrosystems. More specifically, we will construct and justify an equilibrium model using the social state idea as the fundamental principle for the interaction and mutual influence of the three macrosystems. This model is based on Berge equilibrium, revealing the Golden Rule of ethics ("Do to others as you would like them to do to you"), and Nash equilibrium, revealing rational relations, in the complex metasystem of the three macrosystems.

The new strategic decision methodology for administering the social sphere will be formed by constructing and justifying a hierarchical social sphere management model under uncertainty, consisting of two models: a model for managing the dynamics of complex social-economic systems and a formal game-theoretic model for decision-making under uncertainty (a guaranteed solution based on an appropriate modification of Savage's principle of minimax regret).

Chapter 2

Equilibrium Models of the Complex National Metasystem

Introduction

In Section 2.1, we present the basic concepts for constructing a game-theoretic model of the three national macrosystems (economic, legal, and social). The concepts of Nash and Berge equilibria for the economic, legal, and social macrosystems are defined in Sections 2.2 and 2.3, respectively. Section 2.4 justifies and formalizes a balanced equilibrium model based on Berge equilibrium (altruistic decision-making according to the GR) and Nash equilibrium (rational decision-making) to balance the three macrosystems of the complex metasystem.

Section 2.5 gives an illustrative example of one application of the Berge equilibrium model: we study the dynamics of family structures and relations affecting the life system of the population as well as the state, prospects, and possibilities of public administration of sociodemographic processes in Russia. Mathematical models of family relations based on the concepts of Berge and Nash equilibrium are constructed.

2.1. The Golden Rule of Ethics in Game Theory

The GR is one of the most ancient, specific, and widespread moral generalizations expressing the experience accumulated by mankind. It instructs: "Do to others as you would like them to do to you."

Academician A.A. Guseinov noted:

a) Relations between people are moral only if they are interchangeable as the subjects of individually responsible behavior.
b) The culture of moral choice is the ability to put oneself in the place of another.

c) One must commit only the acts approved by the objects of activity. See [68] and [269].

The essence of the GR and its connections with philosophy, morality, duty, ethics, and politics were considered in the recent books [269] and [270]. Note that they were devoted to the static and dynamic cases of Berge equilibrium, respectively. The GR shows how to be moral, and not why an individual should be moral. Hence, this rule can be assumed one of the main ethical adjusters of social relations. Within a general philosophical approach, ethics and humanity underlie the culture of strategic decision-making: this principle is a main prerequisite and ultimate goal when developing the national economic system and increasing the population's welfare. The social state is treated as a state serving the interests of society [8]. With such an interpretation, the operation of the economic, legal, and social systems should be balanced and aimed at increasing the population's welfare. In this context, a balanced equilibrium based on the concept of Berge equilibrium (the GR) [269] structurally reflects the social state's essence and changes the constitutional doctrine in this part; as a mathematical theory of optimal decision-making under conflict, game theory allows balancing the three macrosystems under consideration.

The gradual development of economic-mathematical modeling of decision processes at the macrolevel of complex systems accordingly changes the requirements to the performance of controlled systems. In the course of modeling, researchers should consider several main factors: two or even more criteria measuring the controlled system's performance and various types of interval uncertainties with given limits (without any statistical characteristics). In this book, uncertainty is understood as incomplete or inaccurate information at different hierarchy levels for implementing decisions in the economic and social macrosystems.

Most of the strategic decisions in socio-economic systems are accompanied by the conflict of interests between individual control systems with appropriate power and influence groups defending their own interests and various additional factors inherent in the decision process. *A conflict is understood as a situation* in which the parties have different interests and opportunities to choose appropriate actions for their benefit.

As a rule, the conflicting nature of processes does not imply any open confrontation between the parties but indicates their different interests (mostly economic). In such situations, traditional optimization methods become almost impracticable. Moreover, the generally accepted mathematical theories of market equilibrium do not reflect real socio-economic processes. For example, in real economic and social macrosystems, the same decisions can be optimal for one party and nonoptimal for the other. The resulting decisions can depend on all parties with different interests (conflicting ones). Game theory is a mathematical framework that studies such situations, representing a branch of the general theory for describing and analyzing optimal decision processes with one or several participants under uncertainty and conflict.

Note that games differ from real conflicts: they are played according to certain rules. Real conflicts are usually difficult to simulate economically and mathematically. Therefore, any game is a simplification of the original real problem that covers only the main (primary) factors reflecting the essence of the process or phenomenon studied.

In modern conditions, *the management of complex socio-economic systems at the macrolevel* should be treated as multicriteria decision-making under uncertainty, considering the interconnections and mutual influence of economic, legal, and social processes. *Strategic decisions* are understood as mechanisms for transforming social requirements into public and generally binding norms and mechanisms that adjust interrelations and allocate economic resources for solving public problems (particularly the social ones).

In this book, *the economic macrosystem* is a set of interconnected economic agents that form a definite economic structure of society and public relations that develop during the production, distribution, exchange, and consumption of economic and social benefits. *The legal macrosystem* is a set of interconnected, coordinated, and interacting legal institutions that administer public relations and the agents of these institutions that characterize the level of the national legal state. *The social macrosystem* is a set of interconnected and mutually sectors of the social sphere.

The economic, legal, and social macrosystems interact in many aspects and at various levels.

The economy as a macrosystem has several features. For example, its state and operation are determined, among other things, by both objective and subjective factors. One of the main instruments is government regulation (public administration) through national legislation: a certain order of economic and entrepreneurial activity is established, and various economic criteria and indicators are adopted (e.g., tax rates, fees, tariffs, duties, prices for certain categories of goods, etc.). On the other hand, the law as a macrosystem is determined by the economy, structure, and economic relations, which are reflected in legal relations and fill them with economic content.

The correlation of the economic and legal systems, manifested in their mutual influence and interaction, is that the legal order of economic relations corresponds to the laws and trends of economic development. This interaction can be positive, contributing to the normal operation of the economic macrosystem and its growth, or negative, inhibiting its development. This mutual influence can be assessed by analyzing and synthesizing the existing national law enforcement practice and the current economic situation. As already noted, the legal system fixes the existing economic relations. Therefore, the interaction between the economic and legal spheres is complex since the economic macrosystem is determined by the volume and nature of the rights of economic agents.

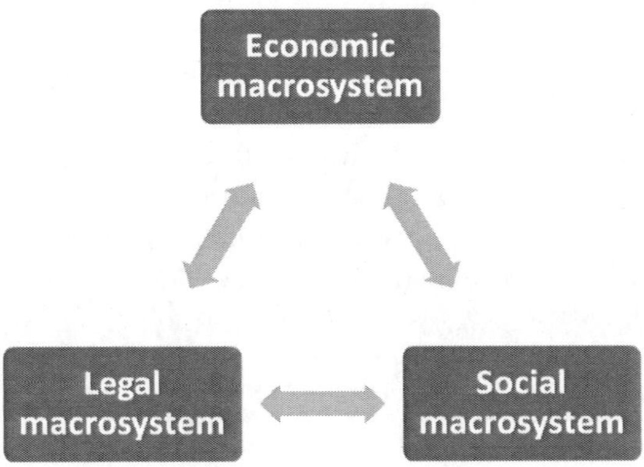

The country's economic development determines the state of the social sphere in particular and society as a whole. Economic patterns are mediated by legal and social factors affecting the individual's behavior in society. The transformation processes in the economic and social macrosystems are mostly concentrated in the structure of individual relations and property relations. According to the neoliberal economic doctrine, property relations evolve along an individual private path. This evolution associates the economic status of an individual with that of the owner of production means. However, note that there are other ways to ensure this status, e.g., strengthening the legal status of the population and improving the relevant legal institutions.

Presently, the legal institutions guaranteeing the population's quality of life need filling with real economic and social content. The complex of rights defining the citizen as a participant of social production should be improved as well: the subjective right to work should be legally diversified considering socio-economic factors. Under the inevitable transformation of society, the law should synthesize economic efficiency and social security of the population.

It is also necessary to develop and augment legal means of adapting the population to the negative effects of the economic macrosystem. National social programs should not hinder economic incentives for the population to work. The existing system of state guarantees should be economically and socially filled and flexible, covering all life risks.

The use of economic and legal mechanisms in strategic decision-making on the quality and structure of the national social macrosystem cannot deprive the population of its social rights.

The current legal regulation of the social sphere aims to denationalize its sectors through developing privatization processes in the infrastructure of the social macrosystem. This reason explains the expanding poverty zone and the thesis about the population's social insecurity. Thus, the following doctrinal regulations included in the Constitution of the Russian Federation are violated: Russia is "a social state, the policy of which is aimed at creating conditions for a decent life and free human development" [38]. Decision-making on the population's social and legal security is mechanical: the sphere and density of the action of law are enlarged around the individual during the operation of society [192]. Meanwhile, legal security should have a social aspect with appropriate economic content, patterns, and restrictions.

Under the growing nonstationarity of the economic macrosystem, it is necessary to increase the population's legal and social security means and strengthen the individual's status in the sphere of social rights of citizens with the corresponding economic content. At the same time, the population's social security should not cause the unjustified extension of the legal infrastructure that hinders the country's economic development. Some public trends that are currently taking shape, on the one hand, stimulate the growing economic and social infantilism of certain population groups (e.g., through manual control and the "ideal adjuster" image); on the other hand, they increase social tension, thereby contributing to the dysfunctionality and nonstationarity of the economic and social macrosystems.

These facts call for transforming the existing approaches to the public administration of socio-economic systems, which can become prerequisites for designing a mechanism of the national legal system focused on the population's interests and the real implementation of the social state idea. This problem can be solved by strategic decision-making on a new structure of the national legal system that adjusts the economic and social macrosystems and provides the economic and socio-legal security of the population: from revising the existing norms defining the list and minimum amount of social guarantees to designing a new, meaningful, and multifunctional organizational infrastructure of universal social security.

This idea cannot be implemented without replacing the currently applied neoliberal economic doctrine based on the principles of individual rationality with a new philosophical and moral concept, e.g., the GR, mathematically expressed by the concept of Berge equilibrium.

The game-theoretic approach of this book proceeds from the assumption that all participants in economic, legal, and social relations incline to some equilibria. Note that the antisocial policy of post-reform Russia led to a conflict as a phenomenon, concerning which we can speak about the participants, their actions, the outcomes resulting from these actions, the parties, interested somehow in these outcomes, and the essence of this interest [112].

The game-theoretic framework below logically rests on three postulates:

- The conflict under consideration has specific features.
- Appropriate decisions are made for resolving this conflict.
- Some decisions are optimal.

This section is restricted to conflicts where the parties strive to achieve the individual goals of each macrosystem. This approach is justified since the model reflects real processes. *Noncooperative games* are a class of games dealing with such conflicts. It has several features as follows:

1) All decisions are made not by a single person but by a group of persons (individuals or legal entities) who form a control system (the so-called players). Are they competitors? Yes: they operate under limited resources.
2) Each player (control system) has appropriately defined specific strategic goals, which are interconnected and affect each other.
3) Each player disposes of specific tools and mechanisms to achieve its goal.

For example, according to Article 13 of the Federal Constitutional Law no. 2-FKZ of December 17, 1997, "On the Government of the Russian Federation" (as amended on December 28, 2016), the Government as a control system "carries out administration in the socio-economic sphere; ensures the unity of the executive power system in the Russian Federation, directs and controls the activities of its bodies; forms federal target programs and ensures their implementation; exercises the right of legislative initiative granted to it."

Article 14 of the Law mentioned above defines the powers in the economic sphere: "The Government of the Russian Federation exercises administration of economic processes in accordance with the Constitution of the Russian Federation, federal constitutional laws, federal laws, and normative decrees of the President of the Russian Federation; ensures the unity of economic space and freedom of economic activity, free movement of goods, services, and financial resources; predicts the social and economic development of the Russian Federation, elaborates and implements development programs for the priority sectors of the economy; designs state structural and investment policies and takes measures to implement them; manages federal property..."

Along with the listed functions of the Government, the ministries included in its structure determine, among other things, the activities of regional and municipal bodies of state power (public authorities) at the appropriate levels. National goals are identified with the corresponding federal target programs formulated and approved by a formal procedure.

Thus, the complex control systems are institutionally formed. The legal system determines the goals, strategies, and behavioral rules of the players.

In game theory, the controlled factors of each player are identified with his (its) strategies, and the choice of a particular strategy is a solution of the corresponding noncooperative game.

As a rule, the mathematical model of a noncooperative game consists of the following elements: the set of players (in our case, control systems); the set of admissible strategies for each player; *a scalar functional for each player, defined on the set of admissible strategies of all players, which measures the achievement of his (its) goal.* In game theory, this functional is called *the player's payoff function.*

As previously shown, the economic, legal, and social macrosystems are interconnected and influence each other. Each system is governed by an institutionally determined control system (player) that makes decisions based on available information and performs actions considering the relevant goals. In the economic, legal, and social macrosystems, the heads of the appropriate public authorities are endowed with management and administration functions.

Within the currently used economic doctrine ("help yourself" and "every man for himself"), assume that they play a noncooperative game and, at the same time, have to be in the mainstream of national tasks, formed jointly with the control system of a higher hierarchy level (e.g., by the Government).

Let each player be assigned a number: the first, second, and third. The set of all players will be denoted by $\square = \{1, 2, 3\}$. Each player chooses and uses its particular strategy.

A strategy will be understood as a rule that assigns to the player's state a certain action (behavior) from the supposed admissible ones under the available information [275]. Thus, player *i* in the game Γ_3 chooses and uses a strategy x_i, where X_i denotes the set of its strategies. *Each player's performance is assessed using its payoff function: the latter's value (called payoff or outcome) quantifies the performance.*

There is no clear definition in the literature for *the performance of control systems*. Based on the general conceptualization, it can be defined as *the degree to which the characteristics of the results of the control system's operation meet the requirements established by all interested parties involved.* Obviously, the interested parties include society, the controlled system itself, and other control and controlled systems of the lower hierarchy levels. Concerning *the performance of control systems*, the key criterion is control effectiveness, which cannot be completely equated with the performance of the entire macrosystem: effectiveness refers primarily to what should be achieved (the consistency between the goal and result). In reality, good goals lead to the opposite results since the control and controlled systems conflict.

In terms of game theory: if players implement their strategies and simultaneously obtain outcomes, then a static noncooperative game is considered. If the system evolves over time, and thus the players get the opportunity to vary their strategies, then a dynamic noncooperative game arises.

The next section is devoted to static noncooperative games.

2.2. Nash Equilibrium of Economic, Legal, and Social Macrosystems

Nowadays, the generally accepted approach in decision-making is to use the concept of Nash equilibrium [153-156]. We construct a noncooperative three-player game of the form

$$\Gamma_3 = \left\langle \{1,2,3\}, \{X_i\}_{i=1,2,3}, \{f_i(x)\}_{i=1,2,3} \right\rangle, \tag{2.1}$$

where the players are public authorities (control systems) of the three interconnected macrosystems: economic, legal, and social.

They choose strategies $x_i \in X_i \subseteq R^{n_i}$ *to increase their performance,* i.e., *their payoffs* $f_i(x)$ in a given strategy profile $x = (x_1, x_2, x_3) \in X_1 \times X_2 \times X_3 = X \subseteq R^3$.

A Nash equilibrium $(x^e, f^e = (f_1(x^e), f_2(x^e), f_3(x^e))) \in X \times R^3$ is given by the three equalities

$$\begin{aligned} f_1(x^e) &= \max_{x_1 \in X_1} f_1(x_1, x_2^e, x_3^e), \\ f_2(x^e) &= \max_{x_2 \in X_2} f_2(x_1^e, x_2, x_3^e), \\ f_3(x^e) &= \max_{x_3 \in X_3} f_3(x_1^e, x_2^e, x_3). \end{aligned} \tag{2.2}$$

According to (2.2), each player (control system) seeks to achieve its goals, not necessarily realizing those of the other systems. The goals of the control system, e.g., in the economic sphere, can be realized with prejudice to the interests of the social sphere by legal tools.

For example, presently, the budget deficits of pension funds (a function of the economic macrosystem) are supposed to be covered at the expense of the population (the subject of the social macrosystem) by adopting new legislation in the pension sphere (using mechanisms of the legal macrosystem). Is it possible to justify the Nash equilibrium in this example? Yes! Most of the population born in 1969 and later will be forced to adopt new rules for calculating pensions and other measures related to raising the retirement age. By choosing a different behavioral strategy, they can lose the opportunity to receive pensions and social state support at an older age. The individual's alternative behavior—a conflict with the control systems of the economic and legal sphere—will go beyond the legal field with the corresponding negative consequences for the individual. This paternalistic approach contributes to achieving a Nash equilibrium in the example under consideration. In other words, the resulting strategy profile of the three-player game will satisfy the following property: no participant can increase its payoff by a unilateral deviation if the other participants continue using the same strategies.

This concept of equilibrium was proposed by J. Nash in 1949. After 45 years, J. Nash, R. Selten, and J. Harsanyi were awarded the Nobel Prize in Economic Sciences "for their pioneering analysis of equilibria in the theory of non-cooperative games." The concept of Nash equilibrium has been widely used in various fields. Moreover, the Nobel committee bestowed eight prizes for Nash equilibrium-related research. Note that in contrast to Berge equilibria [269], Nash equilibria satisfy individual rationality, not facilitating the peaceful resolution of conflicts.

2.3. Berge Equilibrium of the Complex Metasystem

A mathematical model of the GR based on Berge equilibrium was developed and justified in the recent monographs [269, 270]. Also, see [15, 16]. In particular, the existence of Berge equilibrium was established under standard assumptions of mathematical game theory (the compact strategy sets and continuous payoff functions of players). A practical method for designing Berge equilibria was proposed; Berge equilibria under uncertainty were investigated; finally, several simplified applications to competitive economy models were presented. Note that the authors did not consider the issues of designing metasystem equilibrium.

Let us construct a formal mathematical model for the interaction of the economic, legal, and social macrosystems based on Berge equilibrium.

A Berge equilibrium $(x^B, f^B = (f_1(x^B), f_2(x^B), f_3(x^B))) \in X \times R^3$ is given by the three equalities

$$
\begin{aligned}
f_1(x^B) &= \max_{(x_2,x_3)\in X_2\times X_3} f_1(x_1^B, x_2, x_3),\\
f_2(x^B) &= \max_{(x_1,x_3)\in X_1\times X_3} f_2(x_1, x_2^B, x_3),\\
f_3(x^B) &= \max_{(x_1,x_2)\in X_1\times X_2} f_3(x_1, x_2, x_3^B).
\end{aligned}
\tag{2.3}
$$

Unlike (2.2), each player (control system) in (2.3) strives to increase the payoff functions of the other two, i.e., to improve their performance. Such an aspiration of the players has moral foundations (the GR) and matches the equilibrium desired by most society members: the economic system operates only in the legal field and aims to satisfy the interests of the social system. At the same time, the operation of the social system, ensured by the norms of law, stimulates the development of the economic system. In turn, the legal system is not an institutional barrier to the progress of the economic and social systems. In this case, economic development is intended to improve the quality and state of the social sphere by improving the population's quality of life without legislative gaps and excessive administration of economic activities. This is the principle of balancing the three macrosystems through the prism of the social state idea.

Returning to the pension reform discussed above, we mention other goals and ways of their implementation based on moral categories. For example, to increase the welfare of older people, it is possible to legalize a state rent from the largest industrial oligopolies into the federal budget. The question arises: do such measures correlate with the GR? Yes! Nothing would be withdrawn from the economic macrosystem: superprofits from economic activity would be redistributed. Such measures would improve the performance of the economic macrosystem through additional taxes and reduce the state pension fund deficit through redistribution. The performance of the social macrosystem would also be improved due to the growing welfare of population groups such as working and non-working pensioners.

Berge equilibria do not satisfy individual rationality. The players' payoffs in some Berge equilibria are greater compared to Nash equilibria [269].

2.4. Balanced Berge Equilibrium of the Complex Metasystem

The economic-mathematical model presented below is based on the concept of Berge equilibrium; see the books [269, 270]. The Germeier convolution of the players' payoff functions was constructed therein using the original game; it was proved that the minimax strategy at the saddle point is a Berge equilibrium in the original game. The same technique was adopted to establish an existence theorem for Berge equilibria considering its internal instability. (There may be several Berge equilibria such that the payoffs of all players in one equilibrium exceed those in the other [266, 276]). The requirement of Pareto maximality was therefore added, and the existence of a Pareto-maximal Berge equilibrium was proved in the class of mixed strategies. Below, using the results of earlier research [275], we define Slater-minimal guarantees for each strategy profile in the "game of guarantees" and modify Wald's (maximin) principle to introduce the concept of Slater-guaranteed Berge equilibrium (balanced Berge equilibrium) and prove existence theorems.

In the previous book [275], the saddle point, Wald's principle [234-236], and other techniques of operations research and multicriteria choice were employed to design a Nash equilibrium in an *N*-player game and prove its existence in pure strategies (under strategic uncertainty) and mixed strategies (under information discrimination). In what follows, we use the definitions of a Berge equilibrium and a Pareto-maximal Berge equilibrium [269] in pure and mixed strategies, together with the concepts of Slater-guaranteed Nash equilibria and Slater-minimal uncertainties, the existence of which was proved in [275], to construct a Slater-guaranteed balanced Berge equilibrium as an analog of the saddle point.

2.4.1. Berge Equilibrium in a Noncooperative *N*-Player Game

Further presentation needs some background in operations research. The assertion below was proved in [210].

Assume that:

1) A scalar function $F(x, y)$ is continuous on the product of compact sets $\mathrm{X} \subset \mathbb{R}^n$ and $\mathrm{Y} \subset \mathbb{R}^m$, where Y is convex.
2) For each $x \in \mathrm{X}$, the function $F(x, y)$ is strictly convex in the variable y on the set Y, i.e., the inequality

$$F(x, \alpha y^{(1)} + (1-\alpha) y^{(2)}) < \alpha F(x, y^{(1)}) + (1-\alpha) F(x, y^{(2)})$$

holds for each $x \in \mathrm{X}$, $\forall y^{(1)}, y^{(2)} \in \mathrm{Y}$, and $\forall \alpha = const \in (0,1)$.

Then the *m*-dimensional vector function $y(\cdot): \mathrm{X} \to \mathrm{Y}$ given by

$$\min_{y \in \mathrm{Y}} F(x, y) = F(x, y(x)), \forall x \in \mathrm{X}, \tag{2.4}$$

is continuous as well.

Also, we will use Slater- and Pareto-minimal uncertainties [275] and the following notations of multicriteria choice problems: for two vectors $f^{(j)} = (f_1^j, ..., f_N^j), (j = 1, 2)$:

$$
\begin{aligned}
&\left[f^{(1)} = f^{(2)}\right] \Leftrightarrow \left[f_i^{(1)} = f_i^{(2)} (i \in \mathbb{N})\right];\\
&\left[f^{(1)} \neq f^{(2)}\right] \Leftrightarrow \neg\left(f^{(1)} = f^{(2)}\right);\\
&\left[f^{(1)} \geq f^{(2)}\right] \Leftrightarrow \left[f_i^{(1)} \geq f_i^{(2)} (i \in \mathbb{N})\right];\\
&\left[f^{(1)} \geq f^{(2)}\right] \Leftrightarrow \left(f^{(1)} \geq f^{(2)}\right) \wedge \left(f^{(1)} \neq f^{(2)}\right);\\
&\left[f^{(1)} \not\geq f^{(2)}\right] \Leftrightarrow \neg\left(f^{(1)} \geq f^{(2)}\right);\\
&\left[f^{(1)} > f^{(2)}\right] \Leftrightarrow \left[f_i^{(1)} > f_i^{(2)} (i \in \mathbb{N})\right];\\
&\left[f^{(1)} \not> f^{(2)}\right] \Leftrightarrow \neg\left(f^{(1)} > f^{(2)}\right).
\end{aligned}
\tag{2.5}
$$

Let the n-dimensional vector $x \in \mathrm{X}$ be a alternative, the m-dimensional vector $y \in \mathrm{Y}$ be an uncertain factor, and $y(\cdot) \in \mathrm{Y}^{\mathrm{X}}$ be a counteralternative, where Y^{X} denotes the set of all m-dimensional vector functions $y(x)$ with the domain of definition X and the codomain Y. The analysis below will be confined to the counteralternatives $y(\cdot): \mathrm{Y} \to \mathrm{X}$ continuous on X.

Definition 2.1. Consider the N-criteria choice problem $\Gamma = \langle \mathrm{Y}, f(x, y) \rangle$ with a fixed alternative $x^* \in \mathrm{X}$. An uncertainty $y_S \in \mathrm{Y}$ is said to be Slater-minimal in the problem Γ if $f(x^*, y) \not< f(x^*, y_S)$ for all $\forall y \in \mathrm{Y}$. An uncertainty $y_P \in \mathrm{Y}$ is said to be Pareto-minimal in the problem Γ if $f(x^*, y) \not\leq f(x^*, y_P)$ for $\forall y \in \mathrm{Y}$.

Consider the N-criteria choice problem $\Gamma(x) = \left\langle \mathrm{Y}^{\mathrm{X}}, f(x, y) \right\rangle$ defined $\forall x \in \mathrm{X}$. A counteralternative $y_S(x) \in \mathrm{Y}^{\mathrm{X}}$ is said to be *Slater-minimal* if for each $x \in \mathrm{X}$, $f(x, y) \not< f(x, y_S(x))$ $\forall y \in \mathrm{Y}$. A counteralternative

$y_P(x) \in \mathrm{Y}^{\mathrm{X}}$ is said to be *Pareto-minimal* if for each $x \in \mathrm{X}$, $f(x, y) \not\leq f(x, y_P(x)) \ \forall y \in \mathrm{Y}$.

Proposition 2.1. Consider the multicriteria choice problem $\Gamma(x^*) = \langle \mathrm{Y}, f(x^*, y) \rangle$.

1) If the set Y is compact, and the function $f(x^*, y)$ is continuous on Y, then the set Y_S of all Slater-minimal uncertainties y_S is non-empty and compact [164].

2) The uncertainty $y_S \in \mathrm{Y}$ given by

$$\min_{y \in \mathrm{Y}} \sum_{i \in \square} \alpha_i f_i(x^*, y) = \sum_{i \in \square} \alpha_i f_i(x^*, y_S) \tag{2.6}$$

$\forall \alpha_i = const \geq 0$, where $\sum\limits_{i \in \square} \alpha_i > 0 \ (i \in \square)$, is Slater-minimal in the problem $\Gamma(x^*)$ [275].

3) The uncertainty $y_P \in \mathrm{Y}$ given by

$$\min_{y \in \mathrm{Y}} \sum_{i \in \square} \alpha_i f_i(x^*, y) = \sum_{i \in \square} \alpha_i f_i(x^*, y_P) \tag{2.7}$$

$\forall \alpha_i = const > 0 \ (i \in \square)$ is Pareto-maximal in the problem $\Gamma(x^*)$ [162, 275].

4) Due to (2.6), the sets of Slater-minimal y_S and Pareto-minimal y_P uncertainties in the problem $\Gamma(x^*)$ satisfy the relation $\mathrm{Y}_S \supseteq \mathrm{Y}_P$.

2.4.1.1 Nash Equilibrium in the Noncooperative N-Player Game

Consider a noncooperative N-player game of the form

$$\langle \square, \{X_i\}_{i \in N}, Y, \{f_i(x, y)\}_{i \in N} \rangle, \tag{2.8}$$

where:

$\square = \{1, \ldots, N\}$ denotes the set of players,

$X_i \subseteq R^{n_i}$ is the set of admissible strategies x_i of player i, and

$Y \subseteq R^{m_i}$ is the set of strategic uncertainties y.

In the game (2.4), all players independently and simultaneously choose their strategies x_i without creating coalitions. As a result, a strategy profile $x = (x_1, \ldots, x_N) \in \prod_{i \in N} X_i$ is formed in this game. An uncertainty $y \in Y$ is realized independently of the players' strategies. For each player $i \in \square$, a payoff function $f_i(x, y)$ is defined on the pairs $(x, y) \in X \times Y$. Each player $i \in \square$ seeks to maximize his (its) payoff $f_i(x, y)$ using an appropriately chosen strategy $x_i \in X_i$. Note that the players expect any (a priori unknown) realization of the uncertainty $y \in Y$.

A Nash equilibrium $x^e = (x_1^e, \ldots, x_N^e) \in X$ was defined in [[275]], and its positive and negative properties were explored. As is known, a Nash equilibrium $x^e = (x_1^e, \ldots, x_N^e) \in X$ of the noncooperative game (2.8) is stable to unilateral deviations of players and satisfies individual rationality [[275]]. Several existence theorems in pure and mixed strategies were established in [275]. In particular, the set of Nash equilibria is internally unstable and improvable; unlike the saddle point, such equilibria are neither interchangeable nor equivalent [[275]]. A modification of this concept, the Slater-optimal Nash equilibrium, was studied in [[275]]. Using these auxiliary results, we introduce the following equilibrium.

Definition 2.2. A strategy profile $x^B = (x_1^B, \ldots, x_N^B) \in X$ is called a Berge equilibrium [269] in the game (2.8) if $\max_{x \in X} f_i(x \| x_i^B) = f_i(x^B)$ $(i \in \square)$, where $(x \| x_i^B) = (x_1, \ldots, x_{i-1}, x_i^B, x_{i+1}, \ldots, x_N)$.

The Berge equilibrium of the noncooperative game (2.8) with $\square = \{1,2\}$ will coincide with the Nash equilibrium if the players exchange their payoff functions and choose their strategies based on the latter concept; see [269]. This fact, together with the existence theorem of Nash equilibrium [[275]], proves the existence of a Berge equilibrium in the game (2.8) with $\square = \{1,2\}$.

Next, we define the concept of Pareto–optimal Nash equilibrium in the game (2.8) as a strategy profile $x^* \in \mathrm{X}$ such that:

$x^* \in \mathrm{X}$ is a Berge equilibrium in the game (2.8), i.e.,

$$\max_{x\in \mathrm{X}} f_i(x \| x_i^B) = f_i(x^B) \ (i \in \square),$$

and $x^* \in \mathrm{X}$ is a Pareto-maximal alternative in the *N*-criteria choice problem

$$\left\langle \mathrm{X}^B, \{f_i(x)\}_{i\in\urcorner} \right\rangle,$$

i.e., the system of inequalities $f_i(x) \geq f_i(x^*)$ $(i \in \square)$, with at least one strict inequality, is inconsistent [269].

2.4.2. Slater-Guaranteed Balanced Berge Equilibrium of the Complex Metasystem

Using the auxiliary results from subsection 2.4.1 and the guaranteed solution [275] (see the proof of existence in [275]), we introduce the concept of balanced Berge equilibrium.

Definition 2.3. A pair $(\tilde{x}^B, \tilde{f}^S) \in \mathrm{X} \times \square^N$ is called *a Slater-guaranteed balanced Berge equilibrium* [269] in the game (2.8) if there exists an uncertainty $y_S \in \mathrm{Y}$ such that:

1) The strategy profile x^B is a Berge equilibrium in the game

$$\left\langle \mathbb{N}, \{X_i\}_{i \in \mathbb{N}}, \{f_i(x, y_S)\}_{i \in \mathbb{N}} \right\rangle, \tag{2.9}$$

which is obtained from (2.8) with $y = y_S$, i.e., by Definition 2.2,

$$\max_{x \in X} f_i(x \| x_i^B, y_S) = f_i(x^B, y_S) \ (i \in \mathbb{N}). \tag{2.10}$$

2) The uncertainty y_S is a Slater-minimal alternative in the N-criteria choice problem

$$\left\langle Y, \{f_i(x^B, y)\}_{i \in \mathbb{N}} \right\rangle, \tag{2.11}$$

which is obtained from (2.8) with $x = x^B$, i.e., by Definition 2.1,

$$f(x^B, y) \not< f(x^B, y_S) \ \ \forall y \in Y. \tag{2.12}$$

3) The pair $(\tilde{x}^B, \tilde{f}^S)$ is Slater-maximal in the N-criteria choice problem

$$\left\langle \{x^B, y_S\}, \{f_i(x, y)\}_{i \in \mathbb{N}} \right\rangle, \tag{2.13}$$

where each element (x^B, y_S) of the set $\{x^B, y_S\}$ simultaneously satisfies (2.10) and (2.12), i.e.,

$$\tilde{f}^S = f(\tilde{x}^B, \tilde{y}_S) \not< f(x, y) \ \ \forall (x, y) \in \{x^B, y_S\}. \tag{2.14}$$

Accordingly, the Berge equilibrium x^B is called Slater-guaranteeing in the game (2.8), and $\tilde{f}^S$ is called the guaranteed vector payoff (the vector guarantee, or the guaranteed solution) [275].

This solution of the noncooperative game under uncertainty has the following *advantages*:

1) Using their strategies from the profile $\tilde{x}^B$, the players obtain the vector guarantee $\tilde{f}^S$ since, due to (2.12), for $x^B = \tilde{x}^B$ the components of the vector $f_i(\tilde{x}^B, y)(i \in \square)$ cannot be simultaneously smaller than those of $f_i(\tilde{x}^B, \tilde{y}_S)(i \in \square)$. In addition, by (2.14), this guarantee is Slater-maximal among all other guarantees $f(x^B, y_S)$ achieved on any pairs (x^B, y_S) under conditions 1 and 2 of Definition 2.3.
2) The equilibrium $(\tilde{x}^B, \tilde{f}^S)$ is defined under the worst-case (maximally counteracting) uncertainty, i.e., rests on the principle of guaranteed result [[275]].
3) This concept is quite general and incorporates the basic concepts of game theory and multicriteria choice as special cases. Moreover, it can be equipped with Pareto, Borwein, Joffrion, and A-optimality [[275]]. The connection between such solutions was established in [[244]].
4) The concept of Slater-guaranteed equilibrium is adequate for the practical construction and proof of existence [[269]].

The central result of Chapter 2 is the construction of the balanced equilibrium for the three macrosystems: economic, legal, and social. Consider the control structure of the economic macrosystem as a player that can generate or supply dysfunctional processes and uncertainties in the complex metasystem. It chooses strategies $y \in \mathrm{Y}$ and has a payoff function of the form

$$\psi_{econ}(y, x) = -\sum_{i \in \square} \alpha_i f_i(y, x),$$

where $\alpha_i = const \geq 0 (i \in \square) \wedge \sum_{i \in \square} \alpha_i > 0$. The other players are the control structures of the social and legal macrosystems with the payoff functions

$$\psi_{Soc}(y, z, x) = \max\{f_i(y, z_i \| x) - f_i(y, z)(i \in \square), \sum_{j \in \sqcup} f_j(y, x) - \sum_{j \in \lrcorner} f_j(y, z)\}$$

and

$\psi_{leg}(y,z,x) = -\psi_{soc}(y,z,x) = \psi(y,z,x)$, respectively.

Well, player 1 is the control structure of the economic macrosystem, further referred to as *Econ*, with the payoff function $\psi_{econ}(y,x)$. Players 2 and 3 are the control structures of the legal (*Leg*) and social (*Soc*) macrosystems with the payoff functions $\psi_{leg}(y,z,x)$ and $\psi_{soc}(y,z,x)$, respectively.

Let the strategies of players *Soc* and *Leg* be $x \in \mathrm{X}$ and $z \in \mathrm{Z} = \mathrm{X}$, respectively, in the game (2.8). As repeatedly mentioned above, the economic macrosystem determines the specifics of the national legal and social macrosystems and causes transformation processes. Hence, let the strategy of player *Econ* be $y \in \mathrm{Y}$. Consider the auxiliary three-player game

$$\left\langle \{Econ, Leg, Soc\}, \{\mathrm{Y}, \mathrm{Z}, \mathrm{X}\}, \{\psi_i(y,z,x)\}_{i=1,2,3} \right\rangle. \tag{2.15}$$

A Nash equilibrium in the game (2.15) is given by the three equalities

$$\begin{aligned} &\max_{y \in \mathrm{Y}} \psi_{Econ}(y, z^e, x^e) = \psi_{Econ}(y^e, z^e, x^e), \\ &\max_{z \in \mathrm{Z}=\mathrm{X}} \psi_{Leg}(y^e, z, x^e) = \psi_{Leg}(y^e, z^e, x^e), \\ &\max_{x \in \mathrm{X}} \psi_{Soc}(y^e, z^e, x) = \psi_{Soc}(y^e, z^e, x^e). \end{aligned} \tag{2.16}$$

Due to the form of $\psi_i(y,z,x)$ $(i = 1,2,3)$ in the first equality, we obtain $y^e = y_S$, and the pair (z^e, x^e) is a saddle point of the zero-sum two-player game [269]:

$$\left\langle \psi(y_S, z, x) = \psi_{Soc} = (y_S, z, x), \mathrm{Z} = \mathrm{X}, \mathrm{X} \right\rangle.$$

Recall that if there exists a saddle point in the zero-sum two-player game, then the minimal strategy is a Pareto-maximal Berge equilibrium in the noncooperative game [269]. Therefore, if the game (2.15) has a Nash equilibrium, then $(z^e, f^S = f(y^e, z^e, x^e))$ is the Slater-guaranteed balanced

Berge equilibrium under the nonmandatory requirement (2.13) of Definition 2.3.

The balanced equilibrium under consideration has a negative property: by condition 1 of Definition 2.3, a strategy profile $\tilde{x}^B \in \mathrm{X}$ is a Berge equilibrium if

$$\max_{x \in \mathrm{X}} f_i(\tilde{x} \| x_i^B, y_S) = f_i(\tilde{x}^B, y_S), \tag{2.17}$$

where the uncertainty is fixed. However, according to the problem statement, the uncertainty y takes arbitrary values from the set Y. The possibility of a particular realization y_S is minimal, and equalities (2.17) do not necessarily hold for other $y \neq y_S$. If $y \in \mathrm{Y}, y \neq y_S$, is realized in the game (2.8), Berge equilibrium actually vanishes: the strategy profile x^B provides the vector guarantee $\tilde{f}^S = f(\tilde{x}^B, \tilde{y}_S)$ only if all players follow their strategies from x^B without any deviations.

This negative property can be eliminated by adopting the guaranteed Berge equilibrium as a solution under uncertainty; see [269] for definition and proof of existence.

As an application and illustrative example of Berge equilibrium, consider a model of family relations in three-person families to analyze the factors affecting matrimonial relations in the modern world.

2.5. Example: Models of Family Relations Based on Berge and Nash Equilibria in Three-Person Families

One of the administrative functions of the state in the social sphere is to strengthen and support the family institution as an important structural component in the system of public relations. The transformation of the family in recent decades has renewed almost all social institutions. Note that the transformation of the family is directly related to the economic, social, and legal aspects of the changes that have taken place. In turn, transformations of family relations directly affect the socio-economic system as a whole and the public administration of sociodemographic processes [252].

There are different theoretical and methodological approaches to the study and administration of family relations [168]. They are often developed within the humanities; such studies are much less common in the natural sciences. As expected, an interdisciplinary approach proposed in this book will yield very interesting results in family relations research [252].

As stated earlier, the family is a fundamental structural element of private and public life [175]. Several global trends characterize the family institution in modern Russia:

1) Nuclearization (in nuclear families, not the desire for procreation but the relationship between spouses is crucial) [175, 176].

2) A higher number of divorces with respect to the number of marriages and an increased number of incomplete families.

Table 2.1. Divorces vs. marriages

Year	Divorces		Marriages	
	Absolute number	Relative rate per 100 people	Absolute number	Relative rate per 100 people
2014	693 730	4.7	1 225 985	8.4
2015	611 646	4.2	1 161 068	7.9
2016	608 336	4.1	985 836	6.7

Source: Federal State Statistics Service http://www.gks.ru/wps/wcm/connect/rosstat_main/rosstat/ru/statistics/population/demography/#.

As follows from Table 2.1, the increased number of divorces with respect to the number of marriages is not due to a higher number of divorces: in 2016, there were 608.3 thousand divorces, which is slightly below the level of 2015 (611.6 thousand). According to the Federal State Statistics Service, there was a significant drop in marriages in 2016: from 1161.1 thousand (2015) to 985.8 thousand (2016), only 84.8% of the previous year. Marriage preservation also declined. In 2016, the number of divorces was 61.7% of the total number of marriages; in 2015, 52.7%. For details, see [252].

According to the 2010 All-Russian Population Census (as refined on 2014), the number of single-parent families in the structure of family cells with children below the age of 18 is 5 742 017, constituting 48.6% of the total number of married couples with children; see Table 2.2 and [252].

3) Lower reproduction. Compared to 2015, the total fertility rate (the number of births per woman) significantly decreased in 2016: by

0.015 (51 850 children). The birth rate decreased accordingly; see Table 2.3 and [252].

Table 2.2. Structure of family cells

Russia	Number of families
Families with children below the age of 18	17 555 160
including:	
married couples with children	11 813 143
single mother with children	5 087 048
single father with children	654 969
incomplete family cells	5 742 017

Source: Federal State Statistics Service http://www.gks.ru/wps/wcm/connect/rosstat_main/rosstat/ru/statistics/population/motherhood/#.

Table 2.3. Births and total fertility rate

Year	Total fertility rate	Births
2015	1.777	1 940 579
2016	1.762	1 888 729

Source: Federal State Statistics Service http://www.gks.ru/wps/wcm/connect/rosstat_main/rosstat/ru/statistics/population/demography/#.

4) The reduced role of exogenous ethical and public factors. Significant signs of the modern transformation of family relations are violating moral family values and changing the importance of intrafamily regulators of behavior after marriage, particularly the degradation of relations between parents and children and between spouses [7].

The Russian family has qualitative features caused by the environment: under the growing economic inequality, the stratification of the population, and gradual changes in the status of previously established social groups, the processes of transformation of the family institution in Russia show dysfunctionality and bifurcations. The idea of returning to traditional values becomes popular among Russian experts and researchers of family relations.

According to N. Rimashevskaya [175], there are three main sociodemographic models of the family: "... patriarchal, or traditional; child-centered, or modern; spousal, or postmodern. In modern society, they are present simultaneously, each with a particular weight (50%, 40%, and 10%, respectively). In dynamics, the first model gradually loses its advantage, while the range of the third, on the contrary, expands. The socio-economic reforms led to radical changes in the functions and role of the family, its life cycles, and intrafamily relations." In the course of more than twenty-five years of research, Rimashevskaya and her followers identified the factors characterizing the change in the family institution: "The sovereignty of the family and its role in the development of society are increasing; the economic function of the family has expanded significantly; other spheres of its activity have weakened; the woman's "retreat" in the private sphere has caused persistent conflicts within the family, destabilization, and the development of domestic violence."

In turn, matrimonial, self-preserving, and reproductive relations formed in the family at all levels of society's life affect the demographic and socio-economic development of the country. Therefore, changes in family relations are usually considered using a systematic approach: from the perspective of macroeconomics, social relations, and law development. When the need arises to administer sociodemographic processes, the state should identify the mechanisms operating at the family level: the household life of the population is carried out within family structures of various forms and models. The social mechanisms operating at the microlevel, manifested in the family, are reflected at the macrolevel in the quantity, quality, and dynamic trends of human potential. In the social sphere, the public administration of the family's internal mechanisms allows controlling (at least, influencing) the upbringing and demographic reproduction processes. Thereby, the state tries to solve the problems of sociodemographic and economic development. Many researchers and experts emphasize that the present-stage trends lead to the transformation of family structures, naturally changing over time, and the corresponding transformation of society.

F. Engels [53-55] analyzed the history of the origin and development of marriage and the family and showed their prospects. He wrote that the family has an active origin; it never remains unchanged but passes from lower to higher forms as society develops from lower to higher stages. He indicated the three main forms of marriage that generally correspond to the three main stages of human development: wildness (group marriage), barbarism (pair marriage), and civilization (monogamy, complemented by adultery and prostitution). The dominance of men over female slaves and polygamy lies between paired marriage and monogamy. For details, see the book [53].

Note that for tens of thousands of years, the evolution of society took place within diverse forms of the polygamous family. Historians, ethnographers, and archaeologists recorded the disintegration of polygamous clan communities and the formation of monogamous patriarchal families in the written sources that survived our time. For resolving "the riddle of polygamy" (or "the riddle of monogamy"), many socio-humanitarian studies were carried out, and various explanations were proposed. For many decades of analyzing polygyny, researchers of family relations have failed to answer why part of the population abandoned the once very widespread polygamy long before the appearance of socio-economic legal, moral, cultural, and religious factors in favor of monogamy. After all, from the perspective of evolution and natural selection, polygamy is the optimal form of intergender relations that maximizes the reproductive success of parents.

In an international study of 2017—see [184]—it was shown that the necessary and sufficient condition for the existence and development of polygamy is a high level of resource provision for a man to support more than one wife and children. The authors of a new complex interdisciplinary research based on a game-theoretic approach [177] constructed a mathematical model explaining why the population living in European countries abandoned polygamy. Moreover, they tested the model's accuracy on an example of the Kipsig agrarian and pastoralist people (Kenya). The new formal mathematical model of family relations simultaneously resolves the riddle of polygyny and hypothesized the presence of other human development mechanisms in society, which are of higher level and power than the main mechanism of evolution (natural selection). In the cited study, polygyny was defined as a form of long-term relations between men and women in which a man has long-term unions simultaneously with two more women, and children from each union inherit through the male line.

When analyzing the constructed model of family relations, the authors traditionally used the concept of Nash equilibrium [153-156]. (This is a point of contact of players' interests where each player will benefit nothing by a unilateral deviation, i.e., changing his (its) strategy if the other players do not change theirs). For both men and women, the optimal strategy to win the game was defined as a marriage choice that would maximize the expected reproductive success. The model covered two types of inherited wealth: competing and non-competing. The second type of wealth, e.g., the parents' gene pool, is somehow inherited by all children. The first type, e.g., money or land, was traditionally not divided among all and therefore passed on to one or a narrow group of heirs. According to the authors, competing wealth becomes the main factor in choosing the form of union between a man and a woman. If they both strive to maximize the expected reproductive success, they agree to choose monogamy according to the game solution. In other words, if there is no (or not enough) competing wealth in the family, the evolution of this family structure is determined by natural selection against the background of polygamy. If competing wealth is in abundance (especially among the rich minority of the population, whom the poor majority dreams to join), then the factors of biological evolution are inferior to those of well-being, and society tends to monogamy. Thus, the cited researchers presented an experimentally confirmed mathematical explanation for the riddle of polygyny and, most importantly, proved the presence of higher-level and more powerful mechanisms of civilization development than natural selection.

The state's viability is determined, among other things, by the demographic factor and the new forms of the monogamous family, which are not always progressive. The family institution remains the main reproduction mechanism. Therefore, special attention in this book will be paid to the moral foundations of family relations. G. Hegel [78] wrote that the family is a natural society whose members are bound by love and trust; see [175, 201]. The family institution performs such socially significant functions as reproduction and regulation; historically, property, social experience, and moral standards are inherited through the family mechanism. The GR is one of the most ancient, specific, and widespread moral generalizations expressing the experience accumulated by mankind. Hence, this rule is one of the main moral regulators of family relations.

Let us construct a formal mathematical *model of family relations based on Berge equilibrium*, which reveals the Golden Rule of ethics and demonstrates the mechanisms of traditional family values. First, consider a model of family relations based on the widely used concept of Nash equilibrium.

Nowadays, the family is performing its main social functions worse and worse, transferring them to other social institutions [175, 201] with the development of social services, health care, and the pension system. The family's social functions include reproduction, upbringing, communication, education, emotion, households, economics, etc. [7]. Most of the listed functions belong to moral categories that should be reproduced in the family from generation to generation. So how does the transformation of intrafamily relations take place? For example, the main function of the family is reproduction and upbringing. It still holds, but the number of children varies between 1 and 2, and their upbringing is increasingly delegated to professional educators, preschool institutions, and schools. A woman raising children of preschool age is often forced to work because of increasing poverty; in many cases, this transforms the relations between her, her children, and her husband. The employment rate of women aged 20-49 with at least one preschool child is growing; see Table 2.4 and [175, 176, 252].

Table 2.4. The employment rate of women aged 20-49 with at least one preschool child (in percentage)

Category of women	Year		
	2014	2015	2016
Women with at least one preschool child (aged 0–6)	64.0	64.0	64.9
including those with at least one child aged:			
0–2	47.7	47.1	47.2
3–6	78.5	77.6	77.8

Source: Federal State Statistics Service http://www.gks.ru/wps/wcm/connect/rosstat_main/rosstat/ru/statistics/population/motherhood/#.

At the same time, family functions related to the individualized and selfish behavior of family members gradually become more significant. Many researchers underline that such changes in the family institution are caused by urbanization, industrialization, the prolonged terms of study (the increased level of education, especially for children and women), the development of the pension system, the growth of employment, the emancipation of women, and the global socio-economic processes considered progressive and irreversible. D. Caldwell [36] mentioned all these factors back in 1976; also, see [175, 201].

How should family members behave to each other? What are the grounds of intrafamily relations? We believe that the positive development and stability of family relations are based on moral categories inherent in each family member to some degree [252].

Consider a common family structure consisting of three persons: father (*man*), mother (*woman*), and their child (*kid*). Let all family members make independent decisions. We construct a noncooperative three-player game of the form

$$\Gamma_3 = \left\langle \{1,2,3\}, \{\mathrm{X}_i\}_{i=m,w,k} \{f_i(x)\}_{i=m,w,k} \right\rangle,$$

where each family member $i = \{m, w, k\}$ chooses his (her) strategy $x_i \in \mathrm{X}_i \subseteq \mathrm{R}^{n_i}$ to improve his (her) performance $f_i(x = (x_m, x_w, x_k))$, i.e., the payoff $f_i(x)$, in a current strategy profile $x = (x_m, x_w, x_k) \in \mathrm{X}_m \times \mathrm{X}_w \times \mathrm{X}_k = \mathrm{X}$.

In modern decision-making, the concept of Nash equilibrium dominates the other approaches. For this example, it is described by a strategy profile $(x^e = (x_m^e, x_w^e, x_k^e), f^e = (f_m(x^e), f_w(x^e), f_k(x^e))) \in X \times R^3$ such that

$$\begin{cases} f_m(x^e) = \max\limits_{x_m \in X_m} f_m(x_m, x_w^e, x_k^e), \\ f_w(x^e) = \max\limits_{x_w \in X_w} f_w(x_m^e, x_w, x_k^e), \\ f_k(x^e) = \max\limits_{x_k \in X_k} f_k(x_m^e, x_w^e, x_k). \end{cases}$$

In other words, each family member seeks to satisfy his (her) selfish ambitions (improve his (her) performance only), putting the personal interests above the rest. Such selfish behavior of family members, among other factors, transforms the family as a social institution. In fact, the system of three equalities is *a mathematical model of selfish relations in a three-person family* [252].

The antipode of selfishness is altruism, which includes such a moral category as self-sacrifice. It can be negative for family relations. The concept of Berge equilibrium reflects the Golden Rule of ethics only in its positive interpretation: as the desire to act for the benefit of others, the desire to benefit one's neighbor [68]. It is described by a strategy profile $(x^B = (x_m^B, x_w^B, x_k^B), f^B = (f_m(x^B), f_w(x^B), f_k(x^B))) \in X \times R^3$ such that

$$\begin{cases} f_m(x^B) = \max\limits_{x_w, x_k \in X_w \times X_k} f_m(x_m^B, x_w, x_k), \\ f_w(x^B) = \max\limits_{x_m, x_k \in X_m \times X_k} f_w(x_m, x_w^B, x_k), \\ f_k(x^B) = \max\limits_{x_m, x_w \in X_m \times X_w} f_k(x_m, x_w, x_k^B). \end{cases}$$

According to these equalities, the father chooses an appropriate strategy x_m^B to satisfy the interests of the mother and child maximally:

$$\max_{x_m, x_k \in X_m \times X_k} f_w(x_m, x_w^B, x_k) = f_w(x^B),$$

$$\max_{x_m, x_w \in X_m \times X_w} f_k(x_m, x_w, x_k^B) = f_k(x^B).$$

In turn, the mother and child maximize the father's payoff function via appropriately chosen strategies $x_w = x_w^B$ and $x_k = x_k^B$:

$$\max_{x_w, x_k \in X_w \times X_k} f_m(x_m^B, x_w, x_k) = f_m(x^B).$$

The mother's behavior is as follows: by maximizing the performance of the father and child through the choice of x_w^B, thanks to their actions, she receives the greatest satisfaction of her interests. The child raised on the parents' example, who maximize his payoff function:

$$\max_{x_m, x_w \in X_m \times X_w} f_k(x_m, x_w, x_k^B) = f_k(x^B),$$

seeks to choose x_k^B so that:

$$\max_{x_w, x_k \in X_w \times X_k} f_m(x_m^B, x_w, x_k) = f_m(x^B),$$

$$\max_{x_m, x_k \in X_m \times X_k} f_w(x_m, x_w^B, x_k) = f_w(x^B).$$

Consequently, in the Berge equilibrium-based model of family relations, each of the three family members improves the performance of the other two, experiencing the same effect on him(her)self. This model clearly illustrates the Golden Rule of ethics, characteristic of traditional family values [252].

In [269, 270], the internal instability of the set of Berge equilibria was discovered. To eliminate this negative property, we propose a method for designing a Pareto-maximal Berge equilibrium; see Chapter 5. The method reduces to finding the saddle point of an auxiliary zero-sum two-player game constructed from the original noncooperative one. The existence of a Berge equilibrium in mixed strategies is also established under standard assumptions of mathematical game theory (the compact strategy sets and continuous payoff functions of players). The static game is considered.

Let us return to the public administration of sociodemographic processes. A priority direction of current social policy is supporting the family, motherhood, and childhood [174]. The set of measures used by the adjuster (the Government of the Russian Federation) in the social sphere is represented by several documents: the Concept of Long-Term Socio-Economic Development of the Russian Federation up to 2020; The Concept of Demographic Development of the Russian Federation up to 2025; The National Action Strategy in the Interests of Children for 2017-2022; The Concept of Family Policy in the Russian Federation up to 2025; other regulatory legal acts of ministries and departments in the social sphere. The social policy of the state, aimed at supporting families with children, implies the development and implementation of state and federal target programs to provide these categories of the population with social state guarantees. The quantitative dynamics of the main minimum social guarantees established in accordance with the legislation of the Russian Federation are presented in Table 2.5; also, see [252].

Table 2.5. The main minimum social guarantees in the Russian Federation (in percentage of the minimum subsistence level on January 1, 2018)

Minimum social guarantees	Year		
	2015	2016	2017
Minimum wage	57.3	59.0	70.1
Child care allowance below the age of 1.5:			
first child	28.6	30.1	31.4
second and subsequent children	57.3	60.1	62.8
Double child care allowance below the age of 3 (the citizens exposed to radiation during the Chernobyl disaster)	57.3	60.1	62.8
Child care allowance (conscripts)	103.7	108.8	113.7
Child care allowance for disabled persons below the age of 18 or child care allowance for persons disabled since childhood (group 1):			
provided to parent (adoptive parent) or guardian (custodian)	52.9	52.3	51.4
provided to other persons	11.5	11.4	11.2
Minimum unemployment compensation	8.2	8.1	7.9
Academic scholarship from state budget:			
higher education	12.9	12.7	13.9
intermediate vocational education	4.7	4.6	5.0

Source: Federal State Statistics Service http://www.gks.ru/free_doc/new_site/population/urov/garan.htm.

Social support for families with children differs by forms (monetary and in-kind; services, benefits, and allowances) and recipients (children, large families, pregnant women, the poor, orphans, and children left without parental care). The major support falls on the monetary form, mainly through benefits and allowances, monthly cash payments and compensations, and the implementation of state target programs. For example, the program "Social support of citizens" (http://programs.gov.ru/Portal/programs/passport/03) includes the subprogram "State support for families with children," consisting of several measures: social programs such as state support on the occasion of pregnancy and childbirth and assistance to citizens with children; monthly benefits and allowances (compensations) for the summer recreation of children; social support to large families; maternity (family) capital. This subprogram is intended to overcome negative demographic trends, stabilize and increase the population size, provide benefits, allowances, and compensations to citizens with children, and improve the latter's health. Such social programs are based on the declarative principle and, to a large extent, depend on the activity of families with children and their awareness in matters of exercising legal rights [252].

Analysis of state programs implemented in the social sphere shows the following:

- Support for families is neither comprehensive nor systemic, differing in fragmentation. Such measures mainly stimulate the birth of a child and support the family until the child reaches the age of 1.5 years.
- There is a serious problem of compensations, benefits, and allowances for families with children: their underdevelopment and nondifferentiation, the poor endowment of the designed and tested payment mechanisms, and numerous benefits of scanty amounts [52].
- The most acute issue is related to the complexity of the legislative sphere, which must ensure the payment of benefits to the population. In Russia, more than 200 regulatory legal acts have been developed for family policy measures at the federal level and more than 2000 regulatory documents at the regional level that relate to family and demographic regulation measures [52]. Benefits and allowances for families with children are differentiated by 190 items [174]. Systematized legislation in the field of family policy is a prerequisite for the stabilization and strengthening of the family institution. This measure would increase the efficiency of administration in the social sphere (family and demographic policy) and the availability of social support measures for families with children [252].

Conclusion

Game theory is a mathematical apparatus for analyzing and developing strategies and making optimal decisions under uncertainty. The application of game-theoretic tools to the socio-economic problems of society allows solving complex strategic problems, in particular, balancing the three macrosystems that are significant from the society's perspective: economic, legal, and social. Chapter 2 has presented *a new concept of equilibrium for the economic, legal, and social macrosystems* based on Slater-guaranteed balanced Berge equilibrium. This type of equilibrium has been designed and justified. The equilibrium model considers the effect of uncertain factors: the modern economic system has such intrinsic properties as uncertainty, inconsistency, multiple criteria, and incomplete information.

Thus, we have described a new approach to strategic decision-making to solve the integral problem of balancing the three macrosystems mentioned by constructing and justifying Slater-guaranteed balanced Berge equilibrium. This approach contributes to eliminating the problem of population poverty.

Opposing to the neoliberal economic doctrine and supplementing the individual rationality-based Nash equilibrium, Berge equilibrium suggests a way of balancing based on philosophical and moral principles. Some positive and negative properties of Berge equilibrium have been discussed (particularly internal instability). This property is undoubtedly important but not critical: it serves as a driver for the transition from one stage of system operation to another. Moreover, the existence theorem (see Chapter 5) deals with internal instability by incorporating Pareto maximality into the concept of Berge equilibrium. The existence of a Pareto-maximal Berge equilibrium is proved in the case of continuous payoff functions and compact sets of mixed strategies of the players.

As an application of the Berge equilibrium model, Chapter 2 considers the dynamics of family structures and relations affecting the population's life system as well as the current state, prospects, and capabilities of public administration of sociodemographic processes in Russia. Mathematical models of family relations are based on the concepts of Berge and Nash equilibria in a three-person family.

Chapter 3

Modelling Decision Processes in the Social Sphere at the Macrolevel

Introduction

This chapter develops a new scientific approach to improving decision processes in the social sphere at the macrolevel using a hierarchical model of social sphere management and decision-making at each hierarchy level. For this purpose, we construct a multilevel mathematical model for managing the dynamics of complex socio-economic macrosystems under uncertainty (the incomplete and nonidentical structures and volumes of information) at various hierarchy levels. In addition, Chapter 3 proposes a new approach to managing the dynamics of the social sphere using an example of the population's social security and support system. We present a new method for formalizing guaranteed solutions of multicriteria choice problems under interval uncertainty with given limits. The guaranteed solution is based on a modification of Savage's principle of minimax regret with the following pair: the set of social state guarantees for the population and life risks in case of which definite categories of the population exercise their constitutional right to obtain appropriate social guarantees. An existence theorem for the guaranteed solution is proved under standard assumptions of multicriteria choice problems, and a method to find this solution is suggested.

3.1. Systems Analysis of the Transformation of the Population's Social Security and Support System

This section considers an approach to managing the dynamics of complex socio-economic systems under uncertainty, which is understood as the incomplete and (or) nonidentical information (by the structure and volume) at different hierarchy levels. Systems analysis is carried out for the population's social security and support sphere that undergoes current transformations as an integral part of the socio-economic macrosystem. We propose game-theoretic methods and technologies to improve the population's quality of life and eliminate the poverty of its socially unsecured and vulnerable segments.

According to general systems theory [101, 113, 172, 225], socio-economic systems belong to the class of complex dynamic macrosystems composed of interacting and mutually influencing systems and have a pronounced hierarchical structure. For example, the hierarchical structure includes three levels normatively defined by the state power levels. In turn, socio-economic macrosystems are components of society as a whole. In a special case, a complex socio-economic macrosystem consists of social and economic systems that perform definite functions. The economic system—the set of all economic relations realized in society—continuously interacts with the elements of the social system. On the other hand, the social system is also a component of society with a definite structure, human capital, and socio-economic and sociodemographic phenomena.

During the operation of the complex socio-economic macrosystem, management functions are often substituted by social design tools: the subjects and objects of social relations included in this macrosystem begin to perform uncharacteristic functions. In particular, the management of socio-economic processes for improving the population's quality of life and overcoming economic inequality is currently implemented through social engineering tools instead of developing industrial potential aimed at economic growth. In this case, social design mechanisms underlie the management of socio-economic processes, thereby replacing economic policy tools. As a result, the systems and their elements lose operational balance, and the macrosystem becomes dysfunctional. In the final analysis, dysfunction or nonstationarity [122] expands the poverty zone, increases economic inequality, reduces the amount of social support for the population, and raises social tension.

Note that nonstationarity is often caused by uncertainty, conflict, and external and internal risks. Under these factors, the value of making managerial decisions in the complex socio-economic macrosystem is proportional to the cost of resources for resolving difficult conflicts and critical situations.

Therefore, appropriate tools are needed for describing socio-economic phenomena and processes when constructing models of complex macrosystems that consider various types of internal interaction and the influence of the environment [162]. In this book, socio-economic processes are described using game theory and multicriteria choice.

Game theory is a set of mathematical models and tools for analyzing and developing short- and long-term strategies, e.g., behavioral rules for private socio-economic systems and optimal managerial decisions under conflict and uncertainty at the microanalysis level [163].

Will the above laws, usually applied to the microeconomic level, remain valid for macroanalysis? The answer can be obtained by considering the main trends in the transformation of the social sphere in recent years. The social sphere as a complex socio-economic macrosystem consists of several sectors vital for the population. However, from the 1990s to the present time, strategic decisions related to the social sphere have been implementing *the transition from the universal social security principles to the European social security system, which provides for state support only for definite categories of the population.* Therefore, we study the population's social security and support system and the denationalization processes of social sectors in detail.

In recent years, the amount of budgetary resources allocated to the population's social security and support system to improve the quality of life of low-income and socially unsecured and vulnerable citizens has been steadily decreasing. When implementing the social policy at the federal, regional, and municipal levels, the emphasis is shifted towards reducing the amount of targeted revenues. With a decrease in the amount of federal budgetary funding, state institutions are being squeezed out of the social sphere through their reorganization into autonomous institutions, which are commercial structures. In parallel, a system of socially oriented non-profit organizations is being formed through presidential grants. At the moment, such organizations have several funding sources: the contract system (targeted funds of the federal budget, i.e., tenders for the subjects of socially oriented non-profit organizations), the provision of paid social services to the population, and donation agreements from organizations of the corporate sector of the economy and individuals. *Thus, the social sphere undergoes a gradual denationalization.*

Instead of an organized and rigidly structured hierarchical system with a single coordinating Center (Principal), there are many separate organizations of various types and legal forms of ownership, making decisions and acting in the market of social services and products independently of each other. The former social security and support system of the population is being transformed into a semi-structured, non-stationary, and decentralized system based on the principle of individual rationality. Also, note that with the systematic application of social design tools, the mass media limit and distort the information field about the social reforms implemented by the state: pensions, social support for low-income citizens, and other social security issues.

The nonstationarity of the complex socio-economic macrosystem is determined by its inherent dynamism and uncertainty [122]. Uncertainty is understood as incomplete and (or) inaccurate information about the conditions for implementing decisions in socio-economic systems at different hierarchy levels [258, 262].

When considering decision problems in complex socio-economic macrosystems, game theory is used to construct economic-mathematical models of the corresponding decision processes under certain assumptions about the exogenous and endogenous variables, analyze these macrosystems, and design their parameters and control actions [258, 262].

Modelling complex socio-economic macrosystems as integral sets of interconnected and interacting social and economic institutions is complicated by the need for realistic solutions, which increases the model's dimension due to the refinement of its parameters. Therefore, it is necessary to decompose the model and develop a hierarchy of interconnected mathematical models, especially since the structure of controlled systems is institutionally determined by three levels of the hierarchy [258].

Management of socio-economic macrosystems poses the following problems:

1) development of stabilizing controls,
2) the consistency of decision criteria in the socio-economic macrosystem,
3) the consistency of hierarchical interaction,
4) the need to consider the factors of uncertainty and the corresponding risks.

The stable operation of such macrosystems is determined by the dynamic property of controllability and includes several requirements:

1) an almost monotonic increase of some performance criteria of the system (the standard of living, income level, employment rate, the level of savings of the population, etc.),
2) the asymptotic stability (stabilizability) of the macrosystem,
3) the harmonization of all hierarchy levels.

Below, we present a hierarchical problem statement and possible solution methods on an example of the population's social security and support system [258].

3.2. A Multilevel Dynamic Model for Managing the Population's Social Security and Support System

The current state of control theory, management, and game theory allows studying complex socio-economic non-stationary macrosystems. In the case of large-dimension models, analytical methods are combined with numerical modeling, and model decomposition is applied. Due to the above-mentioned attributes of complex systems (openness, hierarchy, nonlinearity, dynamism, etc.), nonlinear analysis, differential games, and rational control methods can be used. Models of hierarchical interaction [144] are applied jointly with the harmonization of interests of all parties to eliminate conflicts [112].

Macroeconomic models are a formalized description of various social and economic phenomena and processes for identifying the relationships between them [168]. Such a generalized model helps to determine a set of alternative control methods for the dynamics of a complex socio-economic macrosystem. Note that even rough models can be useful for decision-making if they yield positive results and (or) compensate for possible negative consequences of management.

Consider *a model of a hierarchical three-level socio-economic system* (the federal, regional, and municipal levels of state power) [258].

The policy in the social sphere is implemented by the Ministry of Labor and Social Security of the Russian Federation (hereinafter referred to as the Ministry of Labor). According to the Decree of the Government of the Russian Federation No. 610 of June 19, 2012, "On Approval of the Statute on the Ministry of Labor and Social Security of the Russian Federation," the Ministry of Labor institutionally designs and implements policy and normative and legal regulation in the following fields: demography, labor, living standards and incomes, wages, and pensions, including non-state pensions; social insurance (except for compulsory medical insurance), including tariffs on insurance premiums; labor conditions and safety; social partnership and labor relations; employment and unemployment; labor migration; alternative civil service and state civil service; social security of the population, including social security of families, women and children, elderly citizens and veterans, and citizens affected by emergencies; guardianship and trusteeship for adult citizens that are partially or completely incapable; social services for the population; prosthetic and orthopedic care, rehabilitation of disabled people, and medical and social expertise; the development, implementation, and advisory and methodological support of anti-corruption measures in organizations, including monitoring; methodological measures for developing municipal services; state property management and public services in the established area of activity [258].

Along with these functions, the Ministry of Labor determines the activities of regional and municipal authorities of the corresponding social security levels, social support centers, and institutions and organizations operating in the social sphere [258].

An important goal of public administration in the social sphere is to overcome economic inequality (eliminate poverty imbalance) by increasing the incomes of the poor and socially unsecured and vulnerable population. Since the mid-2000s, new organizational and legal mechanisms began to be adopted into the population's social security practice. They were expressed by state target programs containing a list of social services (products) provided to the population. The goals, tasks, and target indicators were formulated for each target program; their values were determined, and an implementation plan was drawn up [124].

A significant list of budgetary social support programs for certain categories of citizens (disabled people, large families, children left without parental care, etc.) was adopted at the regional level. Note that due to the growing debt burden of different regions, these programs were not properly funded and, therefore, not fully implemented [258].

3.2.1. An Economic-Mathematical Dynamic Model of the Population's Social Security and Support System

In the socio-economic system under consideration, the Ministry of Labor selects a list of different social services (products) $P_1, P_2, \ldots, P_M$ provided to the population. The social services (products) of the Program must be provided during a given period and in given amounts $P_j^*(t)(j=1,\ldots,M)$. At a time instant t, the Program is characterized by a system of some indicators $r_j(t)=P_j(t)/P_j^*(t)$, and the Program's performance (the effectiveness of providing service j) during a certain period $[0,T]$ can be assessed by $\overline{r}_j = \min_{t\in[0,T]} r_j(t)$. Suppose that the better the Ministry of Labor implements the Program, the higher value the functional

$$J^{Gov}(P) = \min_j \overline{r}_j = \min_j \min_i P_j(t) / P_j^*(t) \quad (3.1)$$

will have in the variables $P = (P_1(t), ..., P_M(t))$; for details, see [256, 258].

According to this formula, we maximize the share of social services (products) provided in the GDP structure. Recall that the complex socio-economic macrosystem is characterized by a hierarchical structure and the subordination of levels.

Assume that the corresponding Centers (Principals) operate in the complex socio-economic macrosystem under consideration. The Principals are understood as regional authorities, e.g., regional ministries and (or) departments of the population's social security that manage the social sphere. They coordinate the activities of Organizations, i.e., commercial and non-commercial structures of any organizational and legal form that operate in the social sphere at the regional level.

The Principals have the following tasks:

1) the allocation of funds from the federal and regional budgets (state investments) to the fixed assets $U_i (i = 1, ..., N_i)$ of Organizations operating in the social sphere;
2) the allocation of public funds to the wages $Q_i(t)(i = 1, ..., N_i)$ of social workers.

The Principal independently develops the Program $P_j^{i^*}(t)(i = 1, ..., N; j = 1, ..., M)$ of social services provided to the population. (Also, the Principal may receive the Program from the upper hierarchy level).

The amount of federal subsidies received depends on the amount of services provided. Hence, Principal *i* seeks to maximize the functional

$$J_i^{Cen}[U, Q] = \min_j \min_i P_j^i(t) / P_j^{i^*}(t)(i = 1, ...N_i). \quad (3.2)$$

in the variables $U = (U_1(t), ..., U_{N_i}(t))$ and $Q = (Q_1(t), ..., Q_{N_i}(t))$; see [256].

To cover a wider class of problems, let the goals of Principal *i* be described by some functional depending on the results of the social activities of the regional Organizations [256]:

$$I_i^{Cen}[U,Q] = I_i^{Cen}(J_1^{Cen}(U,Q),\dots,J_{N_i}^{Cen}(U,Q)). \tag{3.3}$$

The budgetary policy of the state, particularly the allocations to social obligations, is carried out by the Ministry of Finance of the Russian Federation (hereinafter referred to as the Ministry of Finance). Let $z(t)$ denote the amount of funding from the federal budget (monetary resource) allocated by the Ministry of Finance for implementing the social policy at a time instant *t*. The following components can be treated as the budget revenues in the social sphere.

1. The unit-time tax on the fixed assets of Organization *k* in region *i*, further denoted by $x_{ik}(t)$. Organization $x_{ik}(t)$ deducts the amount $\lambda_x x_{ik}$ to the Ministry of Finance through the tax system [256, 258]. In other words, the Ministry of Finance receives the amount

$$z_x^{(t)} = \lambda_x \sum_{i=1}^{N} \sum_{k=1}^{N_i} x_{ik}(t). \tag{3.4}$$

2. The value added tax (VAT) [256, 258]. Assume that Organization (i,k) provides social services (products) $\{P_1^{ik}(t),\dots,P_M^{ik}(t)\}$ in unit time. Let c_j be the price of service (product) $P_j^{ik}(t)$, and c_j^* be the amount deducted to the state as a tax. Then Organization (i,k) obtains the amount

$$\sum_{j=1}^{M} \left(c_j - c_j^*\right) P_j^{ik}(t). \tag{3.5}$$

Hence, all Organizations pay the total tax

$$z_p^t = \sum_{i=1}^{N} \sum_{k=1}^{N_i} \sum_{j=1}^{M} c_j^* P_j^{ik}(t) = \sum_{j=1}^{M} c_j^* P_j(t), \qquad (3.6)$$

where P_j is the total service (total product) j.

Due to the negative transformation processes in the economic system and the growing social burden of recent years, the revenues of the budgets of all levels have decreased. Besides subsidies for leveling the budgetary load of the regions and compensating the expenses on social obligations partially, the Ministry of Finance provides budgetary loans for regions at some interest. Therefore, the Ministry of Finance also obtains a percentage of budgetary loans as its income. Let $y_i(t)$ be the amount provided to Principal i on loan. Then it pays an amount $\lambda_{y_i} y_i(t)(\lambda = const)$ per unit of time. In this case, the Ministry of Finance obtains the amount

$$z_y(t) = \sum_{i=1}^{M} y_i(t)\lambda_{y_i} \qquad (3.7)$$

in the form of a percentage of the loan per unit of time; see [[256], [258]].

Due to the social decision practice established in recent decades, some Organizations in the social sphere, if institutionally allowed to, are also forced to take loans. Let $y_{ik}(t)$ be the loan provided to the Organization at an interest rate $\lambda_{y_{ik}}$. Then the state, represented by the Ministry of Finance, obtains the following amount per unit of time:

$$z_{yy} = \sum_{i=1}^{N} \sum_{k=1}^{N_i} \lambda_{y_{ik}} y_{ik}(t). \qquad (3.8)$$

The coefficients λ_{y_i} and $\lambda_{y_{ik}}$ are adjusted by the Ministry of Finance.

Assume that the budget revenues are spent on the population's social security and support as follows:

1) Expenses on social obligations to the population (non-production expenses) per unit of time, denoted by $R(t)$, are fixed functions of time.
2) Budgetary subsidies allocated to the social sphere, denoted by $R_u(t)$, are obtained by summing $U_i(t)$ up:

$$R_u(t) = \sum_{i=1}^{N} U(t). \tag{3.9}$$

3) The wages of social workers are given by

$$Q(t) = \sum_{i=1}^{N} Q_i(t); \tag{3.10}$$

They are bounded above by the amount of social services (products) provided to the population:

$$Q(t) \leq \sum_{j} c_j P_j(t), \tag{3.11}$$

where summation is performed over all j corresponding to the list of social services (products) [[256], [258]].

4) The total amount of budgetary loans issued to the Principals, $R_y(t)$, consists of the loans for social activities:

$$R_y(t) = \sum_{i=1}^{N} v_i(t). \tag{3.12}$$

5) The total amount of loans to the Organizations is given by

$$R_{yy}(t) = \sum_{i=1}^{N} \sum_{k=1}^{N_i} v_{ik}(t). \tag{3.13}$$

Assume that the maximum amount of loans is limited by the state:

$$0 \le v_i(t) \le v_i^+(t, y_i), \tag{3.14}$$

$$0 \le v_{ik}(t) \le v_{ik}^+(t, y_{ik}, x_{ik}, P_j^{ik}). \tag{3.15}$$

In the general and simplified statements, the Ministry of Finance's control action therefore depends on the budgetary loans of all Principals and the activities of all Organizations.

Besides the constraints (3.14) and (3.15) on the current loans, additional restrictions on the total amount of the borrower's loan should be introduced to prevent the growth of the total credit indebtedness of the regions [[256], [258]]:

$$\begin{aligned} &y_i(t) \le y_i^+(t), \\ &y_{ik}(t) \le y_{ik}^+(t). \end{aligned} \tag{3.16}$$

The financial resources at the disposal of the Ministry of Finance have the dynamics described by the scalar differential equation

$$\dot{z} = z_x + z_p + z_y + z_{yy} - R - R_u - Q - R_y - R,$$

where the terms in the right-hand side have the forms (3.4), (3.6)—(3.13) [256, 258].

The paradox of the present time is as follows: in the non-profit sphere of public administration, the Ministry of Finance seeks to maximize the functional (3.1), using the control actions $U_i(t), Q_i(t), \lambda_x, c_j^*, \lambda_y, \lambda_{yy}, v_i^+, v_{ik}^+, y_i^+$ and y_{ik}^+ to obtain the maximum amount from the lower hierarchy levels.

The model is organized as follows.

Making strategic decisions, the Ministry of Labor develops a policy model in the social sphere and coordinates the activities of all Principals and Organizations, particularly by sending normative legal acts for their implementation at all hierarchy levels. Thus, we propose a centralized management model for the social sphere, excluding several negative trends, such as the transfer of social obligations from the federal authorities to the regions without providing adequate funding and a whole set of related problems for the population.

Note that each Principal i has a certain amount of budgetary funds $U_i(t)$ and credit funds within the limits (3.14) and (3.16). They are spent on the fixed and circulating funds of the Organizations and the loan payments [[256], [258]]:

$$U_i(t)+v_i(t)=\sum_{k=1}^{N_i}U_{ik}(t)+\lambda_{y_i}y_i(t), \tag{3.17}$$

where y_i satisfies the equation

$$\dot{y}_i=v_i(t). \tag{3.18}$$

The Principal's control consists in allocating financial resources at its hierarchy level and choosing the amount of budgetary loans within the limits.

The Principal allocates these resources among the wages funds of the Organizations:

$$Q_i(t)=\sum_{k=1}^{N_i}Q_{ik}^*(t)+q, \tag{3.19}$$

where q is a strictly adjusted (fixed) value or a single-valued function of J_i^{Cen} [256, 258].

The Principal should also determine the measures of disciplinary impact on the Organizations: reward or punishment functions $\varphi_{ik}^j(P_j^{ik})(j=1,\ldots,M;i=1,\ldots,N;k=1,\ldots,N_i)$ such that

$$\sum_{j=1}^{M}\sum_{k=1}^{N_i}\varphi_{ik}^j(P_j^{ik})+\delta_i=0, \tag{3.20}$$

where δ_i is some share of the Principal's welfare.

The problem of Principal i is to choose appropriate control actions $U_{ik}(t), Q_{ik}(t), \varphi_{ik}^{j}$ and $y_i(t)$ under the constraints (3.17)—(3.20) to maximize the functional (3.3) [256, 258].

Organizations are located at the lower level of this complex socio-economic dynamic hierarchical macrosystem.

Each Organization has a budget and (or) fund x_{ik} for providing the social services (products) P_j^{ik}. The dynamics of funds are described by the differential equation

$$\dot{x}_{ik} = -\chi_{ik} x_{ik} + u_{ik}(t) + w_{ik}(t),$$

where $w_{ik}(t)$ denotes the internal resources used per unit of time (internal investment), and χ_{ik} is some coefficient.

The provision of social services (products) is described by $P_j^{ik} = F_j^{ik}(x_{ik}^{j}, \gamma_{ik}^{j}, L_{ik}^{j})$, where x_{ik}^{j} specifies the share of x_{ik} used for social service (product) j and $\sum_{j=1}^{M} x_{ik}^{j} = x_{ik}$.

The cost of all social services (products) provided by Organization (i,k) is given by $\sum_{j=1}^{M} c_j P_j^{ik}$.

The amount of funding received by the Organization per unit of time consists of the cost of the social services (products) provided and the indirect loan $v_{ij}(t)$. These funds are spent as follows [[256], [258]]:

1. paying the VAT $\sum_{j=1}^{M} c_j^{*} P_j^{ik}$;
2. paying the tax on fixed assets $\lambda_x x_{ik}$;
3. paying the wages $Q_{ik}(t) = \sum_{j=1}^{M} \gamma_{ik}^{j} L_{ik}^{j}$, where $Q_{ik}(t) \le Q_{ik}^{*}(t)$;

4. making internal investment in Organization's development and paying the fixed assets (rent, leasing, utilities, etc.) $w_{ik}(t)$;
5. paying the penalties or rewards $\varphi_{ik}^{j}(P_{j}^{ik})$.

The difference

$$\psi_{ik} = \sum_{j=1}^{M}(c_j - c_j^*)P_j^{ik} + v_{ik} - \lambda_x x_{ik} - w_{ik} - \sum_{j=1}^{M}\gamma_{ik}^{j}L_{ik}^{j} - \sum_{j=1}^{M}\varphi_{ik}^{j}(P_j^{ik})$$

is the income of Organization (i,k). The Organization seeks to maximize the total income:

$$J_{ik}^{Org} = \int_{0}^{T}\psi_{ik}dt. \tag{3.21}$$

The Principal and the Ministry of Finance provide information on the amount of funding to the Organizations. This information is incomplete by the degree of awareness of the higher hierarchy levels. Therefore, Organizations make their decisions under uncertainty (the incomplete and (or) nonidentical structures and volumes of information).

The same feature applies to the economic relations between the Principals and the Ministry of Finance.

3.2.2. Rules of System Operation and Solution of a Three-Level Hierarchical Game

For the macrosystem under consideration to operate, the game rules must be defined. For this purpose, we establish the sequence of moves.

The three-level operation of executive authorities (federal, regional, and municipal) has been legally defined. The Federal Ministry of Labor makes the first move, choosing the values of all control parameters and functions and reporting them to the regional ministries and departments of the population's social security (the Principals and Organizations in the social sphere).

Thus, the control action is that the adjuster (the Ministry of Labor) uses the administrative and legal resources for compulsory influence on the corresponding institutions (the subjects of legal relations).

Consequently, the problem reduces to analyzing the two-level hierarchy. At this level, the Principals make the next move, informing the Organizations of their control actions. Then each Organization must make its move: choose the values of the control functions and parameters.

According to the behavioral hypothesis Γ_{ik}, Organization (i,k) maximizes the functional (3.21), increasing the amount of social services (products) by expanding the list of paid services (products) and providing additional paid services to the population above the free list. The Organization's decisions (control action) are a functional of the control actions of the corresponding Principals [256, 258] and the Ministry of Labor. The operational decision at the Organization's level is independent but coordinated with the regional Principal. The decisions of all Principals related to the Ministry of Labor and Organizations are made by analogy.

According to the behavioral hypothesis Γ_i, Principal i maximizes the objective functions (3.2), i.e., the results of all Organizations in region i. Choosing its control actions, the Principal rests on the behavioral hypotheses Γ_{ik} of Organizations.

For the social decision-making at the upper (federal) hierarchy level, the control functions of the Principals are some functionals of the Ministry of Labor's control actions. Within this approach, a resource allocation schedule and a budgetary strategy are optimal if they maximize the functional (3.1), i.e., the Program is implemented in the best way under the hypotheses Γ_i and Γ_{ik}.

Next, let us formalize the solution of the three-level differential game played by the Ministry of Labor, the Principals, and the Organizations. Depending on the game conditions, the principles of lower-level interaction are established by the Principal or determined by the corresponding players (Organizations) independently.

Hence, the problem is to choose the game-theoretic principles of optimality for the lower-level players. If these players choose their strategies independently of each other, then the noncooperative game is considered. If they behave jointly and coordinate their actions, then the cooperative game arises. In the former case, the players are divided into disjoint groups (coalitions): a cooperative game is played within each coalition and a noncooperative game between coalitions [256, 258].

For avoiding a cumbersome model, assume that there will be only one player at the second and third levels. Let the dynamics of the three-level hierarchical game be described by the system of differential equations [256, 258]

$$\dot{x} = f(t, x, u_{Gov}, u_{Cen}, u_{Org}), x(t_0) = x_0, \tag{3.22}$$

where $x \in E^n$ denotes the state vector, and $u_{Gov} \in \Im_{Gov}, u_{Cen} \in \Im_{Cen}$ and $u_{Org} \in \Im_{Org}$ are the strategies of the Ministry of Labor, the Principal, and the Organization, respectively. The parameters, functions, and sets used here and below satisfy the standard constraints of differential games [[264]].

The payoff functions of the players are defined by the functionals

$$J_i(u_{Gov}, u_{Cen}, u_{Org}) = \Phi_i\left[T, x(t)\right] + \int_{t_0}^{T} F_i(t, x, u_{Gov}, u_{Cen}, u_{Org})dt \tag{3.23}$$

$$(i = Gov, Cen, Org).$$

Suppose that the mappings R_i introduced below are single-valued.

Also, we make the following assumptions:

1. There exists a mapping $R_{Org} : \Im_{Gov} \times \Im_{Cen} \to \Im_{Org}$ such that

$$\max_{u_{Org} \in \Im_{Org}} J_{Org}(u_{Gov}, u_{Cen}, u_{Org}) = J_{Org}(u_{Gov}, u_{Cen}, R_{Org}(u_{Gov}, u_{Cen}))$$

   for each fixed pair $\{u_{Gov}, u_{Cen}\} \in \Im_{Gov} \times \Im_{Cen}$.

2. There exists a mapping $R_{Cen} : \Im_{Gov} \to \Im_{Cen}$ such that

$$\max_{u_{Org} \in \Im_{Org}} J_{Cen}\left(u_{Gov}, u_{Cen}, R_{Org}(u_{Gov}, u_{Cen})\right) =$$

$$J_{Cen}\left(u_{Gov}, R_{Cen}(u_{Gov}), R_{Org}\left[u_{Gov}, R_{Cen}(u_{Gov})\right]\right)$$

   for each fixed $u_{Gov} \in \Im_{Gov}$.

3. There exists an admissible strategy of the Ministry of Labor, $u_{Gov}^{0} \in \Im_{Gov}$, such that

$$\max_{u_{Org} \in \Im_{Org}} J_{Gov}\left(u_{Gov}, R_{Cen}(u_{Gov}), R_{Org}\left[u_{Gov}, R_{Cen}(u_{Gov})\right]\right) =$$

$$J_{Cen}\left(u_{Gov}^{0}, R_{Cen}(u_{Gov}^{0}), R_{Org}\left[u_{Gov}^{0}, R_{Org}(u_{Gov}^{0})\right]\right).$$

The strategy u_{Gov}^{0} *defined in items 1-3 will be called the guaranteeing strategy of the state (the Ministry of Labor). The triple* $\{u_{Gov}^{0}, R_{Cen}(u_{Gov}), R_{Org}(u_{Gov}, u_{Cen})\}$ *will be called the solution of the three-level hierarchical game (3.22) and (3.23).* The guaranteeing strategy applied by the Ministry of Labor increases the amount of social security and support, thereby improving the population's quality of life.

Thus, we have constructed an economic-mathematical dynamic model of the population's social security and support system that differs from the currently used one by the centralized hierarchical structure and elements of the market economy. This model underlies a new decision methodology in the social sphere.

Below, we introduce a new theoretical approach to improving decision processes in the social sphere at each hierarchy level. We formalize new guaranteed solutions of multicriteria choice problems for managing complex socio-economic macrosystems under interval uncertainty with given limits.

3.3. Formalization of Social Guarantees as the Guaranteed Solutions of Complex Socio-economic Macrosystems under Uncertainty

This section considers a new method for formalizing guaranteed solutions of multicriteria choice problems under interval uncertainty with given limits. The guaranteed solution is based on a modification of Savage's principle of minimax regret [181, 182]. In addition, the definition involves the concept of the following pair: the set of social state guarantees for the population and life risks in case of which definite categories of the population exercise their constitutional right to obtain appropriate social guarantees. The results presented below express a new approach to design decision support systems under uncertainty for social sphere management.

The current theoretical and practical problems of social sphere management include the formalization and justification of a socially effective administration mechanism. The dynamics of social reality is characterized by structural socio-economic transformations and the increasing complexity of the economic, legal, and social institutions and their interaction processes. From the systems analysis perspective, the social sphere can be represented as a set of interconnected and mutually influencing nonstationary complex socio-economic systems with uncertainty. Their operation determines the population's size, quality of life, health, and education and aims for its well-being [89].

Complex socio-economic systems involve multicriteria administration processes of the social sphere as a whole and its components, determining the corresponding socio-economic processes in society. In turn, these processes form the corresponding reality, and its dynamics have signs of uncertainty.

This book treats uncertainties as uncontrolled or poorly controlled factors described by deterministic or random variables with given ranges (intervals) or a given class of possible distributions. (In other words, no statistical characteristics are available [275]). Such an approach refines the previous definition of uncertainty without any contradictions.

Nowadays, strategic decision-making to prevent the dysfunctional nature of socio-economic processes and uncertainty in the social sphere is based on target programs and comprehensive state programs, which are developed and implemented to increase the population's quality and standard of living and recovery. The large scale and complexity of such programs in the social sphere, limited resources, and reduced budgetary funding are the main obstacles towards their preparation, coordination, and approval [258].

Programs in the social sphere should be aimed at "the availability of services of the required quality in education and health care; achieving the required level of housing; support of socially unsecured and vulnerable segments of the population; accessibility to physical culture, sports, and cultural benefits; integration of migrants and ensuring the standards of personal, informational, and environmental security, etc." Solving these strategic tasks of social sphere administration will decrease risks and losses due to dysfunctional processes and uncertainty and stabilize the social sphere. The programs contain several measures in the social sphere and the corresponding lists of social guarantees for the population.

Social guarantees are socio-economic and regulatory legal tools ensuring minimum living conditions for certain groups and categories of the population in accordance with the requirements of the legislation. Assume that the lists of social guarantees can be formed into a system of social state guarantees financed adequately to the real economic conditions from the federal and regional budgets and extra-budgetary funds.

Note that a flexible and economically filled system of social state guarantees should be formed when developing social Programs aimed, among other things, at securing the population from destructive socio-economic processes and uncertainty. *The system of social guarantees* is understood as a set of measures to satisfy the population's social and economic needs. It implies a purposeful state policy in the social sphere for developing and implementing strategic decisions directly related to the population's quality and standard of living, health, and education, and overcoming economic inequality.

The system of social state guarantees is developed considering the differences between individual groups, segments, and categories of the population. The system of social state guarantees can be based on statistical information and (or) the results of public research. The main *goal of developing the system of social state guarantees* is creating the population's social security system from destructive socio-economic processes and uncertainty.

The relevant public authorities administer the social sphere. Presently, collective and individual decision processes under uncertainty are not fully formalized. At the same time, the existing scientific approaches allow adopting appropriate decisions by analyzing the predictability of the DM's behavior [258, 275]. It is necessary to determine the general action strategy for collective decisions under interval uncertainty with given limits [275].

Therefore, we propose a method for formalizing guaranteed solutions of multicriteria control problems under interval uncertainty with given limits. Also, the system of social state guarantees is formed when developing and implementing federal target programs [258] as an administration tool of the social sphere. A guaranteed solution based on a modification of Savage's principle of minimax regret is formalized, and its existence is proved under standard assumptions of multicriteria choice problems.

3.3.1. Multicriteria Choice under Uncertainty: Problem Statement

When formalizing the problem, we will use a modification of Savage's principle of minimax regret [105]. Suppose that several drafts of social state programs are being developed (a set of draft Programs) aimed at:

1. ensuring the availability of services of the required quality in education and healthcare for the population;
2. achieving the required level of housing for the population;
3. providing the population with cultural benefits and conditions for engaging in physical culture and sports (health improvement of the population);
4. supporting socially unsecured and vulnerable groups of the population.

Each project of a Program generally consists of draft subprograms containing measures intended to increase the population's level, quality of life, and health in terms of target indicators (the indicators of subprograms and draft lists of social guarantees corresponding to each Program in particular and the social sectors in the whole). Social guarantees are provided to certain categories of the population in accordance with the norms of law.

Let a draft list of social guarantees proposed in a Program be bijectively described by a vector parameter $x_i (i \in \square = \{1,\ldots,N\})$.

The value set of the parameter $x = (x_1,\ldots,x_i,\ldots,x_N)$ *will be denoted by* X *and called the set of possible lists of social guarantees; the vector x will be called the draft list of social guarantees in a definite Program.* The set of uncertainties $\mathrm{Y} = \{y_j\}$ consists of the consequences of dysfunctional socio-economic phenomena and processes. Note that y_j are interval uncertainties with given limits: no statistical characteristics are available for them. (For example, the data may be incorrect or even absent [258]).

Due to the nonstationarity of the complex socio-economic system and reduced budget allocations for implementing all Programs, the public authority developing the draft Program seeks to maximize the amount of budgetary funding.

Note that public authorities in the social sphere have to eliminate the causes and consequences of the dysfunctional socio-economic processes: the population's economic inequality and poverty, mortality and ill health, and the decreased level of education; the emergence of new aggressive forms of social relations; the growing social tension, etc. Thus, we define the components $f_i(x, y)(i = 1, \ldots, N)$ of a vector criterion $f(x, y)$ (the vector of social problems to be solved), where x is the draft list of the population's social guarantees provided within the social program under any realization of the interval uncertainty y with given limits.

For the sake of definiteness, assume that the DM chooses an appropriate Program maximizing the components of $f(x, y)$ (e.g., the maximum budgetary funding of the initiated Program) [258]. At the same time, we should consider modern realities, namely, the requirement to reduce the amount of budgetary allocations for implementing state Programs. (This aspect was discussed in the report "On the main directions of increasing the efficiency of federal budget expenditures" by the Ministry of Finance in 2015).

The DM should expect any realization of the uncertainty, e.g., dismissing persons of the third and higher age groups due to the ongoing reform in science and education. This can be described by the inclusion $y \in \mathrm{Y}$. Then the mathematical formalization reduces to the following.

Consider a multicriteria choice problem under uncertainty of the form

$$\langle \mathrm{X}, \mathrm{Y}, f(x, y) \rangle, \tag{3.24}$$

where:

- $x \in \mathrm{X} \subset \mathbb{R}^n$ denotes the list of social guarantees.
- $y \in \mathrm{Y} \subset \mathbb{R}^m$ are the uncertainties characterizing dysfunctional socio-economic processes and phenomena.
- $f(x, y)$ is a vector criterion defined on the Cartesian product $\mathrm{X} \times \mathrm{Y}$.

The components $f_i(x, y)(i \in \mathbb{N} = \{1, \ldots, N\})$ of the vector criterion $f(x, y)$ represent the DM's vector of social tasks [258].

Within the target program approach to social sphere management at the macrolevel, the DM forms a draft Program (solves problem (3.24)) to provide the maximum guaranteed social security of definite population segments, e.g., to get the maximum amount of budgetary allocations for implementing the

Program under the existing limits. Hence, the DM chooses $x \in \mathrm{X}$ to achieve the greatest possible values for all components of $f(x, y)$ considering the inclusion $y \in \mathrm{Y}$, where y are the uncertainties characterizing the dysfunctional socio-economic processes.

Using the maximin-based methodology [244], we associate the vector of the maximum values of $f_i(x, y)$ with each uncertainty $y \in \mathrm{Y}$. This vector determines the point of approximate maximum values. Let a certain amount of funding be allocated for the Programs. At least for the moment, providing all budgetary allocations necessary for developing and implementing the social Programs is an indicative task: the planned maximum values for this indicator will not be achieved due to reduced financing.

When choosing a solution, we will employ *the point of approximate maximum values* described by the vector

$$\bar{\mathfrak{I}} = (\bar{\mathfrak{I}}_1, \dots, \bar{\mathfrak{I}}_N) = \left(\max_{z \in X} f_1(z, y), \dots, \max_{z \in X} f_N(z, y) \right).$$

We construct the vector difference

$$\mathfrak{I}_i(x, y) = \max_{z \in X} f_i(z, x) - f_i(x, y),\ i \in \square = \{1, \dots, N\}, \tag{3.25}$$

which is defined a vector risk function $\mathfrak{I}(x, y) = \left(\mathfrak{I}_1(x, y), \dots, \mathfrak{I}_N(x, y) \right)$. This vector characterizes the difference between the required and received [[258]] budgetary allocations for the Program (e.g., the risk of underfunding and shortage of resources for implementing the Program).

The vector risk in the social sphere can be defined as the difference between the expected and obtained results for all components of the vector of social tasks. Control of this vector allows simulating economic reality using social design tools.

The risks mentioned above objectively exist. They are among the main life risks such as illness, old age, poverty, accidents, and unemployment. In the 2016 Annual report on the implementation and assessment of the effectiveness of the State Program on Social Support for Citizens, the Ministry of Labor noted the following:

- social risks, particularly due to the shortage of social workers, as the difference between the needs and real staffing of the social security system;
- informational risks due to incomplete initial reports and forecasts used in the development and implementation of the Program;
- significant risks of underfunding of the Program, etc.

Analyzing the practical consequences caused by the uncertainty and risks of the Program, the Ministry of Labor predicted further expansion of the poverty zone, social support complications for certain segments of the population in difficult life situations, and the growing social tension in society.

Therefore, we will adopt the concept of social effectiveness: a category that expresses the compliance of the project's results and costs with the goals and interests of its participants, including society and its groups [218].

Following the vector approach [275], we define the *i*th component $\Im_i(x, y)$ of the vector function $\Im(x, y)$ as

$$\Im_i(x,y) = f_i\left(x^S(y), y\right) - f_i(x,y) \ (i \in \square),$$

where the function $x^S(y)$ has the domain Y (the set of all uncertainties y), and for each $y \in \mathrm{Y}$ the value $x^S(y)$ is the Slater-maximal (weakly efficient) solution of the multicriteria choice problem

$$\left\langle \mathrm{X}, \{f_i(x,y)\}_{i\in\square} \right\rangle.$$

Using the vector risk function, we define a guaranteed solution of problem (3.24) and establish its existence under standard assumptions of game theory [258]. This technique allows relating the guaranteed solutions of the mathematical problems under consideration to the social guarantees (the government decisions for the population) when administering the social sphere under uncertainty.

Besides the interval uncertainty with given limits, the DM also deals with multiple criteria. For each uncertainty $y \in \mathrm{Y}$, consider the *N*-criteria choice problem

$$\langle \mathrm{X}, \{f_i(x, y)\}_{i \in \square} \rangle. \tag{3.26}$$

A vector $x^S(y)$ is said to be a Slater-maximal (weakly efficient) solution of problem (3.26) if the following system of inequalities is inconsistent [[164]]:

$$f_i(x^S(y), y) < f_i(x, y), \ \ \forall x \in \mathrm{X} \ \ (i \in \square).$$

We denote by $\mathrm{X}^S(y)$ the set of such solutions $x^S(y)$. Clearly, $\mathrm{X}^S(y) : \mathrm{Y} \to 2^{\mathrm{X}}$ is a multivalued mapping of the points from the set Y into the set of all subsets from X [258, 275].

According to opinion polls, the current level of pension provision does not match the modern requirements to the quality of life of pensioners; see https://iz.ru/news/660330. The pension is a social state guarantee, i.e., a socio-economic standard ensuring a minimum level of living conditions for the specified population group (a generally recognized level of minimum consumption corresponding to the capabilities of the socio-economic system).

We emphasize again that this social guarantee allows receiving only minimum socio-economic benefits to support pensioners' life without satisfying their cultural, educational, and other needs. Hence, the socio-economic efficiency of state projects in the social sphere (e.g., the new federal target program "The Development of the Pension System") is extremely low or even negligible. We therefore employ the concept of a weakly efficient solution to formalize the problem of administering the socio-economic processes.

A scalar criterion $f_i(x, y)$ is said to be strictly concave in $x \in \mathrm{X}$ for each $y \in \mathrm{Y}$ if the set X is convex for any $x^{(k)} \in \mathrm{X}(k = 1, 2)$, $x^{(1)} \neq x^{(2)}$ and

$$f_i\left(\lambda x^{(1)} + (1-\lambda)x^{(2)}, y\right) > \lambda f_i\left(x^{(1)}, y\right) + (1-\lambda) f_i\left(x^{(2)}, y\right)$$
$$\forall \lambda = const \in (0,1).$$

For problems (3.24) and (3.26), the well-known Hurwitz theorem [[164]] can be formulated as follows.

Assume that:

1. The set X is convex and compact, and the set Y is compact.
2. Each scalar criterion $f_i(x, y)(i \in \square)$ is continuous on $\mathrm{X} \times \mathrm{Y}$ and strictly concave in $x \in \mathrm{X}$ for each $y \in \mathrm{Y}$.

A solution $x^S(y)$ of problem (3.26) is Slater-maximal (weakly efficient) if and only if there exists a constant *N*-dimensional vector

$$\alpha = (\alpha_1, \ldots, \alpha_2) \in \Omega = \left\{ \alpha \in R^N \mid \alpha_i \geq 0 (i \in \mathrm{N}), \sum_{i \in \mathrm{N}} \alpha_i = 1 \right\} \quad (i \in \square)$$

such that

$$\max_{x \in X} \sum_{i \in \mathrm{N}} \alpha_i f_i(x, y) = \sum_{i \in \mathrm{N}} \alpha_i f_i(x^S(y), y). \tag{3.27}$$

Lemma 3.1. Under the assumptions of the Hurwitz theorem for problem (3.24), the vector function $x^S(y) : \mathrm{Y} \to \mathrm{X}$ given by (3.27) is unique and continuous on Y.

Really, the strict concavity of each criterion $f_i(x, y)(i \in \square)$, in x for each $y \in \mathrm{Y}$ implies the concavity of their linear convolution with nonnegative coefficients $\alpha_i > 0(i \in \square)$ that do not vanish simultaneously:

$$\psi(x, y) = \sum_{i \in \mathrm{N}} \alpha_i f_i(x, y).$$

Hence, the maximum in (3.27) is achieved at a single point; according to (3.26), the components of the vector function $x^S(y)$ are continuous on Y [[258]].

Decision-making in the social sphere under uncertainty often involves a probabilistic approach to reduce the negative impact of uncertainty. For this purpose, we introduce the concept of mixed, or probabilistic, uncertainty [217] as a probability measure $\mu(\cdot)$ defined on the compact set Y. The set of all mixed uncertainties $\mu(\cdot)$ will be denoted by M.

Under the assumptions of the Hurwitz theorem for problem (3.24), we consider the vector risk function

$$\begin{aligned} &\Im(x,y) = (\Im_1(x,y),\ldots,\Im_N(x,y)), \\ &\Im_i(x,y) = f_i(x^S(y),y) - f_i(x,y) \\ &(i \in \square), \end{aligned} \tag{3.28}$$

where $x^S(y)$ is given by (3.27), and $\Im_i(x,y)$ is a scalar risk function for the i th criterion.

Lemma 3.2. Under the assumptions of the Hurwitz theorem for problem (3.24), the risk function for the i th criterion, $\Im_i(x,y)$, is continuous on $\mathrm{X}\times\mathrm{Y}$.

Really, the continuity of $\Im_i(x,y)$ on $\mathrm{X}\times\mathrm{Y}$ follows from the continuity of $x^S(y)$ (Lemma 3.1) and $f_i(x,y)$ and the continuity of the superposition $f_i(x^S(y),y)$ of the continuous functions $f_i(x,y)$ and $x^S(y)$.

Under the assumptions of the Hurwitz theorem, we associate the auxiliary N-criteria choice problem under uncertainty

$$\langle \mathrm{X}, \mathrm{Y}, \Im(x,y) \rangle \tag{3.29}$$

with the original problem (3.24). In (3.29), the DM chooses an alternative $x \in \mathrm{X}$ to minimize all components $\Im_i(x,y)$ of the vector risk function $\Im(x,y)$; see (3.28) and [258].

In a practical interpretation, each criterion $\Im_i(x,y)$ of the risk function (3.28) characterizes the difference (regret) that when an uncertainty $y \in \mathrm{Y}$ is realized, the DM chooses an alternative $x \in \mathrm{X}$ instead of the “best” alternative $x^S(y)$ in the vector sense. In other words, this is the difference between the approximate indicators (when developing the Program) and the achieved ones. The DM in problem (3.29) seeks to reduce all the components $\Im_i(x, y)$ of the vector risk function as much as possible. Note that any realization of the uncertainty $y \in \mathrm{Y}$ is considered [258]. When selecting the guaranteed solution, the DM expects the "worst-case" uncertainty, which corresponds to the greatest values of the vector risk function in the vector sense [258].

Problems (3.29) and (3.24) differ:

1. The criteria in (3.29) are the risk functions for the i th criterion $\Im_i(x, y)$, unlike the vector of social tasks $f_i(x, y)(i \in \square)$ in (3.24).
2. The DM in (3.29) seeks to decrease all $\Im_i(x, y)$ simultaneously by choosing $x \in \mathrm{X}$ (forming a list of social state guarantees in the Program reduces, e.g., the risks of growing poverty among vulnerable groups of the population); in (3.24), the DM seeks to increase $f_i(x, y)(i \in \square)$.

Up to this point, we have considered interval uncertainties y, elements of a set Y, with given limits only (no statistical characteristics) [275]. It seems reasonable to study mixed, or probabilistic, uncertainties $\mu(\cdot) \in M$.

Well, we associate with problem (3.29) its quasi-mixed extension

$$\langle \mathrm{X}, M, \Im(x, \mu) \rangle. \tag{3.30}$$

Choosing an alternative $x \in \mathrm{X}$ in (3.30), the DM seeks to minimize all components $\Im_i(x, \mu)$ of the vector risk function $\Im(x, \mu)$, where

$$\Im_i(x, \mu) = \int_Y \Im_i(x, y)\mu(dy), (i \in \square).$$

This integral exists due to the compactness of Y and the continuity of the risk function for the i th criterion, $\Im_i(x, y)$ on $\mathrm{X} \times \mathrm{Y}$. When choosing $x \in \mathrm{X}$, the DM considers any realization of the probabilistic uncertainty $\mu(\cdot) \in M$.

Under the assumptions of the Hurwitz theorem for problem (3.24), we define its guaranteed solution as follows.

A pair $(x^*, \Im^*)$ *is called the guaranteed solution of problem (3.24) if there exists a probabilistic uncertainty* $\mu(\cdot) \in M$ *such that* $\Im^* = \Im(x^*, \mu^*)$, *the system of inequalities*

$$\Im_i(x, \mu^*) < \Im_i(x^*, \mu^*)(i \in \square) \qquad (3.31)$$

is inconsistent $\forall x \in \mathrm{X}$, *and the system of inequalities*

$$\Im_i(x^*, \mu^*) < \Im_i(x^*, y)(i \in \square) \qquad (3.32)$$

is inconsistent for all pure uncertainties $y \in \mathrm{Y}$. *In this case, the vector* $\Im_i(x^*, \mu^*)$ *is called the guaranteed risk.*

Let us comment on the guaranteed solution and guaranteed risk.

As a guaranteed solution, we have proposed a pair composed of the alternative x^* and the vector risk $\Im^*$. The list of social guarantees x^* is legally established for the population in case of socio-economic losses (total or partial disability, health, breadwinner, etc.) described by the guaranteed risk $\Im^*$. For any uncertainty $y \in \mathrm{Y}$, the resulting value of the vector risk function $\Im(x^*, y)$ cannot exceed the guaranteed vector risk $\Im(x^*, \mu^*)$: this property explains the multicriteria sense of the inconsistent system (3.32). The guaranteed risk gives an upper bound for the vector risk $\Im(x^*, y)$ in problem (3.24); see [258].

Therefore, the guaranteed risk is a general socio-economic measure for an undesired deviation of an individual or a group of individuals from full-fledged life conditions (e.g., in case of loss of health and (or) a source of livelihood). The guarantee of social risks is determined by biological and socio-economic life factors of an individual or a group of individuals in society.

Presently, a list of Programs has been developed for securing the population against some life risks using social state guarantees with an economic content. For example, in case of partial or complete loss of earnings with total or partial disability, various Programs in the social sphere imply the following social guarantees: during pregnancy and motherhood, maternity leave and benefits for the second and any subsequent child; upon reaching retirement age, pensions, benefits, and subsidies.

The inconsistency of (3.31) means that the alternative x^* is Slater-minimal in the multicriteria choice problem $\langle \mathrm{X}, \mathfrak{I}(x, \mu^*) \rangle$. This problem is obtained from (3.30) under a fixed (mixed or probabilistic) uncertainty $\mu(\cdot) = \mu^*(\cdot) \in M$.

The inconsistency of

$$\mathfrak{I}_i(x^*, \mu^*) < \mathfrak{I}_i(x^*, \mu), \forall \mu(\cdot) \in M \, (i \in \square)$$

implies the inconsistency of (3.32), which means that the uncertainty $\mu(\cdot) \in M$ is a Slater-maximal alternative in the *N*-criteria choice problem $\langle M, \mathfrak{I}(x^*, \mu) \rangle$. This problem is obtained from (3.30) under a fixed alternative $x = x^* \in \mathrm{X}$.

Consider the scalar criterion case of problem (3.24), where $\square = \{1\}$. Then the guaranteed solution $(x^*, \mathfrak{I}_1(x^*, \mu^*))$ of the corresponding problem $\left\langle X, Y, \mathfrak{I}_1(x, y) = \max_{z \in \mathrm{X}} f_1(z, y) - f_1(x, y) \right\rangle$ satisfies the chain of equalities

$$\min_{x \in \mathrm{X}} \mathfrak{I}_1(x, \mu^*) = \mathfrak{I}_1(x^*, \mu^*) = \max_{\mu(\cdot) \in \mathrm{M}} \mathfrak{I}_1(x^*, \mu). \tag{3.33}$$

Hence, the pair $(x^*, \mu^*) \in \mathrm{X} \times M$ is a saddle point of the scalar function $\mathfrak{I}_1(x, \mu)$ [258].

3.3.2. An Existence Theorem and One Method to Find the Guaranteed Solution

Theorem 3.1. Consider problem (3.24) under the following assumptions:

1. The set X is convex and compact, and the set Y is compact.

2. Each payoff function $f_i(x, y)(i \in \mathbb{N})$ is continuous on $\mathrm{X} \times \mathrm{Y}$ and strictly concave in x $\forall y \in \mathrm{Y}$.

Then *there exists the guaranteed solution* $(x^*, \Im^*, \mu^*)$ of this problem [258].

Proof. According to Lemma 3.2, each function $\Im_i(x, y)(i \in \mathbb{N})$ (3.28) is continuous on $\mathrm{X} \times \mathrm{Y}$. We associate with problem (3.24) the multicriteria choice problem (3.29) and its quasi-mixed extension (3.30).

For (3.30), we construct the scalar function

$$\psi(x, \mu) = \sum_{i \in \mathbb{N}} \beta_i \Im_i(x, \mu), \tag{3.34}$$

with arbitrary $\beta_i = const \geq 0 (i \in \mathbb{N})$ such that $\sum_{i \in \mathbb{N}} \beta_i > 0.$ Recall a sufficient condition of Slater optimality [275]:

1. If an alternative x^* satisfies the relation

$$\min_{x \in \mathrm{X}} \psi(x, \mu^*) = \psi(x^*, \mu^*), \tag{3.35}$$

then x^* is the Slater-minimal solution of the multicriteria choice problem $\langle \mathrm{X}, \Im(x, \mu^*) \rangle$ [262, 275], i.e., the system of inequalities (3.31) is inconsistent for all $x \in \mathrm{X}$.

2. If a mixed uncertainty $\mu^*(\cdot) \in M$ satisfies the relation

$$\max_{\mu \in \mathrm{M}} \psi(x, \mu^*) = \psi(x^*, \mu^*), \tag{3.36}$$

Then $\mu^*(\cdot) \in M$ is the Slater-maximal solution of the multicriteria choice problem $\langle X, \Im(x^*, \mu) \rangle$, i.e., the system of inequalities

$$\Im_i(x^*, \mu^*) < \Im_i(x^*, \mu)(i \in \square) \tag{3.37}$$

is inconsistent $\mu^*(\cdot) \in M$.

Since the Dirac function $\delta(y - y^*)dy$ is a "probabilistic" uncertainty, the inconsistency of (3.37) $\mu^*(\cdot) \in M$ implies the inconsistency of (3.32) $\forall y \in \mathrm{Y}$.

Due to (3.35) and (3.36), if there exists a pair $(x^*, \mu^*) \in \mathrm{X} \times M$ such that

$$\max_{\mu \in M} \psi(x^*, \mu) = \psi(x^*, \mu^*) = \min_{x \in X} \psi(x, \mu^*), \tag{3.38}$$

where the function $\psi(x, \mu)$ is given by (3.34), then there exists the guaranteed solution $(x^*, \Im^* = \Im(x^*, \mu^*))$ [258, 267, 275, 278]. The pair (x^*, μ^*) satisfying the chain of equalities (3.38) is a saddle point of the zero-sum two-player game

$$\langle X, M, \psi(x, \mu) \rangle. \tag{3.39}$$

(For details, see [258, 262, 267, 268, 275]).

In the game (3.39), player 1 (minimizer) [254, 258, 262] chooses strategies $x \in \mathrm{X}$ to reduce $\psi(x, \mu)$ as much as possible; player 2 (maximizer) chooses mixed strategies $\mu(\cdot) \in M$ to increase $\psi(x, \mu)$ as much as possible. The solution (3.39) is given by the saddle point (x^*, μ^*) using the chain of equalities (3.38) [258, 262, 267, 268, 275].

Now, we show that under the hypotheses of the existence theorem, the game (3.39) has the saddle point (x^*, μ^*).

For this purpose, note the following:

1. By Lemma 3.2, the continuity of $f_i(x, y)(i \in \square)$ on $\mathrm{X} \times \mathrm{Y}$ implies the continuity of $\Im_i(x, y)(i \in \square)$ and, consequently [231], the continuity of the linear convolution of these functions with constant coefficients,

$$\psi(x,\mu)=\sum_{i\in]}\alpha_i\int_{Y}\Im_i(x,y)\mu(dy), \tag{3.40}$$

on X.

2. The strict concavity of $f_i(x,y)$ in y $\forall x\in X$ implies the (strict) convexity of $f_i(x,y)$ in x $\forall y\in Y$. Since $\max_{x\in X} f_i(x,y)$ does not depend on x, the difference (3.28) is convex in x as well.

As a result, the function (3.40) is convex in x on the convex set X for each $\forall y\in Y$ [230, 231]. According to [231, 258, 262], the zero-sum two-player game (3.39) has the saddle point (x^*,μ^*) given by (3.38).

This proof suggests *the following method to find the guaranteed solution* $(x^*,\Im^*)$ of problem (3.24) [258, 262].

1. Select a set of numbers $\alpha_i>0(i\in\Box)$ such that $\sum_{i\in||}\alpha_i=1$, and find the vector function $x^S(y)$ from the condition

$$\max_{x\in X}\sum_{i\in L}\alpha_i f_i(x,y)=\sum_{i\in|}\alpha_i f_i(x^S(y),y)\forall y\in Y.$$

2. Construct the functions

$$\Im_i(x,y)=f_i(x^S(y),y)-f_i(x,y)(i\in\Box),$$

and then calculate

$$\Im_i(x,\mu)=\int_{Y}\Im_i(x,y)\mu(dy)(i\in\Box).$$

3. Construct the function

$$\psi(x,\mu) = \sum_{i \in \sqsubset} \beta_i \Im_i(x,\mu)$$

$$\forall \beta_i = const > 0 (i \in \square)$$

such that $\sum_{i \in I} \beta_i > 0.$

4. Find a pair (x^*, μ^*) satisfying the equalities

$$\max_{\mu \in M} \psi(x^*, \mu) = \psi(x^*, \mu^*)$$

$$\min_{x \in X} \psi(x, \mu^*) = \psi(x^*, \mu^*).$$

The resulting pair (x^*, μ^*) determines the guaranteed solution $(x^*, \Im^* = \Im(x^*, \mu^*))$ of problem (3.24).

Conclusion

Section 3.1 has considered models, methods, and technologies for managing the dynamics of complex socio-economic systems under uncertainty (the incomplete and nonidentical structures and volumes of information) at three hierarchy levels, using an example of the population's social security and support system.

The solution of a three-level hierarchical game has been obtained, and the control action of the state on socio-economic processes has been described. This action is determined by the functions that the state (represented by the Ministry of Labor) performs for the citizens.

A centralized management model of the social sphere has been constructed. This model is a prerequisite for changing the current strategic decision processes in the social sphere and terminating the denationalization of social sectors gradually. The research results can be used for developing and applying new legal institutions to administer the population's social security and support system and streamline relations between economic agents operating in the social sphere and the population. As expected, this would facilitate the fulfillment of tasks by socio-economic systems.

The systems analysis above is based on game-theoretic tools. As established, public administration of the population's social security and support should increase the quality of life of the poor and socially unsecured segments and overcome economic inequality.

Sections 3.2 and 3.3 have shown that in modern economic reality, decision processes in the social sphere at the macrolevel should be formalized considering several important factors:

1. The controlled system's performance is assessed by multiple criteria; therefore, decision processes in the social sphere should be described by multicriteria choice problems.
2. There are dysfunctional processes (interval uncertainties with given limits but without any statistical characteristics) causing risks; they should be taken into account when making decisions in the social sphere [258].

In Section 3.2, these factors have been considered for the socio-economic and mathematical models. Note that most of the studies in this area involve modifications of Wald's maximin principle (the worst case). According to current evidence, social and economic breakdowns occur infrequently even when applying social design methods. They are unlikely under the systemic administration of the social sphere [258].

The maximin principle yields underestimated guarantees in formal models. In the game-theoretic models of socio-economic processes, it may increase social discontent among the most vulnerable categories of the population.

To avoid these negative properties of Wald's approach, we have formalized a guaranteed solution by modifying Savage's principle of minimax regret; see Section 3.3. As a result, the concepts of a guaranteed solution and guaranteed risk have been justified, and their existence has been proved.

The guaranteed solution formalized through the concept of social guarantees, in particular, suggests a new approach to the design of analytical decision support systems for managing the social sphere.

Adjusting the system of social state guarantees with the "guarantee–risk" methodology allows considering the social tension-inducing uncertainties when developing state programs in the social sphere.

Thus, we have introduced a new theoretical approach to improving decision processes in the social sphere at the macrolevel. Also, we have developed and justified a hierarchical model of social sphere management and decision-making at each hierarchy level.

More specifically:

- A multilevel dynamic model of complex socio-economic systems under uncertainty in the social sphere has been constructed.
- A new approach to managing the dynamics of complex socio-economic systems under uncertainty has been proposed on an example of the population's social security and support system.
- A new guaranteed solution of multicriteria choice problems for managing complex socio-economic systems under interval uncertainty with given limits has been introduced.
- The concept of a guaranteed solution has been formalized by modifying Savage's principle of minimax regret. The following pair has been considered: the set of social state guarantees for the population and life risks in case of which definite categories of the population exercise their constitutional right to obtain appropriate social guarantees.
- An existence theorem for the guaranteed solution has been proved under standard assumptions of multicriteria choice problems, and a method to find this solution has been proposed.

At the end of Chapter 3, we can quote V. Lucas: It can be argued that the theory of n-person games is, by all accounts, the area of the most active development in game theory and that significant mathematical achievements have appeared here in recent years. This is the most appropriate theory for solving many problems in the social sciences...

Chapter 4

Guaranteed Solutions and Risks in Multicriteria Choice and Conflict Systems under Uncertainty

Introduction

Here, we present the mathematical rationale for Chapter 3 and discuss new approaches to modelling decision processes based on game-theoretic tools increasing the outcomes and simultaneously reducing the associated Savage risk. Section 4.1 is devoted to multicriteria choice problems; Section 4.3, to noncooperative games. In Section 4.4, we consider Savage risk functions and payoffs in a noncooperative game under uncertainty and propose an approach for constructing guaranteed solutions and risks and investigating the features of Nash equilibrium.

The economic-mathematical modeling of decision processes in complex socio-economic macrosystems aims to improve the controlled system's performance. Two main factors are often considered: the presence of multiple criteria measuring the controlled system's performance and the presence of various-type interval uncertainties with given limits but without any statistical characteristics. Most of the strategic decisions in socio-economic systems are accompanied by the conflict of interests between individual control systems with appropriate power and influence groups defending their own interests and various additional factors inherent in the decision process at the macrolevel.

As a rule, the conflicting nature of processes does not imply any open confrontation between the parties but indicates their different interests (mostly economic). In real economic and social macrosystems, the same decisions can be optimal for one party and nonoptimal for the other. Under the principle of checks and balances, the resulting decisions depend on all parties with different interests (conflicting ones) [275]. Game theory is a mathematical framework that studies such situations. It represents a branch of the general theory for describing and analyzing optimal decision processes with one or several participants under uncertainty and conflict of interests. *A conflict is understood as a situation in which the parties have different interests and opportunities to choose appropriate actions for their benefit* [258].

Conflict-related issues have been considered since the 17th century by many mathematicians. American scientists J. von Neumann and O. Morgenstern pioneered game theory as a mathematical approach to the competitive economy phenomena. Their fundamental book on game theory [227] was first published in 1944; also, see [228].

Over time, game theory has outgrown this framework and transformed into a general mathematical theory of conflicts. Within game theory, any conflicts can be, in principle, described mathematically, including economic, legal, and social ones [150-152]. Game-theoretic tools mathematically justify important aspects of decision-making in the economic, legal, and social macrosystems. In addition, game theory gives a promising approach to control, planning, and forecasting [160]. Among other things, game theory is intended to recommend a rational course of actions for conflict participants, that is, to determine an optimal strategy for each of them [57].

The practical significance of this theory is the simulation of game experiments (e.g., business games) for determining optimal behavior in complex socio-economic systems at the micro- and mesolevels [211, 212, 282]. Some examples of practical [227, 228] (particularly economic) content were considered by economists in the financial [232], industrial [205], insurance and business areas [137, 138, 146, 147]. We emphasize again that games differ from real conflicts: they are played in accordance with well-defined rules. Real conflicts are usually difficult to describe formally. Therefore, any game is a simplification that reflects only the main (essential) factors of the corresponding process or phenomenon. The terminology borrowed from the practice of such games applies to other conflicts considered in game theory [275].

Nowadays, the management of complex socio-economic systems at the macrolevel should be treated as decision-making under multiple criteria and uncertainty. Also, the interconnection and mutual influence of economics, law, and sociology should be considered.

The theory of multicriteria choice problems under uncertainty is one possible remedy going back to the 1950s. Numerous publications in this area of research are based on modifying Wald's maximin utility principle [235, 236]. This is a pessimistic principle (often called extreme pessimism): it considers only the "worst" outcome among all admissible ones. The maximin criterion expecting the worst values of the uncertain factor is extremely conservative. It should be used when failures are unacceptable, regardless of what other (favorable) outcomes of an operation may be [275].

According to this principle, decisions under uncertainty are made by interacting with a rational, aggressive opponent who applies every effort to prevent success. Then the control system's optimal strategy guarantees a payoff not smaller than "allowed by the opponent" [275]. In modern realities, this approach is hardly acceptable.

An attempt to describe the dynamics of control systems under uncertainty in mathematical terms leads to the formalization of their behavioral principles. Decision-making is defined as the process of choosing alternatives (strategies) to achieve the desired result. Researchers traditionally distinguish between normative decision-making (the theory of rational decisions, reflecting logical decision processes) and descriptive (behavioral, psychological) decision-making. Each theory provides many decision technologies.

4.1. A New Approach to Optimal Solutions of Multicriteria Choice Problems under Uncertainty Using the Savage Principle

Let us construct a risk management model for a socio-economic system with multiple criteria and uncertainty. For most socio-economic processes, it is often impossible to construct a single scalar criterion that describes the interests and behavior of participants [275] since the performance of such processes is usually assessed by several criteria.

The corresponding models are investigated within the theory of multicriteria choice problems, where each decision corresponds to a unique value of each criterion [275]. However, this requirement is often violated in real conditions. A typical situation is when some system parameters take arbitrary (a priori unpredictable) values within given intervals. For example, in the strategic planning of socio-economic development of the state, it is necessary (but not always possible) to fully determine the internal and external conditions, trends, constraints, imbalances, imbalances, the evolutionary capabilities of the system and its subsystems, and other types of uncertainty. In this case, only the range of their variation has to be considered.

One mathematical model for such problems is an ordered set

$$\Gamma = \langle \square, \mathrm{X}, \mathrm{Y}, f(x, y) \rangle$$

with the following notations: $\mathbb{N} = \{1,...,N\}$ is the number set of the components $f_i(x,y)$ of a vector criterion $f(x,y) = (f_1(x,y),...,f_N(x,y))$ that measures the effect of a chosen strategy $x \in X$ under a fixed value of the uncertainty $y \in \mathrm{Y}$;

$\mathrm{X} \subset \mathbb{R}^n$ and $\mathrm{Y} \subset \mathbb{R}^m$ are the sets of admissible strategies and uncertainties, respectively; finally, $y(x): \mathrm{X} \to \mathrm{Y}$ is a strategic uncertainty from the set Y^{X} [275].

4.1.1. Savage's Principle of Minimax Regret

In a multicriteria choice problem under uncertainty, the control system's goal can be *increasing the guaranteed values of each criterion and reducing the guaranteed Savage risks simultaneously*. Let the uncertainty be of interval type with given limits but without any statistical characteristics [275].

In the single-criterion problem $\Gamma_1 = \langle \mathrm{X}, \mathrm{Y}, f(x,y) \rangle$, the principle of minimax regret consists in constructing a pair $(x^*, R_f^*) \in \mathrm{X}$ that satisfies the chain of equalities [[275]]

$$R_f^* = \max_{y \in Y} R_f(x^*, y) = \min_{x \in X} \max_{y \in Y} R_f(x,y), \tag{4.1}$$

where *the Savage risk function* is given by

$$R_f(x,y) = \max_{z \in X} f(z,y) - f(x,y), \tag{4.2}$$

and the value R_f^* (4.1) is called the Savage risk in the problem Γ_1. The value R_f^* quantifies the regret for the control system: the extent to which the realized value of $f(x,y)$ *does not* reach the best one $\max_{z \in X} f(z,y)$ in the problem Γ_1. Based on the realities, the DMs seek to minimize $R_f(x,y)$.

For each component $f_i(x,y)(i \in \mathbb{N})$ of the vector criterion $f(x,y)$ in the problem Γ, the control system constructs the Savage risk function

$$R_i(x,y) = \max_{z \in X} f_i(z,y) - f_i(x,y)(i \in \mathbb{N}). \tag{4.3}$$

By analogy, its value is called the Savage risk. Note that each criterion $f_i(x,y)(i \in \mathbb{N})$ has a particular risk $R_i(x,y)$, and the control system chooses appropriate strategies for reducing all risks as much as possible, expecting any realization of the strategic uncertainty $y \in \mathrm{Y}$, $y(x): \mathrm{X} \to \mathrm{Y}$; for details, see [275].

This formal definition is interpreted as follows: *risk measures the deviation of the realized values from the planned or expected ones.*

4.1.2. Formalization of Guarantees

Formalizing the risk function $R_i(x,y)$ (4.3) for each criterion $f_i(x,y)(i \in \mathbb{N})$, we pass to the following extension of the problem Γ:

$$\left\langle \mathbb{N}, X, Y, \{f_i(x,y), -R_i(x,y)\}_{i \in \mathbb{N}} \right\rangle, \tag{4.4}$$

with the following notations: $\mathbb{N} = \{1,...,N\}$ is the number set of the components $f_i(x,y)$ of the vector criterion $f(x,y) = (f_1(x,y),...,f_N(x,y))$ that measures the effect of a chosen strategy $x \in X$ under a fixed value of the uncertainty $y \in Y$;

$\mathrm{X} \subset \mathbb{R}^n$ and $\mathrm{Y} \subset \mathbb{R}^m$ are the sets of admissible strategies and uncertainties, respectively; $y(x): \mathrm{X} \to \mathrm{Y}$ is a strategic uncertainty from the set Y^{X} [269]; finally, $-R(x,y) = (-R_1(x,y),...,-R_N(x,y))$ is an additional vector criterion of dimension *N*. The minus sign indicates the control system's desire to reduce the risks realized in the decision process, unifying the action of strategies $x \in \mathrm{X}$ and uncertainties $y \in \mathrm{Y}$ on the vector criteria $f(x,y)$ and $-R(x,y)$. In (4.4), the control system chooses appropriate strategies $x \in \mathrm{X}$ for maximizing each component $f_i(x, y)$ and $-R(x, y)(i \in \square)$ of the *N*-dimensional vectors $f(x, y)$ and $-R(x, y)$, respectively, expecting any realization of the strategic uncertainty $y \in \mathrm{Y}$. Note that an increase of $-R(x, y)$ is equivalent to a decrease of $R(x, y)$ and $R_i(x, y) \geq 0$.

In the economic literature, a guarantee is understood as a secured obligation of one party interested in a transaction or as a result of decision-making secured by economic and other resources. The guarantee of a criterion $f_i(x, y)$ can be formalized by analogy.

Definition 4.1. A scalar function $f_i[x]$ is called *the guarantee of a criterion* $f_i(x, y)$ if the inequalities $f_i[x] \leq f_i(x, y)(i \in \square)$ hold for each strategy $x \in \mathrm{X}$ and each fixed value of the uncertainty $y \in \mathrm{Y}$, $y(x) : \mathrm{X} \rightarrow \mathrm{Y}$.

Proposition 4.1. The functions $f_i[x] = \min\limits_{y \in Y} f_i(x, y) \forall x \in \mathrm{X}$ are the guarantees of $f_i(x, y)$.

Proof. Consider a three-stage procedure yielding guarantees for all criteria of problem (4.4):

1. Determine $\varphi_i(y) = \max\limits_{z \in \mathrm{X}} f_i(z, y) \forall y \in \mathrm{Y}\ (i \in \square)$.
2. Construct the Savage risk function $R_i(x, y) = \varphi_i - f_i(x, y)(i \in \square)$.
3. Find the guarantee $\min\limits_{y \in \mathrm{Y}}[-R_i(x, y)]$, i.e.,

$$R_i[x] = \max_{y \in \mathrm{Y}} R_i(x, y)(i \in \square).$$

The control system seeks to reduce the risk $R_i(x, y)(i \in \square)$ as much as possible by choosing $x \in \mathrm{X}$ under any realization of the uncertainty $y \in \mathrm{Y}$.

If the functions $f_i[x]$ and $-R_i[x]$ exist, they are the guarantees of $f(x,y)$ and $-R(x,y)$, respectively: for each $x \in \mathrm{X}$, we have the implications

$$\left[f_i[x] = \min_{y \in Y} f_i(x,y) \right] \Rightarrow \left[f_i[x] \le f_i(x,y) \right] (\forall y \in \mathrm{Y})$$

and

$$\left[-R_i[x] = \min_{y \in Y} (-R_i(x,y)) \right] \Rightarrow \left[-R_i[x] \le -R_i(x,y) \right] (\forall y \in \mathrm{Y}).$$

The existence follows from the book [268].

Remark 4.1. If the sets X and Y are compact, and the function $f_i(x,y)$ is continuous on $\mathrm{X} \times \mathrm{Y}$, then the functions $f_i[x] = \min_{y \in \mathrm{Y}} f_i(x,y)$ and $\varphi_i(y) = \max_{z \in \mathrm{X}} f_i(z,y)$ are continuous on X and Y, respectively.

Let $comp\square^k$ denote the set of compact sets from the space $\square^k$, where $k = n, m.$ Also, let $f_i(x,y) \in comp(\mathrm{X} \times \mathrm{Y})$ indicate that the function $f_i(x,y)$ is continuous.

Remark 4.2. If in the problem $\Gamma = \langle \square, \mathrm{X}, \mathrm{Y}, f(x,y) \rangle$, $f_i(x,y) \in comp(\mathrm{X} \times \mathrm{Y}), x \in comp\square^n$ and $y \in comp\square^m$, then the Savage risk function $R_i(x,y)$ (4.3) is continuous on $\mathrm{X} \times \mathrm{Y}$. Really, $\varphi_i(y) = \max_{z \in \mathrm{X}} f_i(z,y)$ is continuous by Remark 4.1, and $R_i(x,y) = \varphi(y) - f_i(x,y)(i \in \square)$ (4.3) has the same property as the difference of continuous functions.

Remark 4.3. The Savage risk function (4.3) characterizes the deviation of the criterion $f_i(x,y)$ from the desired one $\max_{z \in \mathrm{X}} f_i(z,y)$. Choosing its strategy $x \in \mathrm{X}$, the control system seeks to minimize $R_i(x, y)$ (equivalently, to maximize $-R_i(x, y)$).

We will associate with the original problem Γ problem (4.4). Here, the control system's goal is to choose an appropriate strategy $x \in \mathrm{X}$ so that the vector criteria $f(x, y)$ and $-R(x, y)(i \in \square)$ take as great values as possible. The control system has to expect any realization of the uncertainty $y \in \mathrm{Y}$.

4.2. Formalization of the Guaranteed Solution. Necessary and Sufficient Conditions for Its Existence

Considering the guarantees $f_i[x]$ and $-R_i[x]$ of the criteria $f_i(x, y)$ and $-R_i(x, y)$, respectively, we pass from the multicriteria choice problem under uncertainty (4.4) to the multicriteria choice problem

$$\Gamma_g = \langle \mathrm{X}, \{f_i[x], -R_i[x]\}_{i \in \mathrm{I}} \rangle$$

(the problem of guarantees). Note that the criteria $f_i[x]$ and $-R_i[x]$ are interconnected in the optimization and economic sense: the value $R_i[x]$ measures the control system's risks when obtaining the outcome $f_i[x]$. Increasing (decreasing) the difference $f_i[x] - R_i[x]$ implies a greater (smaller) guarantee $f_i[x]$ under a lower (higher) risk $R_i[x]$.

Let the control system's goal be increasing the guarantee $f_i[x]$ and reducing the risk $R_i[x]$ simultaneously for each $i \in \square$. We associate with the problem $\Gamma_g = \langle \mathrm{X}, \{f_i[x], -R_i[x]\}_{i \in \square} \rangle$ another auxiliary problem [[262], [278]] of the form

$$\Gamma_a = \langle \mathrm{X}, \{G_i[x] = f_i[x] - R_i[x]\}_{i \in \mathrm{I}} \rangle. \tag{4.5}$$

For solving the multicriteria choice problem under uncertainty $\Gamma = \langle \square, \mathrm{X}, \mathrm{Y}, f(x,y) \rangle$, we will employ the concept of Slater maximality. (It covers Pareto maximality as a special case [275, 278]).

Definition 4.2. A strategy $x^S \in \mathrm{X}$ is said to be *Slater-maximal (weakly efficient)* in problem (4.5) if the system of inequalities $G_i[x] > G_i[x^S]\,(i \in \square)$ is inconsistent for all $x \in \mathrm{X}$.

Remark 4.4. According to Definition 4.2, $\overline{x} \in \mathrm{X}$ is not Slater-maximal in problem (4.5) if there exists a strategy $\tilde{x} \in \mathrm{X}$ such that $G_i[\tilde{x}] > G_i[\overline{x}]\,(i \in \square)$.

Proposition 4.2 (sufficient conditions). If

$$\min_{i \in \square} G_i[x^S] = \max_{x \in X} \min_{i \in \square} G_i[x], \tag{4.6}$$

then the strategy $x^S \in \mathrm{X}$ is a Slater-maximal alternative in problem (4.5).

Proof. Due to (4.6) and Remark 4.4, for any strategy $x \in \mathrm{X}$ there exists $k \in \square$ such that the following implication holds:

$\left[G_k[x] \le G_k[x^S] \right] \Rightarrow$ [the system of inequalities $G_k[x] > G_k[x^S]$ $(k \in \square)$ is inconsistent] $\Rightarrow$ [x^S is Slater-maximal in (4.5)].

Theorem 4.1 (existence). If $f_i(\cdot) \in comp(\mathrm{X} \times \mathrm{Y})$, and the sets X and Y are compact, then there exists a Slater-maximal alternative $x^S \in \mathrm{X}$ in the multicriteria choice problem (4.5).

Proof. By Remark 4.1, $[f_i(\cdot\ ) \in c\ o\ m\ \times X\ \square\ ]\ \mathrm{Y} \in$ $[f_i[\ x]\ \ c\ \ o\ (\in m X]$, According to Remark 4.2, $R(\cdot) \in comp(\mathrm{X} \times \mathrm{Y})(i \in \square)$. Hence, due to Remark 4.1,

$\min_{i\in\square} G_i[x] = \min_{i\in\square}(f_i[x] - R_i[x]) \in comp(\mathrm{X}), i \in \square$, and the function $\min_{i\in\square} G_i[x]$ continuous on the compact set X achieves maximum at some point $x^S \in \mathrm{X}$. In other words, equality (4.6) holds, and the conclusion follows by Proposition 4.2.

Definition 4.3. A triple $(x^S, f[x^S], R[x^S])$ is called *the guaranteed solution in outcomes and risks of the multicriteria choice problem under uncertainty* $\Gamma = \langle \square, \mathrm{X}, \mathrm{Y}, f(x,y) \rangle$ if there exist $f_i[x] = \min_{y\in \mathrm{Y}} f_i(x,y), R_i[x] = \max_{y\in \mathrm{Y}} R_i(x,y) (i \in \square)$, where

$$\begin{aligned} &f_i[x] = (f_1[x], ..., f_N[x]), R[x] = (R_1[x], ..., R_N[x]), \\ &R_i[x] = \max_{y\in \mathrm{Y}} R_i(x,y), R_i(x,y) = \max_{z\in \mathrm{X}} f_i(z,y) - f_i(x,y) (i \in \square), \end{aligned} \tag{4.7}$$

and the strategy x^S is a Slater-maximal alternative in (4.5).

Why is the solution from Definition 4.3 proposed? How does it differ from others? The control system is recommended to choose the strategy x^S from the triple $(x^S, f[x^S], R[x^S])$ for the following reasons:

1. For all $i \in \square$, the strategy x^S ensures the outcomes $f_i(x^S, y)$ *not smaller than* x^S with the risk $R_i(x^S, y)$ *not exceeding* $R_i[x^S]$ under any realization of the uncertainty $y \in \mathrm{Y}$. *Thus,* x^S *establishes lower bounds for the outcomes and upper bounds for the associated risks.*
2. The strategy x^S implements the Slater-maximal outcomes and the corresponding minus risks: no other strategy $x \neq x^S$ would increase *all* guaranteed outcomes $f_i[x^S]$ and *simultaneously* reduce all guaranteed risks $R_i[x]$ [[275]].

A promising line of further research is to replace Slater optimality, e.g., with Pareto, Borwein, Joffrion, or A-optimality, using the previously discovered relationship [275]. Replacing scalar minima (Definition 4.2) by the vector ones can also increase the guarantees. However, this issue goes beyond the book.

Remark 4.5. Definition 4.2 suggests a *four-stage procedure to construct the guaranteed solution.* The first three stages are as follows:

1. For $f_i(x,y)$, find $\max_{z\in X} f_i(z,y)=\varphi_i(y)$, and construct the Savage risk function $R_i(x,y)=\varphi(y)-f_i(x,y)(i\in\mathbb{N})$.
2. Determine the guaranteed outcomes $f_i[x]=\min_{y\in Y} f_i(x,y)$ and the guaranteed risks $R_i[x]=\max_{y\in Y} R_i(x,y)(i\in\mathbb{N})$.
3. Using Proposition 4.2, calculate the Slater-maximal strategy x^S in the auxiliary *N*-criteria problem of guarantees Γ_α.

Note that the concept of Pareto maximality can be adopted as well.

Definition 4.4. An alternative $x^P\in X$ is said to be *Pareto-maximal (efficient)* in the multicriteria choice problem (4.5) if the system of inequalities $G_i[x]\geq G_i[x^P](i\in\mathbb{N})$, with at least one strict inequality, is inconsistent $\forall x\in X$ [266-275].

According to [275] and Definition 4.2, any Pareto-maximal alternative is Slater-maximal. (Generally speaking, the converse does not hold). By Karlin's theorem [[91], [99]], an alternative $x^P\in X$ satisfying

$$\max_{x\in X}\sum_{i\in\mathbb{N}}\alpha_i G_i[x]=\sum_{i\in\mathbb{N}}\alpha_i G_i[x^P]\ \forall\alpha_i=const>0, \qquad (4.8)$$

is Pareto-maximal in problem (4.5). Letting $\alpha_1=\alpha_2=1$ for the bi-criteria problem, we obtain the following relation to construct the Pareto-maximal (hence, Slater-maximal) alternative $x^S\in X$:

$$\max_{x\in \mathrm{X}}(G_1[x]+G_2[x]) = G_1[x^S]+G_2[x^S]. \tag{4.9}$$

4. Using x^S, determine the guarantees $f_i[x^S]$ and $R_i[x^S](i\in\mathbb{N})$, and construct the two vectors $f[x^S]=(f_1[x^S],...,f_N[x^S])$ and $R[x^S]=(R_1[x^S],...,R_N[x^S])$, respectively.

The triple $(x^S, f[x^S], R[x^S])$ yielded by this four-stage procedure forms the guaranteed solution in the sense of Definition 4.4. For each criterion $f_i(x,y)(i\in\mathbb{N})$, the strategy $x^S\in \mathrm{X}$ implements the guaranteed outcome $f_i[x^S]$ with the associated Savage risk $R_i[x^S]$ [247, 266-273].

4.3. Modelling Decision Processes under Uncertainty by Combining Nash Equilibrium with Minimax Regret

Like in Section 4.2, the control system's goal is increasing the outcome (payoff) with simultaneously reducing the risk. Also, it is necessary to consider any realization of the interval uncertainty with given limits. In this section, we formalize and justify the concept of a guaranteed Nash equilibrium in payoffs and risks.

Consider a noncooperative *N*-player game under uncertainty of the form

$$\left\langle \mathbb{N}, \{\mathrm{X}\}_{i\in\mathbb{N}}, \mathrm{Y}, \{(f_i(x,y)\}_{i\in\mathbb{N}} \right\rangle, \tag{4.10}$$

where: $\mathbb{N}=\{1,2,\ldots,N\geq 2$ denotes the set of players; each player $i\in\mathbb{N}$ chooses and uses a *strategy* $x_i\in \mathrm{X}_i\subset\mathbb{R}^{n_i}(i\in\mathbb{N})$, thereby forming a *strategy profile* $x=(x_1,...,x_N)\in \mathrm{X}=\prod_{i\in\mathbb{N}}\mathrm{X}_i\subseteq\mathbb{R}^n(n=n_1+\ldots+n_N)$. Any uncertainty $y\in \mathrm{Y}\subset\mathbb{R}^m$ is realized regardless of the players' actions in the game (4.10). *The payoff function of player* i, $f_i(x,y)$ is defined for all pairs

$(x, y) \in \mathrm{X} \times \mathrm{Y}$. The value of this function is called *the payoff of player* i [[275]].

We give the definition of a Nash equilibrium: a strategy profile x^e is called a Nash equilibrium in the game $\langle \square, \{\mathrm{X}_i\}_{i \in \square}, \{f_i[x]\}_{i \in \square} \rangle$ if $\max_{x_i \in \mathrm{X}_i} f_i[x^e \| x_i] = f_i[x^e] (i \in \square)$, where $[x^e \| x_i] = [x_1^e, \ldots, x_{i-1}^e, x_i, x_{i+1}^e, \ldots,$ $\ldots, x_N^e]$. Using the principle of minimax regret, we define the Savage risk.

For the single-criterion choice problem under uncertainty $\Gamma_1 = \langle \mathrm{X}, \mathrm{Y}, f(x, y) \rangle$, let

$$\min_{x \in \mathrm{X}} \max_{y \in \mathrm{Y}} R(x, y) = \max_{y \in \mathrm{Y}} R(x^e, y\} = R, \tag{4.11}$$

where

$$R(x, y) = \max_{z \in \mathrm{X}} f(z, y) - f(x, y) \tag{4.12}$$

is the Savage risk function [244]. The value of $R(x, y)$ is called the Savage risk in the single-criterion problem $\Gamma_1 = \langle \mathrm{X}, \mathrm{Y}, f(x, y) \rangle$. It characterizes the control system's risk when choosing a strategy $x \in \mathrm{X}$ (the deviation between the actual value of $f(x, y)$ and its expected best value $\max_{x \in \mathrm{X}} f(x, y)$). The control system seeks to minimize this risk by choosing $x \in \mathrm{X}$.

The new approach proposed in Section 4.3 combines Nash equilibrium with the principle of minimax regret.

4.3.1. Savage Risk Functions and Payoffs in a Noncooperative Game under Uncertainty

According to Savage's principle of minimax regret (see the previous sections), the risk function of player i is given by

$$R_i(x, y) = \max_{z \in \mathrm{X}} f_i(z, y) - f_i(x, y) (i \in \square), \tag{4.13}$$

where $f_i(x, y)$ is the payoff function of player i in the game (4.10).

To construct the risk function $R_i(x, y)$, we find $\max\limits_{x \in X} f_i(x, y) = f(y)$ $\forall y \in Y$. For determining $f(y)$, suppose the information discrimination of the lower-level player. (This is a standard assumption in the theory of two-level hierarchical games; see [267, 275]). This player forms the uncertainty $y \in Y$ and transfers information to the upper level when constructing a corresponding counterstrategy $x^{[i]}(y): Y \to X$ such that $\max\limits_{x \in X} f_i(x, y) = f_i(x^{[i]}(y), y) = f_i(y), \forall y \in Y$.

The set of such counterstrategies will be denoted by X^Y. It consists of *n*-dimensional vector functions $x(y): Y \to X$ with the domain of definition Y and the codomain X. To construct the minuend in (4.13), for each uncertainty $y \in Y$, the upper hierarchy level has to solve *N* single-criterion choice problems $\langle X^Y, Y, f_i(x, y) \rangle (i \in \mathbb{N})$, where X^Y is the set of counterstrategies $x(y): Y \to X$, and Y is the set of uncertainties. The problem is to find the scalar functions $f_i(y) = \max\limits_{x \in X^Y} f_i(x, y)$ $\forall y \in Y$ and construct the Savage risk functions (4.13).

4.3.2. Guaranteed Solutions and Risks

Proposition 4.3. If $X \in comp\,\mathbb{R}^n$, $Y \in comp\,\mathbb{R}^m$ and $f_i(x, y) \in comp(X \times Y)$, then:

1. The function $\max\limits_{x \in X} f_i(x, y)$ is continuous on Y.
2. The function $\min\limits_{y \in Y} f_i(x, y)$ is continuous on X.

Corollary 4.1. In the noncooperative game under uncertainty (4.10) with $X \in comp\,\mathbb{R}^n, Y \in comp\,\mathbb{R}^m$ and $f_i(x, y) \in comp(X \times Y)$, the Savage risk function $R_i(x, y)(i \in \mathbb{N})$ is continuous on $X \times Y$.

Really, by Proposition 4.3, the minuend in (4.13) is continuous on Y, and the difference of continuous functions is continuous for all $(x, y) \in (\mathrm{X} \times \mathrm{Y})$ [267, 275].

We now turn to guaranteed payoffs and risks in the game (4.10). The method to consider uncertainties when making decisions in conflict systems is as follows: the guarantee $f_i[x] = \min\limits_{y \in \mathrm{Y}} f_i(x, y)(i \in \mathbb{N})$ is associated with each payoff function $f_i(x, y)$ in the game (4.10).

Hence, choosing the strategies $x \in \mathrm{X}$, the players obtain the payoffs $f_i[x] \leq f_i(x, y) \forall y \in \mathrm{Y}$.

Proposition 4.3, Corollary 4.1, and the continuity of the functions $f_i(x, y)$ and $R_i(x, y)$ on $\mathrm{X} \times \mathrm{Y}$ lead to the following result.

Proposition 4.4. If in the game (4.10), the sets X and Y are compact, and the payoff function $f_i(x, y)(i \in \mathbb{N})$ is continuous on $\mathrm{X} \times \mathrm{Y}$, then the guaranteed payoffs

$$f_i[x] = \min_{x \in \mathrm{X}} f_i(x, y)(i \in \mathbb{N}) \tag{4.14}$$

and the guaranteed risks

$$R_i[x] = \max_{y \in \mathrm{Y}} R_i(x, y)(i \in \mathbb{N}) \tag{4.15}$$

are scalar functions continuous on X.

Remark 4.6. *The practical interpretation of the guaranteed payoff* $f_i[x](i \in \mathbb{N})$ is as follows: the payoffs $f_i(x, y)$ realized during the game will be no smaller than $f_i[x]$ $\forall y \in \mathrm{Y}$. Thus, using his (its) strategy from the profile $x \in \mathrm{X}$ in the game (4.10), each player obtains the payoff $f_i(x, y)$ no smaller than $f_i[x](i \in \mathbb{N})$. Consequently, the guaranteed payoff is a lower bound for all possible payoffs of the players under any realization of the uncertainty.

The practical interpretation of the guaranteed risk $R_i[x]$ is an upper bound for all possible Savage risks $R_i(x,y)$ realized $\forall y \in \mathrm{Y}$.

Indeed, (4.15) implies the inequality $R_i(x,y) \le R_i[x] (i \in \mathbb{N})$.

Thus, following the strategy x_i *from* $x \in \mathrm{X}$, *player* $i \in \mathbb{N}$ *obtains the guarantee in payoff* $f_i[x]$ *since* $f_i[x] \le f_i(x,y) \forall y \in \mathrm{Y}$, *simultaneously the guarantee in risk* $R_i[x]$ *since* $R_i(x,y) \le R_i[x] (i \in \mathbb{N})$.

4.3.3. A Noncooperative Game with Two-Component Payoff Function

To investigate the problem further, we pass from the noncooperative *N*-player game under uncertainty (4.10) to the noncooperative *N*-player game under uncertainty with the two-component payoff function:

$$\langle \mathbb{N}, \{\mathrm{X}_i\}_{i \in \mathbb{N}}, \mathrm{Y}, \{f_i(x,y), -R_i(x,y)\}_{i \in \mathbb{N}} \rangle \tag{4.16}$$

Here, the notations $\mathbb{N}, \mathrm{X}_i$, and Y are the same as in the game (4.10), $\{f_i(x,y), -R_i(x,y)\}$ is the two-component payoff function of player *i*, and $R_i(x,y)$ is the Savage risk function $(i \in \mathbb{N})$. The minus sign at $R_i(x,y)$ can be explained as follows: choosing an appropriate strategy $x_i \in \mathrm{X}_i$, player *i* seeks to maximize both criteria *simultaneously*: since $R_i(x,y) \ge 0$ for any $(x,y) \in \mathrm{X} \times \mathrm{Y}$, increasing $-R_i(x,y)$ is equivalent to reducing $R_i(x,y)$. Recall that any uncertainty $y \in \mathrm{Y}$ can be realized.

Due to the interval uncertainty $y \in \mathrm{Y}$ with given limits in the game (4.16), each player $i \in \mathbb{N}$ expects the guaranteed payoffs $f_i[x]$ (4.14) and the guaranteed risks $R_i[x]$ (4.15). With this approach, we pass from the game (4.16) to the game of guarantees $G = \langle \mathbb{N}, \{\mathrm{X}_i\}_{i \in \mathbb{N}}, \{f_i[x], -R_i[x]\}_{i \in \mathbb{N}} \rangle$, where each player $i \in \square$ chooses a strategy $x_i \in \mathrm{X}_i$ to maximize the criteria $f_i[x]$ and $-R_i[x]$ simultaneously.

"Freezing" the strategies of all players in G, except player $x_i \in \mathrm{X}_i$, we arrive in the bi-criteria choice problem

$$G_i = \langle \mathrm{X}_i, \{f_i[x], -R_i[x]\} \rangle \tag{4.17}$$

for each player. In the problem G_i, player i seeks to choose his (its) strategy $x_i \in \mathrm{X}_i$ to maximize the criteria $f_i[x]$ and $-R_i[x]$ simultaneously for $x_i = x_i^e$.

The following question arises: *how can the payoff be increased simultaneously with reducing the risk using only one criterion*? The answer is provided by the concept of vector Pareto optimum [161].

Denoting $f_i[x_i] = f_i[x]$ and $R_i[x_i] = R_i[x]$, we write the problem G_i as

$$\langle \mathrm{X}_i, \{f_i[x_i], -R_i[x_i]\} \rangle. \tag{4.18}$$

Proposition 4.5. Assume that there exist a strategy $x_i^e \in \mathrm{X}_i$ and a number $\tau \in (0,1)$ such that x_i^e maximizes the scalar function

$$F_i[x_i] = f_i[x_i] - \tau R_i[x_i], \tag{4.19}$$

i.e.,

$$F_i[x_i^e] = \max_{x_i \in \mathrm{X}_i} (f_i[x_i] - \tau R_i[x_i]). \tag{4.20}$$

Then x_i^e is the Pareto-maximal strategy in problem (4.18): the system of two inequalities $f_i[x_i] \geq f_i[x_i^e]$, $-R_i[x_i] \geq -R_i[x_i^e]$, with at least one strict inequality, is inconsistent $\forall x_i \in \mathrm{X}_i$.

Proof. Assume on the contrary that the strategy x_i^e (4.20) is not Pareto-maximal in problem (4.18). Hence, there exists a strategy $x_i^* \in \mathrm{X}$ of player i such that the system of two inequalities $f_i[x_i^*] \geq f_i[x_i^e]$ and $-R_i[x_i^*] \geq -R_i[x_i^e]$, with at least of strict inequality, is inconsistent. We multiply both sides of the first inequality by $(1-\tau_i) > 0$ and the second inequality by $\tau_i > 0$. Summing the left- and right-hand sides of the resulting expressions independently, we obtain

$$(1-\tau_i)f_i[x_i^*] - \tau_i R_i[x_i^*] > (1-\tau_i)f_i[x_i^e] - \tau_i R_i[x_i^e].$$

According to (4.19), this means that $F_i[x_i^*] > F_i[x_i^e]$. The latter strict inequality contradicts (4.20), and the proof is complete.

Remark 4.7. The convolution (4.19) of the criteria (4.14) and (4.15) shows the following. If $f_i[x_i^*] \geq f_i[x_i^e]$ for $x_i^* \neq x_i^e$, then by the Pareto maximality of x_i^e and $R_i[x_i] \geq 0$, an improved guaranteed payoff $f_i[x_i^*] \geq f_i[x_i^e]$ leads to a higher guaranteed risk $R_i[x_i^*] > R_i[x_i^e]$. Conversely, decreasing the guaranteed risk $R_i[x_i^*] < R_i[x_i^e]$ also reduces the guaranteed payoff $f_i[x_i^*] < f_i[x_i^e]$. Both scenarios are undesired for the player.

Thus, replacing the bi-criteria choice problem (4.18) with the single-criterion one $\langle \mathrm{X}_i, f_i[x_i] - \tau_i R_i[x_i] \rangle$ gives an answer to the posed question: increases the payoff $f_i[x_i]$ and reduces the risk $R_i[x_i]$ simultaneously. Due to $R_i[x_i] \geq 0$, a higher value of the difference $f_i[x_i] - \tau_i R_i[x_i]$ matches the desire of player i to increase the guaranteed payoff $f_i[x]$ and reduce the guaranteed risk $R_i[x]$ simultaneously using $x_i^* \in \mathrm{X}$.

4.4. Formalization of the Guaranteed Nash Equilibrium in Payoffs and Risks for a Noncooperative *N*-player Game under Uncertainty

This section will answer the following question: how can all actions of the players be combined into a single strategy profile considering the uncertainty? To succeed, we sequentially pass from the original noncooperative N-player game under uncertainty (4.10) to noncooperative games G_1, G_2, and G_3 of the forms

$$G_1 = \langle \mathbb{N}, \{X_i\}_{i\in\mathbb{N}}, Y, \{f_i(x,y), -R_i(x,y)\}_{i\in\mathbb{N}} \rangle,$$
$$G_2 = \langle \mathbb{N}, \{X_i\}_{i\in\mathbb{N}}, \{f_i[x], -R_i[x]\}_{i\in\mathbb{N}} \rangle,$$
$$G_3 = \langle \mathbb{N}, \{X_i\}_{i\in\mathbb{N}}, \{F_i[x] = f_i[x] - \tau_i R_i[x]\}_{i\in\mathbb{N}} \rangle,$$

where:

- $\mathbb{N} = \{1, 2, .., N \geq 2\}$ denotes the set of players;
- $x_i \in X \subset \mathbb{R}^{n_i}$ is the strategy of player i $(i \in \mathbb{N})$;
- $x = (x_1, \ldots, x_N) \in X = \prod_{i\in\mathbb{N}} X_i \subset \mathbb{R}^n (n = \sum_{i\in\mathbb{N}} n_i)$ are the strategy profiles of the games;
- $y \in Y \subset \mathbb{R}^m$ are the uncertainties;
- the payoff function $f_i(x,y)$ of each player $i \in \mathbb{N}$ is defined for all pairs $(x,y) \in X \times Y$;
- the Savage risk function $R_i(x,y)$ is given by (4.13);
- $\tau_i \in (0,1)$ are some constants $(i \in \mathbb{N})$.

In the game G_2, the payoff $f_i(x,y)$ and risk $R_i(x,y)$ functions are replaced by their guarantees $f_i[x] = \min_{x\in X} f_i(x,y)$ and $R_i[x] = \max_{y\in Y} R_i(x,y)$, respectively $(i \in \mathbb{N})$.

In the game G_3, the payoff function of player *i* is replaced by the linear convolution of the guarantees $f_i[x]$ and $-R_i[x]$ (Proposition 4.5).

Consider the game of guarantees

$$G_3 = \langle \mathbb{N}, \{\mathrm{X}_i\}_{i\in\mathbb{N}}, \{F_i[x]\}_{i\in\mathbb{N}} \rangle, \tag{4.21}$$

where $\mathbb{N} = \{1, 2, .., N\}$ is the set of players. Without creating any coalitions, each player $i \in \mathbb{N}$ chooses and uses a strategy $x_i \in \mathrm{X} \subset \mathbb{R}^{n_i}$, thereby forming a strategy profile $x = (x_1, ..., x_N) \in \mathrm{X} = \prod_{i\in\mathbb{N}} \mathrm{X}_i \subset \mathbb{R}^n (n = \sum_{i\in\mathbb{N}} n_i)$. For each player $i \in \mathbb{N}$, the payoff function $F_i[x]$ is defined on the set X. Its value is called the player's payoff [267, 275]. Like before, $[x^e \| x_i] = [x_1^e, ..., x_{i-1}^e, x_i, x_{i+1}^e, x_N^e]$ and $F = (F_1, ..., F_N)$.

Definition 4.5. A strategy profile $x^e = (x_1^e, ..., x_N^e) \in \mathrm{X}$ is called a Nash equilibrium in the game (4.21) if

$$\max_{x_i \in \mathrm{X}_i} F_i[x^e \| x_i] = F_i[x^e]. \tag{4.22}$$

Denoting the set of all profiles $\{x^e\}$ by X^e, we emphasize the following *negative features* of Nash equilibrium:

1. When using Nash equilibrium, even in the game of guarantees, the players need a preliminary agreement regarding the choice of a specific equilibrium from the set X^e.
2. Hence, the player can no longer make independent decisions: agreements with other players are required in advance. This fact contradicts the noncooperative nature of the game, matching the games with coalitions (where such agreements are allowed by definition). Therefore, new approaches to decision-making in noncooperative games should be used, e.g., *the concept of Berge equilibrium* [269].

3. When implementing a pre-selected Nash equilibrium, each player must be sure that the other players in the game will also adhere to their strategies from this equilibrium. (Otherwise, they will not achieve the maximum possible payoff).
4. Such sureness is a problem in real socio-economic conditions: the neoliberal economic doctrine dictates other behavioral principles for economic agents ("every man for himself"). In other words, each player chooses and uses an appropriate strategy based on his (its) interests. There is a vital need to change the economic doctrine, passing to a new philosophical and moral concept (the Golden Rule of ethics) for decision-making.
5. The set of Nash equilibria is internally unstable: there may exist two or more Nash equilibria such that the payoffs of all players in one equilibrium are strictly greater than in the other(s).
6. Such examples were considered in the vast economic literature, and their study goes beyond the scope of this book. Internal instability can be eliminated by adopting as a new solution the so-called active equilibrium (particularly the equilibrium in threats and counterthreats) [24].
7. Nash equilibria are generally improvable. This feature constitutes, e.g., the Prisoner's Dilemma.

The improvability of Nash equilibrium can be eliminated by adopting as new solutions Pareto-maximal strategy profiles or Pareto-maximal Nash equilibria, i.e., Nash equilibria that are simultaneously Pareto-maximal [266, 267].

Nevertheless, the listed features do not diminish the advantages of Nash equilibrium.

We discuss in detail the internal instability of Nash equilibria and possible ways to eliminate it. Also, we construct a Pareto-maximal Nash equilibrium and establish conditions for its existence.

A set $X^e \subset \mathbb{R}^n$ is said to be internally unstable if there are at least two strategy profiles $x^{(1,2)} \in X^e$ such that

$$\left[F[x^{(1)}] < F[x^{(2)}]\right] \Leftrightarrow \left[F_i[x^{(1)}] < F_i[x^{(2)}](i \in \mathbb{N})\right], \tag{4.23}$$

internally stable if condition (4.23) does not hold for any $x^{(1,2)} \in X^e$.

Remark 4.8. Consider the two-player zero-sum modification of the game (4.21), in which $\mathbb{N} = \{1,2\}$ and $f_1 = -f_2 = f^*$. For any two saddle points $x^{(j)} \in \mathrm{X}(j = 1,2)$, we have $f^*(x^{(1)}) = f^*(x^{(2)})$ by the equivalence of saddle points. Therefore, the set of saddle points is internally stable in this game; moreover, a saddle point is a Nash equilibrium [[266], [275]].

Remark 4.9. Internal instability disappears in the game (4.21) with a unique Nash equilibrium.

We associate with the game (4.21) an auxiliary *N*-criteria choice problem of the form

$$\left\langle \mathrm{X}^e, \{F_i[x]\}_{i \in \mathbb{N}} \right\rangle, \tag{4.24}$$

where the set X^e of alternatives x coincides with the set of Nash equilibria x^e in the game (4.21), and the i th criterion $F_i[x]$ is the payoff function (4.19) of player $i \in \mathbb{N}$ [266, 267, 275].

Definition 4.6. An alternative $x^P \in \mathrm{X}^e$ is said to be Pareto-maximal (efficient) in problem (4.24) if the system of inequalities $F_i[x] \geq F_i[x^P]$ $(i \in \mathbb{N})$, with at least one strict inequality, is inconsistent for any $x \in \mathrm{X}^e$. The set of all $\{x^P\}$ will be denoted by X^P [266, 267, 275].

According to this definition, the set $\mathrm{X}^P \subseteq \mathrm{X}^e$ is internally stable.

Also, note the following: if the inequality

$$\sum_{i \in \mathbb{N}} f_i[x] \leq \sum_{i \in \mathbb{N}} f_i[x^P] \tag{4.25}$$

holds for all $x \in \mathrm{X}^e$, then x^P is a Pareto-maximal alternative in problem (4.24).

Definition 4.7. A strategy profile $x^{P_e} \in \mathrm{X}$ is called a Pareto-maximal Nash equilibrium in the game (4.21) if it represents a Nash equilibrium in this game and satisfies Pareto maximality in the sense of Definition 4.6 [266, 267, 275].

Remark 4.10. If the set X^e is non-empty and compact, the sets X_i are compact, and the functions $F_i[x]$ are continuous $(i \in \square)$, the existence of $x^{P_e} \in \mathrm{X}$ in the game (4.21) follows from $\mathrm{X}^e \in comp\mathrm{X} \subset \square^n$.

Sufficient conditions for the existence of a Pareto-maximal Nash equilibrium were established in [275], like an existence theorem in the class of mixed (probabilistic) strategies.

Now we introduce the guaranteed equilibrium in payoffs and risks for the noncooperative N-player game under uncertainty.

Each player in the game (4.10) chooses an appropriate strategy $x \in \mathrm{X}$ to maximize his (its) payoff $f_i(x, y)$ and simultaneously minimize his (its) Savage risk $R_i(x, y) = \max_{z \in \mathrm{X}} f_i(z, y) - f_i(x, y)$ considering any realization of the uncertainty $y \in \mathrm{Y}$. Let $f = (f_1, ..., f_N)$, $R = (R_1, ..., R_N)$, and $F = (F_1, ..., F_N)$ be three N-dimensional vectors, and $\tau_i \in (0,1)$ be N constants $(i \in \square)$.

Definition 4.8. A triple (x^P, f^P, R^P) is said to be *the guaranteed Nash equilibrium in payoffs and risks of the game* (4.10) if the following conditions hold:

1. $f^P = f^P[x]$ and $R^P = R^P[x]$.
2. There exist continuous scalar functions $f_i[x] = \min_{y \in \mathrm{Y}} f_i(x, y)$ and $R_i[x] = \max_{y \in \mathrm{Y}} R_i(x, y)$ on X, where $R_i(x, y) = \max_{z \in \mathrm{X}} f_i(z, y) - f_i(x, y)(i \in \square)$.
3. For at least one constant $\tau_i \in (0,1)$, the set X^e of Nash equilibria x^e is non-empty in the game of guarantees $G_3 = \langle \square, \{\mathrm{X}_i\}_{i \in \mathrm{I}}, \{F_i[x] = f_i[x] - \tau_i R_i[x]\}_{i \in \mathrm{I}} \rangle$, i.e.,

$$\max_{x_i \in X_i} F_i[x^e \| x_i] = F_i[x^e](i \in \mathbb{N}).$$

4. The strategy profile x^P is Pareto-maximal in the *N*-criteria choice problem of guarantees $\langle \mathrm{X}^e, \{F_i[x]\}_{i\in \mathbb{N}} \rangle$, i.e., the system of inequalities

$$F_i[x] \geq F_i[x^P](i \in \mathbb{N}) \forall x \in \mathrm{X}^e$$

is inconsistent.

Finally, we mention *several advantages of this equilibrium*:

1. The solution (x^P, f^P, R^P) takes into account the player's desire to increase the payoff and simultaneously reduce the associated risk.
2. The payoffs satisfy the lower bounds $f_i[x^P] \leq f_i(x^P, y) \forall y \in \mathrm{Y}$, and the risks satisfy the upper bounds $R_i[x^P] \geq R_i(x^P, y) \forall y \in \mathrm{Y}$. The continuity of the guarantees $f_i[x]$ and $R_i[x]$ follows from $\mathrm{X} \in comp\mathbb{R}^n$, $\mathrm{Y} \in comp\mathbb{R}^m$ and $f_i(x, y) \in comp(\mathrm{X} \times \mathrm{Y})$ (Proposition 4.3).
3. Compared to $f_i[x^P]$, improving the player's guaranteed payoff will increase the guaranteed risk above $R_i[x^P]$. Conversely, compared to $R_i[x^P]$, reducing the guaranteed risk will decrease the guaranteed payoff below $f_i[x^P]$.
4. Due to the Pareto optimality of x^P, the difference $F_i[x^P]$ cannot be simultaneously increased.
5. Among all guaranteed solutions, (x^P, f^P, R^P) is the best one maximizing the difference $F_i[x^P]$ in the vector sense.
6. If $\mathrm{X} \in comp\mathbb{R}^n, \mathrm{Y} \in comp\mathbb{R}^m$ and $f_i(x, y) \in comp(\mathrm{X} \times \mathrm{Y})$, then the guarantees $f_i[x]$ and $R_i[x]$ exist and are continuous on X (Proposition 4.3). Therefore, the existence of (x^P, f^P, R^P)

correlates with the existence of a Nash equilibrium in the game of guarantees G_2.

Note that the considerations and proofs of this section [273-275] can be applied to Berge equilibrium.

Conclusion

This chapter has presented new approaches to guaranteed decision-making and risk management in multicriteria choice and conflict problems with uncertain factors. Interval uncertainties with given limits (and without any statistical characteristics) have been considered. The proposed methodology for modelling guaranteed decision processes is based on increasing the outcomes (payoffs) with simultaneously reducing the associated Savage risks under any realization of the interval uncertainty.

Section 4.1 has introduced a new approach to optimal solutions of multicriteria choice problems under uncertainty using Savage's principle of minimax regret. In Section 4.2, the guaranteed solutions and associated risks have been formalized; necessary and sufficient conditions for the existence of these solutions have been established. Section 4.3 has been devoted to noncooperative games. In Section 4.4, a new game-theoretic approach has been proposed to construct the guaranteed solutions and risks, prove their existence, and find a Nash equilibrium and study its properties. Also, the guaranteed equilibrium in payoffs and risks of a noncooperative N-player game under uncertainty has been formalized using Pareto optimality [32], and its advantages have been discussed.

The research of Chapter 4 mainly rests on the author's previous results [20-26, 251-259, 275]. They will be used in the next chapter to construct the balanced Berge equilibrium [15, 16].

Chapter 5

The Guaranteed Berge Equilibrium in Payoffs and Risks for a Noncooperative N-Player Game under Uncertainty

Introduction

Chapter 5 discusses new game-theoretic models of decision processes based on increasing the outcomes (payoffs) and simultaneously reducing the associated Savage risk. They are adopted to construct guaranteed solutions and the corresponding risks and investigate the features of Berge equilibrium.

This chapter involves the approaches and considerations of Chapter 4 applied to the concept of Berge equilibrium. To avoid repetitions, we consider only the specific features of Berge equilibrium and use the results of Section 2.1. To identify the specific features of Berge equilibrium (particularly stability and unimprovability), we formalize the Pareto-guaranteed Berge equilibrium, prove its existence in the class of mixed strategies, and study its properties.

5.1. Modelling Decision Processes under Uncertainty by Combining Berge Equilibrium with Minimax Regret

As repeatedly mentioned, the Golden Rule of ethics (GR) in its positive statement is a widespread philosophical and moral behavioral principle. According to the GR, morality and humanity should underlie decision-making culture at all levels as a main prerequisite and ultimate goal for developing control and controlled systems.

Control systems are usually more complex by content than controlled ones. Control systems fix goals and strategies and determine behavioral rules in the noncooperative game model. Recall that this model consists of the following elements: the set of players (control systems); the set of strategies for each player; a scalar functional for each player, defined on the set of their strategies, which measures the player's performance (the achievement of his (its) goal). This functional is called the player's payoff function.

Following Chapter 4, consider again the noncooperative N-player game under uncertainty:

$$\langle \mathbb{N}, \{X\}_{i\in\mathbb{N}}, Y, \{(f_i(x,y)\}_{i\in\mathbb{N}} \rangle, \tag{5.1}$$

where $\mathbb{N} = \{1,2,\dots,N \geq 2\}$ denotes the set of players. In this game, each player $i \in \mathbb{N}$ independently and simultaneously chooses his (its) *strategy* $x_i \in X_i \subset \mathbb{R}^{n_i} (i \in \mathbb{N})$ without creating coalitions. As a result, a *strategy profile* $x = (x_1,\dots,x_N) \in X = \prod_{i\in\mathbb{N}} X_i \subseteq \mathbb{R}^n$, $n = n_1 + n_2 + \dots + n_N$, is formed in the game. An uncertainty $y \in Y \subseteq \mathbb{R}^m$ is realized independently of the players' strategies.

For each player $i \in \mathbb{N}$, a *payoff function* $f_i(x,y)$ is defined on the pairs $(x,y) \in X \times Y$. Its value is called *the payoff* of player i. In addition, let $X \in comp\mathbb{R}^n, Y \in comp\mathbb{R}^m$ and $f_i(x,y) \in comp(X \times Y)$; see Proposition 4.3 and [267, 275].

Using formula (4.13), we define the Savage risk functions $R_i(x,y) = \max_{z\in X} f_i(z,y) - f_i(x,y) (i \in \mathbb{N})$ and construct the guaranteed payoff $f_i[x] = \min_{x\in X} f_i(x,y)$ and guaranteed Savage risk $R_i[x] = \max_{y\in Y} R_i(x,y)$ of player i, $(i \in \mathbb{N})$; see the expressions (4.14) and (4.15) and [271].

Consequently, we pass to the game of guarantees

$$G_2 = \langle \mathbb{N}, \{X_i\}_{i\in\mathbb{N}}, \{f_i[x], -R_i[x]\}_{i\in\mathbb{N}} \rangle$$

and the auxiliary game

$$\begin{aligned} G_3 &= \langle \mathbb{N}, \{X_i\}_{i\in\mathbb{N}}, \{F_i[x] = f_i[x] - \tau_i R_i[x]\}_{i\in\mathbb{N}} \rangle = \\ &= \langle \mathbb{N}, \{X_i\}_{i\in\mathbb{N}}, \{F_i[x]\}_{i\in\mathbb{N}} \rangle, \end{aligned} \tag{5.2}$$

where $\tau_i \in (0,1)$ is some constant.

Letting $[x \| z_i] = [x_1, ..., x_{i-1}, z, x_{i+1}, ..., x_N]$ and applying the methodology of [275] (also, see Chapter 4), we give the following notion.

Definition 5.1. A strategy profile $x^B = (x_1^B, ..., x_N^B) \in \mathrm{X}$ is called *a Berge equilibrium* in the game (5.2) if

$$f_i(x^B \| x_i) \le f_i(x^B) \forall x \in \mathrm{X} (i \in \square).$$

If the players in the two-player game $(\square = \{1,2\})$ exchange their payoff functions, then the Nash equilibrium of the modified game will become the Berge equilibrium of the original game [269]. Due to this fact, Features 3 and 4 of Nash equilibrium (Section 4.4) will also hold for Berge equilibrium. In particular, *the set of Berge equilibria will be internally unstable and improvable*.

5.2. The Existence of Pareto-Maximal Berge Equilibrium in a Noncooperative *N*-player Game under Uncertainty

To eliminate the negative feature of the game (5.2), we add Pareto optimality to the concept of Berge equilibrium; see Definition 4.7.

Definition 5.2. A strategy profile $x^{P_B} \in \mathrm{X}$ is called a Pareto-maximal Berge equilibrium in the game (5.2) if the following conditions hold:

1. The strategy profile x^{P_B} is a Berge equilibrium in this game, i.e., $\max\limits_{x \in \mathrm{X}} F_i[x \| x_i^B] = F_i[x^B] (i \in \square)$, where $\{x^B\} = \mathrm{X}^B$.
2. The strategy profile x^{P_B} is a Pareto-maximal alternative in the *N*-criteria choice problem $\langle \mathrm{X}^B, \{F_i[x]\}_{i \in \square} \rangle$, i.e., the system of

inequalities $F_i[x] \geq F_i[x^B](i \in \square)$, with at least one strict inequality, is inconsistent $\forall x^B \in \mathrm{X}^B$.

Sufficient conditions for the existence of a Pareto-maximal Berge equilibrium involve the Germeier convolution [63] and the *N*-dimensional vectors $x = (x_1, x_2, ..., x_N) \in \mathrm{X}$, $z = (z_1, z_2, ..., z_N) \in \mathrm{X}$, $f = (f_1, f_2, ..., f_N)$, $R = (R_1, R_2, ..., R_N)$, and $F = (F_1, F_2, ..., F_N)$, and $\tau_i = const \in [0,1](i \in \square)$. Consider the $(N+1)$ scalar functions

$$\begin{aligned} &f_1(x,z) = F_1[z_1, x_2, ..., x_N] - F_1[z], \\ &f_2(x,z) = F_2[x_1, z_2, ..., x_N] - F_2[z], \\ &... \\ &f_N(x,z) = F_N[x_1, x_2, ..., z_N] - F_N[z], \\ &f_{N+1}(x,z) = \sum_{k=1}^{N} F_k[x] - \sum_{k=1}^{N} F_k[z] \end{aligned} \tag{5.3}$$

and their Germeier convolution

$$f(x,z) = \max_{k=1,2,...,N+1} f_k(x,z). \tag{5.4}$$

By analogy with Remark 4.8, we present the following result.

Proposition 5.1. Assume that the two-player zero-sum game

$$\langle \mathrm{X}, \mathrm{Z} = \mathrm{X}, f(x,z) \rangle$$

has a saddle point $(x^0, z^B) \in \mathrm{X} \times \mathrm{Z} = \mathrm{X}$, i.e.,

$$\max_{x \in \mathrm{X}} f(x, z^B) = f(x^0, z^B) = \min_{x \in \mathrm{X}} f(x^0, z).$$

Then the strategy z^B is a Pareto-maximal Berge equilibrium in the game (5.2). Note that the set of saddle points in a zero-sum two-player game is internally stable; hence, *the set of Pareto-maximal Berge equilibria is internally stable*.

Let us prove the existence of Pareto-maximal Berge equilibria in mixed strategies. First, we provide some background on game theory and decision-making.

A pure strategy is a strategy that is *unambiguously* chosen by the player. In applications, such situations are quite rare, and mixed strategies are often used instead. *A mixed strategy can be interpreted as a strategy in which pure strategies alternate randomly.*

Consider the game (5.2) to find a Berge equilibrium that is simultaneously Pareto-maximal in mixed strategies under the following assumptions: the sets of players' strategies are compact, and their payoff functions are continuous. We will apply the methodology of E. Borel [28-31].

Well, $x=(x_1,...,x_N)\in \mathrm{X}=\prod_{i\in \mathbb{N}} \mathrm{X}_i \subseteq \mathbb{R}^n$, and the payoff function of player *i*, $f_i(x,y)$, is defined for all $(x,y)\in \mathrm{X}\times \mathrm{Y}$. Its value gives the payoff of player *i*. In addition, $\mathrm{X}\in comp\,\mathbb{R}^n$, $\mathrm{Y}\in comp\,\mathbb{R}^m$, and $f_i(x,y)\in comp\,\mathrm{X}\times \mathrm{Y}$ (see Proposition 4.3). Now let us pass to the mixed extension of the game (5.2).

We construct a Borel τ-algebra $\Omega(\mathrm{X}_i)$ on each of the *N* compact sets X_i and define probability measures $\mu(\cdot)$ on $\Omega(\mathrm{X}_i)$, i.e., nonnegative scalar functions that are countably additive and normalized to 1. The set of such probability measures will be denoted by $\{\mu_i\}$, and a measure $\mu(\cdot)$ will be understood as a mixed strategy of player *i* [[269]].

For (5.2), we construct mixed strategy profiles as the product measures $\mu(dx)=\mu_1(dx_1)...\mu_N(dx_N)$. Denoting the set of such strategy profiles by $\{\mu_i\}$, we find the mathematical expectations

$$f_i(\mu)=\int_{\mathrm{X}} f_i(x)\mu(dx)(i\in \mathbb{N}). \tag{5.5}$$

Let us associate with the game $G_3 = \langle \mathbb{N}, \{X_i\}_{i\in\mathbb{N}}, \{F_i[x]\}_{i\in\mathbb{N}} \rangle$ (5.2) its mixed extension

$$G_3^* = \langle \mathbb{N}, \{\mu_i\}_{i\in\mathbb{N}}, \{f_i(\mu)\}_{i\in\mathbb{N}} \rangle.$$

The noncooperative *N*-player game G_3^* has the following elements:

$\mu_i(\cdot) \in \{\mu_i\}$ is the mixed strategy of player $i (i \in \mathbb{N})$,

$\mu(\cdot) \in \{\mu\}$ is a mixed strategy profile,

$f_i(\mu)$ is the payoff function of player $i (i \in \mathbb{N})$ given by (5.5).

Consider the *N*-dimensional vectors $x = (x_1, ..., x_N) \in X$ and $z = (z_1, ..., z_N) \in X$, $\mu(\cdot), \eta(\cdot) \in \{\mu\}$, and the mathematical expectations

$$\begin{aligned}
&F_i(\mu) = \int_X F_i(x)\mu(dx),\\
&F_i(\eta) = \int_X F_i(z)\eta(dz),\\
&F_i(\eta \| \mu) = \int_{X_1} \cdots \int_{X_{i-1}} \int_{X_i} \int_{X_{i+1}} \cdots \int_{X_N} F_i(z_1, \dots, z_{i-1}, x_i, z_{i+1}, \dots, z_N)\eta_N(dz_N)\dots\\
&\dots\eta_{i+1}(dz_{i+1})\eta_i(dz_i)\eta_{i-1}(dz_{i-1})\dots\eta_1(dz_1),
\end{aligned} \tag{5.6}$$

where $x_i, z_i \in X_i (i \in \mathbb{N})$ and $x, z \in X$.

In the game (5.2), there is a correspondence between Berge equilibrium in pure strategies (Definition 5.1) and Berge equilibrium in mixed strategies $\mu^B(\cdot) \in \{\mu\}$.

Definition 5.3. A strategy profile $\mu^B(\cdot) \in \{\mu\}$ is called a Berge equilibrium in the game (5.2) if

$$F_i(\mu^B \| \mu_i) \le F_i(\mu^B) \forall \mu(\cdot) \in \{\mu_i\} (i \in \mathbb{N}). \tag{5.7}$$

The profile $\mu^B(\cdot)\in\{\mu\}$ is also called *a Berge equilibrium in mixed strategies* of the game (5.2).

According to [15] and [269], the game (5.2) has a Berge equilibrium in mixed strategies under the conditions $X_i \in comp\mathbb{R}^{n_i}$ and $f_i(x)\in comp(X)$ $(i\in\mathbb{N})$.

We associate with the game $G_3^* = \langle \mathbb{N}, \{\mu_i\}_{i\in\mathbb{N}}, \{F_i(\mu)\}_{i\in\mathbb{N}} \rangle$ the *N*-criteria choice problem

$$\langle \{\mu_i\}_{i\in\mathbb{N}}, \{F_i(\mu)\}_{i\in\mathbb{N}} \rangle. \tag{5.8}$$

In problem (5.8), the control system (DM) seeks to maximize all components of the vector criterion $F(\mu)=(F_1(\mu),...,F_N(\mu))$ by choosing an appropriate strategy profile (alternative) $\mu(\cdot)\in\{\mu\}$. Let us define the concept of a Pareto-maximal alternative.

Definition 5.4. An alternative $\mu(\cdot)\in\{\mu\}$ is said to be Pareto-maximal in problem (5.8) if the system of inequalities

$$F_i[\mu]\geq F_i^P[\mu](i\in\mathbb{N}),$$

with at least one strict inequality, is inconsistent $\forall\mu(\cdot)\in\{\mu\}$ [269].

Due to the results of Chapter 4, the condition $\sum_{i\in\mathbb{N}} f_i[x]\leq\sum_{i\in\mathbb{N}} f_i[x^P]$ (4.25) has the following analog:

If $\sum_{i\in\mathbb{N}} F_i(\mu)\leq\sum_{i\in\mathbb{N}} F_i(\mu^P)$ for all $\mu(\cdot)\in\{\mu\}$, then the mixed strategy profile $\mu^P(\cdot)\in\{\mu\}$ is Pareto-maximal in problem (5.8); see [269, 275].

Definition 5.5. A strategy profile $\mu^{P_B}(\cdot)\in\{\mu\}$ is called a Pareto-maximal Berge equilibrium in mixed strategies of the game (5.2) if:

1. $\mu^{P_B}(\cdot)$ is a Berge equilibrium in the game (5.2) in the sense of Definition 5.3.
2. $\mu^{P_B}(\cdot)$ is a Pareto-maximal alternative in the multicriteria choice problem (5.8) in the sense of Definition 5.4.

Now we establish the existence of a Berge equilibrium in mixed strategies that is Pareto-maximal with respect to all other Berge equilibria.

Proposition 5.2. Consider the noncooperative game (5.2) under the following assumptions:

1. The strategy set of each player *i* is $\mathrm{X}_i \in comp\mathbb{R}^{n_i}\ (i \in \mathbb{N})$.
2. The payoff function $F_i(x)$ of each player $i(i \in \mathbb{N})$ is continuous on the set $\mathrm{X} = \prod_{i \in \mathbb{N}} \mathrm{X}_i$.

Then there exists a Pareto-maximal Berge equilibrium in mixed strategies $\mu^{P_B}(\cdot) \in \{\mu\}$ in this game [269, 275, 276].

Proof. Following the considerations of Chapter 4, we construct the scalar function (5.4):

$$f(x,z) = \max_{k=1,\dots,N+1} f_k(x,z),$$

where

$$f_1(x,z) = F_1[z_1, x_2, \dots, x_N] - F_1[z],$$
$$f_2(x,z) = F_2[x_1, z_2, \dots, x_N] - F_2[z],$$
$$\dots$$
$$f_N(x,z) = F_N[x_1, x_2, \dots, z_N] - F_N[z],$$
$$f_{N+1}(x,z) = \sum_{k=1}^{N} F_k[x] - \sum_{k=1}^{N} F_k[z]$$

are given by formula (5.3), $x=(x_1,...,x_N)\in \mathrm{X}, x_i \in \mathrm{X}_i (i\in \mathbb{N})$ and $z=(z_1,...,z_N)\in \mathrm{X}, z_i \in \mathrm{X}_i (i\in \mathbb{N})$.

According to the proof of Proposition 4.3, the function $f(x,z)$ is defined and continuous on the product $\mathrm{X}\times\mathrm{X}$ of compact sets.

Next, we construct an auxiliary two-player zero-sum game of the form

$$\langle \{\mathrm{I},\mathrm{II}\}, \mathrm{X}, \mathrm{Z}=\mathrm{X}, f(x,z)\rangle. \tag{5.10}$$

In this game, players I and II are opponents: they choose strategies $x\in\mathrm{X}$ and $z\in\mathrm{X}$ to maximize and minimize, respectively, the payoff function $f(x,z)$ continuous on $\mathrm{X}\times\mathrm{Z}=\mathrm{X}$.

We apply to the game (5.10) a special case of Glicksberg's theorem [216]: the saddle point in the game (5.10) coincides with the Nash equilibrium in the noncooperative two-player game

$$\langle \{\mathrm{I},\mathrm{II}\}, \{\mathrm{X},\mathrm{Z}=\mathrm{X}\}, \psi_{\mathrm{I}}(x,z)=f(x,z), \psi_{\mathrm{II}}(x,z)=-f(x,z)\rangle.$$

In this game, player I seeks to maximize $\psi_{\mathrm{I}}(x,z)=f(x,z)$ by choosing $x\in\mathrm{X}$, whereas player seeks to maximize $\psi_{\mathrm{II}}(x,z)=-f(x,z)$ by choosing $z\in\mathrm{X}$. Since the sets X and $\mathrm{Z}=\mathrm{X}$ are compact, and the payoff functions $\psi_{\mathrm{I}}(x,z)=f(x,z)$ and $\psi_{\mathrm{II}}(x,z)=-f(x,z)$ are continuous on $\mathrm{Z}\times\mathrm{X}$, by Glicksberg's theorem there exists a Nash equilibrium (μ^e,η^*) in the mixed extension of this game, written as

$$G_2=\left\langle \{\mathrm{I},\mathrm{II}\}, \{\mu\}, \{\eta\}, \{f_i(\mu,\eta)=\int_{\mathrm{X}}\int_{\mathrm{X}} f_i(x,z)\mu(dx)\eta(dz)\}_{i=\mathrm{I},\mathrm{II}}\right\rangle.$$

Moreover, (μ^e,η^*) is the saddle point of the mixed extension of the game (5.10) [[269], [276]]:

$$\left\langle \{\mathrm{I},\mathrm{II}\},\{\mu\},\{\eta\},\{\psi_i(\mu,\eta)=\int_X\int_X \psi_i(x,z)\mu(dx)\eta(dz)\}_{i=\mathrm{I},\mathrm{II}} \right\rangle.$$

According to Glicksberg's theorem, there exists a pair (μ^e,η^*) representing the saddle point of $\psi(\mu,\eta)$:

$$\psi(\mu,\eta^*)\le\psi(\mu^e,\eta^*)\le\psi(\mu^e,\eta). \tag{5.11}$$

Recall that if the players exchange their payoff functions in the two-player game with □ $=\{\mathrm{I},\mathrm{II}\}$, then the Nash equilibrium of the modified game will be the Berge equilibrium of the original game [269]. Using this fact and Proposition 5.1, we obtain $\mu^e=\mu^B\in\{\mu\}$ and, consequently, $\psi(\mu,\eta^*)\le\psi(\mu^B,\eta^*)\le\psi(\mu^B,\eta)$.

Letting $\eta=\mu^B$ in the right-hand side of this expression yields $\psi(\mu^B,\mu^B)=0$. Therefore, for each $\mu(\cdot)\in\{\mu\}$, we have

$$0\ge\psi(\mu,\eta^*)=\int_X\int_X \max_{k=1,\dots,N=1}\psi_k(x,z)\mu(\mathrm{dx})\eta^*(dz). \tag{5.12}$$

As established in [[266]],

$$\max_{k=1,\dots,N=1}\int_X\int_X \psi_k(x,z)\mu(\mathrm{dx})\eta(dz)\le$$
$$\int_X\int_X \max_{k=1,\dots,N=1}\psi_k(x,z)\mu(\mathrm{dx})\eta(dz). \tag{5.13}$$

(This formula generalizes the well-known property of maximization: the maximum of a sum does not exceed the sum of the maxima).

From (5.12) and (5.13) it follows that

$$\max_{k=1,\dots,N=1}\int_X\int_X \psi_k(x,z)\mu(\mathrm{dx})\eta^*(dz)\le 0,\forall\mu(\cdot)\in\{\mu\}.$$

Hence, for each $k = 1,...,N, N+1$,

$$\int_X \int_X \psi_k(x,z)\mu(\mathrm{dx})\eta^*(dz) \le 0, \forall \mu(\cdot) \in \{\mu\}. \tag{5.14}$$

The mixed strategies and the mixed strategy profile are normalized:

$$\int_X \mu_i(dx) = 1, \int_X \eta_i(dz) = 1, \int_X \mu(dx) = 1, \int_X \eta(dz) = 1 \tag{5.15}$$

For $\mu_i(\cdot) \in \{\mu_i\}, \eta_i(\cdot) \in \{\eta_i\}, \mu(\cdot) \in \{\mu\}, \eta(\cdot) \in \{\eta\} (i \in □)$. Due to this property, we consider two cases, $k \in □$ and $k = N+1$, and refine inequalities (5.14).

1. $k \in □$. With formulas (5.3) and (5.15), for each $i \in □$ inequality (5.14) reduces to:

$$\int_X \int_X [F_i(z\|x_i) - F_i(z)]\mu(dx)\eta^*(dz) =$$
$$\int_X \int_{X_i} [F_i(z\|x_i) - F_i(z)]\mu_i(dx_i)\eta^*(dz) =$$
$$\int_X \int_{X_i} F_i(z\|x_i)\mu_i(dx_i)\eta^*(dz) -$$
$$\int_X F_i(z\|x_i)\eta^*(dz) \int_{X_i} \mu_i(dx_i) \overset{(5.15)}{=}$$
$$[\int_{X_1} \cdots \int_{X_{i-1}} \int_{X_i} \int_{X_{i+1}} \cdots \int_{X_N} F_i(z_1,...,z_{i-1},x_i,z_{i+1},...$$
$$...,z_N)\eta_N^*(dz_N)...\eta_{i+1}^*(dz_{i+1})\mu_i(dz_i)\eta_{i-1}^*(dz_{i-1})...\eta_1^*(dz_1)] - F_i(\eta^*) =$$
$$F_i(\eta^* \| \mu) - F_i(\eta^*) \le 0, \forall \mu_i \in \{\mu_i\}.$$

This result, together with (5.7), implies the inclusion $\eta^*(\cdot) \in \{\eta\}$: by Definition 5.3, the mixed strategy profile $\eta^*(\cdot)$ is a Berge equilibrium of the game (5.2) [266, 269, 276].

2. $k = N+1$. In this case, inequality (5.14) takes the form

$$\int_X \int_X \psi_{N+1}(x,z)\mu(dx)\eta^*(dz) =$$

$$\int_X \int_X \sum_{i\in\mathbb{N}} F_i(x)\mu(dx)\eta^*(dz) - \int_X \int_X \sum_{i\in\mathbb{N}} F_i(z)\mu(dx)\eta^*(dz) =$$

$$\int_X \sum_{i\in\mathbb{N}} F_i(x)\mu(dx)\int_X \eta^*(dz) - \int_X \sum_{i\in\mathbb{N}} F_i(z)\eta^*(dz)\int_X \mu(dx) \overset{(5.9)}{=}$$

$$\sum_{i\in\mathbb{N}} F_i(\mu) - \sum_{i\in\mathbb{N}} F_i(\eta^*) \le 0, \forall \mu(\cdot) \in \{\mu\}.$$

This inequality gives (5.9) for $\mu^P = \eta^*$, i.e., the mixed strategy profile $\eta^*(\cdot)$ is a Pareto-maximal alternative in the *N*-criteria choice problem (5.8).

By items 1 and 2 and Definition 5.5, the profile $\eta^*(\cdot)$ is a Pareto-maximal Berge equilibrium in mixed strategies of the game (5.2). The proof of Proposition 5.2 is complete.

By analogy with Definition 4.8, we formalize the guaranteed (unimprovable) Berge equilibrium in payoffs and risks of the game (5.2).

Definition 5.6. A triple (x^P, f^P, R^P) is said to be *the guaranteed Berge equilibrium in payoffs and risks of the game* (5.2) if the following conditions hold:

1. $f^P = f^P[x]$ and $R^P = R^P[x]$.
2. There exist continuous scalar functions $f_i[x] = \min_{y\in Y} f_i(x,y)$ and

   $R_i[x] = \max_{y\in Y} R_i(x,y)$ on X, where

   $R_i(x,y) = \max_{z\in X} f_i(z,y) - f_i(x,y) (i \in \mathbb{N})$.

3. At least for one constant $\tau_i \in (0,1)$, the set X^B of Berge equilibria x^B is non-empty in the game of guarantees

$$G_3 = \langle \mathbb{N}, \{\mathrm{X}_i\}_{i\in \mathbb{N}}, \{F_i[x] = f_i[x] - \tau_i R_i[x]\}_{i\in \mathbb{N}} \rangle,$$

i.e., $\max\limits_{x_i \in \mathrm{X}_i} F_i[x^B \| x_i] = F_i[x^B](i \in \mathbb{N})$.

4. The strategy profile x^P is a Pareto-maximal alternative in the N-criteria choice problem of guarantees $\langle \mathrm{X}^B, \{F_i[x]\}_{i\in \mathbb{N}} \rangle$, i.e., the system of inequalities

$$F_i[x] \geq F_i[x^P](i \in \mathbb{N}) \forall x \in \mathrm{X}^B$$

is inconsistent [266, 269, 276].

Finally, we emphasize several advantages of this Berge equilibrium:

1. The solution (x^P, f^P, R^P) takes into account the player's desire to increase the payoff and simultaneously reduce the associated risk.
2. The payoffs satisfy the lower bounds $f_i[x^P] \leq f_i(x^P, y) \forall y \in \mathrm{Y}$, and the risks satisfy the upper bounds $R_i[x^P] \geq R_i(x^P, y) \forall y \in \mathrm{Y}$. The continuity of the guarantees $f_i[x]$ and $R_i[x]$ follows from $\mathrm{X} \in comp\mathbb{R}^n, \mathrm{Y} \in comp\mathbb{R}^m$, and $f_i(x,y) \in comp(\mathrm{X} \in \mathrm{Y})$ (Proposition 4.3).
3. Compared to $f_i[x^P]$, improving the player's guaranteed payoff will increase the guaranteed risk above $R_i[x^P]$. Conversely, compared to $R_i[x^P]$, reducing the guaranteed risk will decrease the guaranteed payoff below $f_i[x^P]$.
4. Due to the Pareto optimality of x^P, the difference $F_i[x^P]$ cannot be simultaneously increased.

5. Among all guaranteed solutions, (x^P, f^P, R^P) is the best one maximizing the difference $F_i[x^P]$ in the vector sense.
6. If $\mathrm{X} \in comp\mathbb{R}^n, \mathrm{Y} \in comp\mathbb{R}^m$, and $f_i(x, y) \in comp(\mathrm{X} \in \mathrm{Y})$, then the guarantees $f_i[x]$ and $R_i[x]$ exist and are continuous on X. Therefore, the existence of (x^P, f^P, R^P) correlates with the existence of a Nash equilibrium in the game of guarantees G_2.

Conclusion

We have formalized the Pareto-guaranteed Berge equilibrium, proved its existence in mixed strategies, and revealed its positive and negative properties.

This equilibrium has the following positive features:

1. When using Berge equilibrium, even in the game of guarantees, the players need no preliminary agreements regarding the choice of a specific equilibrium from the set X^B: decision-making is based on the Golden Rule of ethics in its positive statement, and each player independently chooses his (its) strategy without any negotiations with other game participants in advance. This fact matches the noncooperative character of the game.
2. When implementing the chosen Berge equilibrium, each player is sure that the other players will also adhere to their strategies from this equilibrium. (Otherwise, they will not achieve the maximum possible payoff). Such sureness rests on the philosophical and moral paradigm of the Golden Rule of ethics, which underlies decision-making.
3. Like the set of Nash equilibria, the set of Berge equilibria is internally unstable: there may exist two or more Nash equilibria such that the payoffs of all players in one equilibrium are strictly greater than in the other(s) [266, 269, 276]. Internal instability can be eliminated by adopting the followings solutions:
   - active equilibrium (particularly the equilibrium in threats and counterthreats or the equilibrium in sanctions and countersanctions) [21, 24, 248, 279, 281].
   - Pareto-maximal Berge equilibrium (see this chapter of the book).

4. Berge equilibria are generally improvable. This feature can be eliminated by adopting as new solutions Pareto-maximal strategy profiles or Pareto-maximal Berge equilibria, i.e., Berge equilibria that are simultaneously Pareto-maximal (see this chapter of the book). Nevertheless, the listed features do not diminish the advantages of Berge equilibrium.

Thus, Chapter 5 has discussed new game-theoretic models of decision processes based on increasing the outcomes (payoffs) and simultaneously reducing the associated Savage risk. They have been used to construct guaranteed solutions and the corresponding risks and investigate the features of Berge equilibrium. To identify the specific features of Berge equilibrium (particularly stability and unimprovability), we have formalized the Pareto-guaranteed Berge equilibrium, proved its existence in the class of mixed strategies, and studied its properties.

Chapter 6

The Concept of Equilibrium in Sanctions and Countersanctions in a Differential Game of $N \geq 2$ Players

Introduction

This chapter presents a methodology for modelling decision processes in complex controlled dynamic systems. The idea of balancing such systems (driving them to an equilibrium) is implemented, and a new mechanism for the stability of equilibria is proposed. The approach below involves economic-mathematical modeling jointly with methods of systems analysis, economics, law, sociology, game theory, management, and performance measurement. A linear-quadratic positional differential game of several players is considered. Coefficient criteria are derived under which the game has an equilibrium in sanctions and countersanctions and, at the same time, no Nash equilibrium. The economic and legal model of active equilibrium is studied through the legal concept of sanctions, which enlarges the practical application of this class of problems.

6.1. Active Equilibria, Sanctions, and Countersanctions

The current national market system is based on the neoliberal economic doctrine. In differentiated forms, it covers all spheres of public relations and appears in decision processes at all levels of complex control and controlled systems. Various concepts of static [279] and active equilibria [194] are adopted to balance controlled systems [95] in game-theoretic economic-mathematical modeling. If decision-making in a complex system is described by an analytically constructed differential game, then, according to leading researchers, equilibrium as an acceptable solution of a differential game should have the property of stability [263, 272, 281]. In a practical interpretation, stability means that no player will increase his payoff by any unilateral deviation from an equilibrium.

Within the neoliberal economic doctrine, the well-known solution proposed by J. Nash [153-156] meets this requirement in many situations. (In 1994, J. Nash, J. Harsanyi, and R. Selten were awarded the Nobel Prize in Economic Sciences "for the pioneering analysis of equilibria in the theory of non-cooperative games.") Note that this equilibrium does not always exist under certain conditions and (or) has several negative properties. For example, the set of Nash equilibria can be internally and externally unstable. The mathematical problem of ensuring the stability of equilibria can be solved using active equilibria, e.g., the classical equilibrium in threats and counter-threats or the equilibrium in objections and counterobjections [126, 160], simultaneously with imposing the requirement of efficiency (Pareto maximality) [35, 136, 164].

The economic and legal justification of game-theoretic models generally uses the idea of system balancedness: complex controlled systems correlate through interaction, and balancedness means that the legal order of public relations corresponds to the laws and trends of economic development. In a particular case, the economic and legal justification of the equilibrium in sanctions and countersanctions is based on the legal concept of sanctions defining the legal responsibility of subjects (agents). In practical terms, the adjuster implements the principle of inevitable legal liability (particularly sanctions) for an offense and crime (any deviation from the behavioral rules established by legal regulations, e.g., any deviation from the equilibrium mentioned above).

Let us proceed to the conceptual framework used below. At the microlevel, the concept of threat contains both a real action by a market participant and its possibility to compel the latter to comply with the previously established rules; at the macrolevel, the matter concerns "the threat of coercion," i.e., a regulatory definition of the legal inevitability of punishment. In the legal literature, the threat of coercion means a sanction and refers to measures of impact applied in regulation [111, 114]. In mathematical game theory, the terms "threat" and "sanction" can be used as a synonym for the word "objection" to mitigate their "aggressive" nature. The economic content of sanctions in legal sources includes measures of compulsory economic impact for violation of the established procedure for activities and often have preventive, compensatory, and repressive functions. Accordingly, in the macro- and micromodels of decision-making, the player resisting coercion and using countermethods of impact is determined through the concepts of counterobjection, counterthreat, and countersanction.

Like other equilibria, the equilibrium in sanctions and countersanctions can yield stable solutions, but each concept uses different mechanisms. In the case of Nash equilibrium, all players, except for the deviating one, continue using the same strategies as before. In the case of equilibrium in sanctions and countersanctions, the players pass to the legally admissible actions that force the deviating player to follow the equilibrium: the players implement countersanctions. Hence, the inevitability of punishment is a good reason for the players not to deviate from such an equilibrium. From the legislation viewpoint, their actions rest on the concept of legal responsibility for changing the content of a current obligation and future negative consequences due to its violation [114].

As mentioned above, the classical concept of threats and counterthreats is not widespread in mathematical game theory [126] and is restricted either to static games or differential two-player games [19, 50, 61, 173, 203, 259, 263, 279, 280]. The approach presented below is novel for the theory of differential games:

1. We augment the equilibrium in sanctions and countersanctions with the property of Pareto maximality.
2. We identify a fairly large class of differential games of $N \geq 2$ players in which there is an equilibrium in sanctions and countersanctions and, at the same time, there is no Nash equilibrium.
3. We propose an algorithm for constructing the equilibrium in sanctions and countersanctions.

6.2. Problem Statement

To construct a game-theoretic model of equilibrium in sanctions and countersanctions, we consider a noncooperative linear-quadratic differential N-player game in normal form described by an ordered quadruple

$$\Gamma = \left\langle \Box, \Sigma, \{U_i\}_{i\in\Gamma}, \{J_i(U, t_0, x_0)\}_{i\in\Gamma} \right\rangle.$$

In the game Γ, the set of players (e.g., market participants) is $\Box = \{1, \ldots N\}$, where $N \geq 2$. The dynamics of the controlled system Σ (the interacting subjects of market activity, also called agents) obey the vector linear differential equation

$$\Sigma \div \dot{x} = A(t)x + u_1 + \ldots + u_N, x(t_0) = x_0, \tag{6.1}$$

with the following notations: $x \in \mathbb{R}^n$ is the n-dimensional state vector of the system Σ; $t \in [t_0, \vartheta]$ is a finite time interval of the game with a fixed terminal time instant $\vartheta = const > 0$; $u_i \in \mathbb{R}^n$ is the control action of player i $(i \in \mathbb{N})$; $(t, x) \in [0, \vartheta] \times \mathbb{R}^n$ is a pair determining *a current position* in the game Γ; finally, (t_0, x_0) as *an initial position*, where $0 \le t_0 \le \vartheta$. The matrix $A(t)$ of dimensions $n \times n$ is assumed to have continuous elements on $[0, \vartheta]$, which is denoted by $A(\cdot) \in C_{n\times n}[0, \vartheta]$.

The strategy U_i of player i will be identified with an n-dimensional vector function $u_i(t, x)$, and this fact will be denoted by $U_i \div u_i(t, x)$. Then the strategy set of player i can be written as

$$U_i = \{U_i\} = \{U_i \div u_i(t, x), u_i(t, x) = Q_i(t)x \,|\, \forall Q_i(\cdot) \in C_{n\times n}[0, \vartheta]\}.$$

Thus, player i chooses his (its) strategy by specifying a matrix $Q_i(t)$ $(i \in \mathbb{N})$ of dimensions $n \times n$ from the space $C_{n\times n}[0, \vartheta]$.

The game evolves over time under market competition in the following way. Without forming coalitions with other players, each player i chooses a particular strategy $U_i \div Q_i(t)x$, which yields *a strategy profile* $U = (U_1, \ldots U_N) \in U = U_1 \times \ldots \times U_N$ of the game. Next, each player finds the solution $x(t),\ t_0 \le t \le \vartheta,$ of the system (6.1) with $u_i = Q_i(t)x$ $(i \in \mathbb{N})$, i.e.,

$$\dot{x}(t) = [A(t) + Q_1(t) + \ldots + Q_N(t)], x(t_0) = x_0. \tag{6.2}$$

The system of linear homogeneous differential equations (6.2) with continuous coefficients on $[t_0, \vartheta]$ has a continuous solution $x(t)$ that is extendable to $[t_0, \vartheta]\ \forall t_0 \in [0, \vartheta)$. Then each player constructs *the realization* of his (its) strategy $u_i[t] = Q_i(t)x(t)\ (i \in \mathbb{N})$ and the corresponding realization of the strategy profile $u[t] = (u_1[t], ..., u_N[t])$, which consists of the N continuous n-dimensional vectors $u_1[t], ..., u_N[t]$ on $[t_0, \vartheta]$. The payoff function of player i is a quadratic functional

$$J_i(U_1, ... U_N, t_0, x_0) = x'(\vartheta)C_i x(\vartheta) + \int_{t_0}^{\vartheta} \sum_{j \in \mathbb{N}} u_j'[t] D_{ij} u_j[t] dt \quad (i \in \mathbb{N}) \quad (6.3)$$

defined on the continuous pairs $(x(t), u[t]), t \in [t_0, \vartheta]$. Without loss of generality, let the constants matrices C_i and D_{ij} of dimensions $n \times n$ be symmetric. The prime denotes transposition: x' is a row vector. The value of the functional (6.3) is called *the payoff of player i*. The neoliberal economic doctrine assumes that each player in the game Γ seeks to maximize his (its) payoff only.

This research aims to find a rather general class of noncooperative linear-quadratic differential N-player games in normal form Γ that have no Nash equilibrium but simultaneously have an equilibrium in sanctions and countersanctions. To this effect, we will associate with the game Γ the N-criteria dynamic choice problem

$$\Gamma_v = \langle \Sigma, U, \{J_i(U, t_0, x_0)\}_{i \in \mathbb{N}} \rangle.$$

Here, the controlled dynamic system Σ coincides with (6.1); the set of alternatives U coincides with the set of strategy profiles $U = \prod_{i=1}^{N} U_i$ of the game Γ; the N criteria $J_i(U, t_0, x_0) (i \in \mathbb{N})$ are given by (6.3). The DM's goal in the problem Γ_v is to choose an alternative $U^P \in U$ for which the N criteria (6.3) will take the maximum possible values. V. Pareto proposed a conventional approach to such problems in 1909; see [161].

Definition 6.1. An alternative $U^P = (U_1^P, ..., U_N^P) \in U$ is said to be Pareto-maximal in the problem Γ_v if $\forall U \in U$ and $\forall (t_0, x_0) \in [0, \vartheta) \times \mathbb{R}^n$, $x_0 \neq 0_n$, the system of inequalities

$$J_i(U, t_0, x_0) \geq J_i(U^P, t_0, x_0)(i \in \mathbb{N}),$$

with at least one strict inequality, is inconsistent. In this case, the vector $J^P = J^P[t_0, x_0] = (J_1(U^P, t_0, x_0), ..., J_N(U^P, t_0, x_0))$ is called a Pareto maximum in the problem Γ_v.

Note two results, which are immediate from Definition 6.1.

Property 6.1.

$$[J_i(\hat{U}, t_0, x_0) > J_i(U^P, t_0, x_0)] \Rightarrow [J_j(\hat{U}, t_0, x_0) < J_j(U^P, t_0, x_0)]$$

for at least one number $j \in \mathbb{N}$, $j \neq i$.

Property 6.2. If the condition

$$\max_{U \in U}\{\sum_{i \in \mathbb{N}} \alpha_i J_i(U, t_0, x_0)\} = Idem\{U \to U^P\} \tag{6.4}$$

holds for constants $\alpha_i > 0 (i \in \mathbb{N})$, then the alternative U^P is Pareto-maximal in the problem Γ_v. Here, $Idem\{U \to U^P\}$ indicates the bracketed expression from (6.4) with replaced U by U^P.

Consider two concepts of equilibrium for the game Γ, where $J = (J_1, ..., J_N) \in \mathbb{R}^N$.

Definition 6.2. A pair $(U^e, J^e = J(U^e, t_0, x_0)) \in U \times \mathbb{R}^N$ is called *a Nash equilibrium* of the game Γ if

$$\begin{cases} \max\limits_{U_1 \in U_1} J_1(U_1, U_2^e, ..., U_N^e, t_0, x_0) = J_1(U_1^e, U_2^e, ..., U_N^e, t_0, x_0) = J_1^e, \\ \max\limits_{U_2 \in U_2} J_2(U_1^e, U_2, ..., U_N^e, t_0, x_0) = J_2(U_1^e, U_2^e, ..., U_N^e, t_0, x_0) = J_2^e, \\ \ldots \\ \max\limits_{U_N \in U_N} J_N(U_1^e, U_2^e, ..., U_{N-1}^e, U_N, t_0, x_0) = \\ J_N(U_1^e, ..., U_{N-1}^e, U_N^e, t_0, x_0) = J_N^e \end{cases}$$

for any $(t_0, x_0) \in [0, \vartheta) \times \square^n, x_0 \neq 0_n$ (0_n denotes a zero vector of dimension n).

Now we construct the equilibrium in sanctions and countersanctions.

Let $U = (U_1, U_2, ..., U_N)$ be some fixed strategy profile of the game Γ. Player 1 is said to impose a sanction to the strategy profile U if there exists his (its) strategy $U_1^T \in U_1$ such that

$$J_1(U_1^T, U_2, ..., U_N, t_0, x_0) > J_1(U_1, U_2, ..., U_N, t_0, x_0). \tag{6.5}$$

An existing sanction is not necessarily implemented: it means the threat of coercion. Recall that the role of a sanction is revealed through the legal responsibility of players: sanctions make them refrain from violating the established game rules and are implemented in case of "frustration." In terms of game theory, implementing the sanction is beneficial to player 1: according to (6.5), his (its) individual payoff will increase compared to the previous strategy profile U.

The complex of punitive measures taken by one party against the other in response to sanctions is manifested in countersanctions. Player 2 is said to impose *an incomplete countersanction* to a sanction U_1^T of player 1 if there exists a strategy $U_2^C \in U_2$ such that

$$J_1(U_1^T, U_2^C, ..., U_N, t_0, x_0) \leq J_1(U_1, U_2, ..., U_N, t_0, x_0). \tag{6.6}$$

Player 2 is said to impose *a complete countersanction* to U_1^T if there exists a strategy $U_2^C \in U_2$ such that inequality (6.6) is satisfied simultaneously with

$$J_2(U_1^T, U_2^C, \ldots, U_N, t_0, x_0) > J_1(U_1^T, U_2, \ldots, U_N, t_0, x_0). \tag{6.7}$$

Incomplete and complete countersanctions of other players to a sanction U_i^T are formalized by analogy.

In the presence of an incomplete countersanction, player 2 can choose his (its) strategy U_2^C for making the payoff of player 1 (who imposes an original sanction) equal to a value *not exceeding* his (its) original payoff in the strategy profile U; see (6.6). (Note that he (it) may even reduce the payoff of player 1!) Therefore, the presence of an incomplete countersanction negates the implementation of a sanction. In addition, a complete countersanction motivates player 2 to choose U_2^C because his (its) payoff in the resulting strategy prole $(U_1^T, U_2^C, \ldots, U_N)$ yielded by implementing the sanction and countersanction will increase compared to the strategy prole $(U_1^T, U_2, \ldots, U_N)$ yielded by implementing the sanction U_1^T. A sanction U_i^T of player *i* to a strategy profile U and a (complete) countersanction of one of the other players are defined by analogy.

If at least one of the other players has a countersanction to each sanction imposed by any player to U, then it makes no sense for him (it) to implement the sanction: due to the countersanction of another player, his (its) payoff will not increase (but it may even decrease!).

Definition 6.3. A strategy profile $U^P = (U_1^P, U_2^P, \ldots, U_N^P) \in U$ is called an active equilibrium [27] of the game Γ if, for any initial position $(t_0, x_0) \in [0, \vartheta) \times \mathbb{R}^n, x_0 \neq 0_n$:

1. The alternative U^P is Pareto-maximal in the *N*-criteria dynamic choice problem Γ_v.

2. At least one of the other players has an incomplete countersanction to each sanction $U_i^T \in U_i$ of any player.

Definition 6.4. A pair $(U^P, J^P) \in U \times \mathbb{R}^N$ is called *an equilibrium in sanctions and countersanctions* in the differential *N*-player game Γ if, for any initial position $(t_0, x_0) \in [0, \vartheta) \times \mathbb{R}^n, x_0 \neq 0_n$:

1. The alternative U^P is Pareto-maximal in the *N*-criteria dynamic choice problem Γ_v.
2. At least one of the other players has an complete countersanction to each sanction $U_i^T \in U_i$ of any player.

As before, $J^P = (J_1^P, J_2^P, \ldots, J_N^P)$ and $J_i^P = J_i(U^P, t_0, x_0)(i \in \mathbb{N})$. From Denitions 6.3 and 6.4, it follows that any equilibrium in sanctions and countersanctions is at the same time an active equilibrium. Active equilibria and equilibria in sanctions and countersanctions are based on the concept of threats and counterthreats, well known in game theory [160]. They have all the positive properties of Nash equilibria [281]. More specically:

1. They are stable against the deviations of an individual player.
2. They satisfy individual rationality.
3. They coincide with the saddle point in the case of zero-sum two-player games.

At the same time, these equilibria are free from the following disadvantages of Nash equilibrium [281]:

- They exist in several cases when there is no Nash equilibrium (e.g., in the game Γ).
- Unlike Nash equilibrium, they are unimprovable and internally stable due to Pareto maximality.

- The presence of a Nash equilibrium in the game implies the existence of certain types of unimprovable equilibria in which the payoffs of all players are no smaller than in the Nash equilibrium.
- The best Nash equilibria (in the sense of Pareto maximality) are equilibria in sanctions and countersanctions.

Let us emphasize again: the requirement of efficiency (Pareto maximality) has been incorporated into Definitions 6.3 and 6.4 to eliminate some negative properties of Nash equilibrium, such as the internal and external instability of the set of Nash equilibria.

N.N. Krasovskii [104] formalized the concepts of players' strategies and the motions of a dynamic system induced by them for a two-player zero-sum positional differential game. The constructions underlying the positive properties above are valid for a more general class—noncooperative positional differential games [271].

Note that under economic sanctions [158, 159], the methodology for constructing active equilibria, particularly the concept of equilibrium in sanctions and countersanctions, is of utmost importance for economic-mathematical modeling of decision processes and applications.

6.3. Formalization of Efficient Strategy Profiles and Payoffs in the Problem Γ_v

Hereinafter, the notation $D < 0 (> 0)$ means that a quadratic form $x'Dx$ is negative definite (positive definite, respectively).

Consider the auxiliary N-criteria static problem

$$\Gamma_N = \left\langle \mathbb{R}^{Nn}, \{f_i(u) = u_1' D_{i1} u_1 + \ldots + u_N' D_{iN} u_N\}_{i\in\mathbb{N}} \right\rangle, \tag{6.8}$$

in which the DM chooses an alternative $u = (u_1, u_2, \ldots, u_N) \in \mathbb{R}^{Nn}$ for simultaneously maximizing all components of a vector criterion $f(u) = (f_1(u), f_2(u), \ldots, f_N(u))$.

For this problem, Definition 6.1 can be reformulated as follows: an alternative u^P is Pareto-maximal in Γ_N if $\forall u \in \mathbb{R}^{Nn}$ the system of inequalities $f_i(u) \geq f_i(u^P)(i \in \mathbb{N})$, with at least one strict inequality, is inconsistent.

We present some auxiliary properties of the quadratic forms $x'Dx = \sum_{\gamma,\beta=1}^{n} d_{\gamma\beta} x_\gamma x_\beta$ with constant coefficients $d_{\gamma\beta}$ (the elements of a matrix D of dimensions $n \times n$) and the components $x_1, \ldots, x_n$ of an n-dimensional vector $x \in \mathbb{R}^n$.

Lemma 6.1. With the change of coefficients $b_{\gamma\beta} = \dfrac{d_{\gamma\beta} + d_{\beta\gamma}}{2}$, a quadratic form $x'Dx$ is reduced to the form $x'Bx$, where the matrix $B = (b_{ij})$ of dimensions $n \times n$ is symmetric, i.e., $B = B'$.

Without loss of generality, all quadratic forms below are supposed to have symmetric matrices.

Lemma 6.2. If $D_{ii} > 0$, then all n roots of the characteristic equation $\det[D_{ii} - \Lambda E_n] = 0$ are real and positive $(i \in \mathbb{N})$, where E_n denotes an identity matrix of dimensions $n \times n$ [[62]].

Let $\Lambda_{ii} > 0$ be the greatest root under consideration. Then

$$u_i' D_{ii} u_i \leq \Lambda_{ii} \|u_i\|^2 = \Lambda_{ii} u_i' u_i \ \forall u_i \in \mathbb{R}^n. \tag{6.9}$$

Since $D > 0 \Leftrightarrow -D = (-1)D < 0$, for $D < 0$, all n roots $\lambda_{ij} < 0$ of the characteristic equation $\det[D_{ij} - \lambda E_n] = 0$ are negative $(i, j \in \mathbb{N}, i \neq j)$.

Let $-\lambda_{ij}$ be the greatest (smallest by magnitude) root among them. By analogy with (6.9), we have

$$u_j' D_{ij} u_i \leq -\lambda_{ij} u_i' u_j \ \forall u_j \in \mathbb{R}^n. \tag{6.10}$$

Without loss of generality, consider the *N*-criteria choice problem Γ_N in which a sanction is imposed by player 1 and a countersanction by player 2. (The players are numbered subjectively).

The next result follows from Property 6.2.

Lemma 6.3. Assume that in the problem Γ_N:

1. The symmetric matrices D_{ij} of dimensions $n \times n$ satisfy the inequalities $D_{ii} > 0, D_{ij} < 0 \; (i, j \in \square, i \neq j)$ and

$$\Lambda_{11}\Lambda_{22} < \lambda_{12}\lambda_{21}. \tag{6.11}$$

2. The nonzero matrix

$$A = \begin{bmatrix} \Lambda_{11} & -\lambda_{21} & \dots & -\lambda_{N1} \\ -\lambda_{12} & \Lambda_{22} & \dots & -\lambda_{N2} \\ \dots & \dots & \dots & \dots \\ -\lambda_{1N} & -\lambda_{2N} & \dots & \Lambda_{NN} \end{bmatrix}$$

of dimensions $N \times N$ is singular, i.e., its determinant is $\det A = 0$.

Then the system of strict homogeneous linear inequalities

$$\begin{cases} +\alpha_1\Lambda_{11} - \alpha_2\lambda_{21} - \alpha_3\lambda_{31} - \dots - \alpha_N\lambda_{N1} < 0, \\ -\alpha_1\lambda_{12} + \alpha_2\Lambda_{22} - \alpha_3\lambda_{32} - \dots - \alpha_N\lambda_{N2} < 0, \\ -\alpha_1\lambda_{13} - \alpha_2\lambda_{23} + \alpha_3\Lambda_{33} - \dots - \alpha_N\lambda_{N3} < 0, \\ \dots\dots\dots\dots\dots\dots\dots\dots\dots\dots\dots\dots \\ -\alpha_1\lambda_{1N} - \alpha_2\lambda_{2N} - \alpha_3\lambda_{3N} - \dots - \alpha_{N-1}\lambda_{N-1N} + \alpha_N\Lambda_{NN} < 0, \end{cases} \tag{6.12}$$

has a positive solution $\alpha = (1, \alpha_2, \dots, \alpha_N), \alpha_j > 0, j = 2, \dots, N$, where Λ_{ii} and $-\lambda_{ij} \; (i, j \in \square, i \neq j)$ are the greatest roots of the characteristic equations

$\det[D_{ii} - \Lambda E_n] = 0$ and $\det[D_{ij} - \lambda E_n] = 0,$ respectively $(i, j \in \square, i \neq j)$.

Proof. To construct a Pareto-maximal strategy profile in the game Γ, we will apply Property 6.2 and the linear convolution $\sum_{i \in \square} \alpha_i f_i(u)$ of the criteria (6.8) with positive coefficients $\alpha_i > 0$. For (6.8), we construct a quadratic form from the components of the *Nn*-dimensional vector $u = (u_1, ..., u_N)$:

$$f(u) = \sum_{i \in \square} \alpha_i f_i(u) = \sum_{i \in \square} \alpha_i [u_1' D_{i1} u_1 + u_2' D_{i2} u_2 + ... + u_N' D_{iN} u_N].$$

Due to (6.8) – (6.10),

$$\begin{aligned}
&f(u) = u_1'[\alpha_1 \Lambda_{11} - \alpha_2 \lambda_{21} - \alpha_3 \lambda_{31} - ... - \alpha_N \lambda_{N1}] u_1 + \\
&u_2'[-\alpha_1 \lambda_{12} + \alpha_2 \Lambda_{22} - \alpha_3 \lambda_{32} - ... - \alpha_N \lambda_{N2}] u_2 + \\
&\dots\dots\dots\dots\dots\dots\dots\dots\dots\dots + \\
&u_{N-1}'[-\alpha_1 \lambda_{1N-1} - \alpha_2 \lambda_{2N-1} - ... + \alpha_{N-1} \Lambda_{N-1N-1} - \alpha_N \lambda_{NN-1}] u_{N-1} + \\
&u_N'[-\alpha_1 \lambda_{1N} - \alpha_2 \lambda_{2N} - ... - \alpha_{N-1} \lambda_{N-1N} + \alpha_N \Lambda_{NN}] u_N = \\
&d_1 \|u_1\|^2 + .. + d_N \|u_N\|^2 .
\end{aligned}$$

The numbers $\alpha_i = const > 0$ $(i \in \square)$ can be chosen so that all d_i will become negative and

$$\begin{aligned}
&d_1 = [\alpha_1 \Lambda_{11} - \alpha_2 \lambda_{21} - \alpha_3 \lambda_{31} - ... - \alpha_N \lambda_{N1}], \\
&d_2 = [-\alpha_1 \lambda_{12} + \alpha_2 \Lambda_{22} - \alpha_3 \lambda_{32} - ... - \alpha_N \lambda_{N2}], \\
&\dots\dots\dots\dots\dots\dots\dots\dots\dots\dots \qquad (6.13) \\
&d_{N-1} = [-\alpha_1 \lambda_{1N-1} - \alpha_2 \lambda_{2N-1} - ... + \alpha_{N-1} \Lambda_{N-1N-1} - \alpha_N \lambda_{NN-1}], \\
&d_N = [-\alpha_1 \lambda_{1N} - \alpha_2 \lambda_{2N} - ... - \alpha_{N-1} \lambda_{N-1N} + \alpha_N \Lambda_{NN}].
\end{aligned}$$

To prove this fact, we associate with (6.12) the system of strict homogeneous linear inequalities

$$\begin{cases} \alpha_1\Lambda_{11} - \alpha_2\lambda_{21} < 0, \\ -\alpha_1\lambda_{12} + \alpha_2\Lambda_{22} < 0, \\ -\alpha_1\lambda_{13} - \alpha_2\lambda_{23} + \alpha_3\Lambda_{33} < 0, \\ -\alpha_1\lambda_{14} - \alpha_2\lambda_{24} - \alpha_3\lambda_{34} + \alpha_4\Lambda_{44} < 0, \\ \dots\dots\dots\dots\dots\dots\dots\dots\dots\dots\dots\dots \\ -\alpha_1\lambda_{1N-1} - \alpha_2\lambda_{2N-1} - \dots + \alpha_{N-1}\Lambda_{N-1N-1} < 0, \\ -\alpha_1\lambda_{1N} - \alpha_2\lambda_{2N} - \dots - \alpha_{N-1}\lambda_{N-1N} + \alpha_N\Lambda_{NN} < 0. \end{cases} \tag{6.14}$$

This system is obtained from (6.12) by discarding all negative terms, except for $-\alpha_2\lambda_{21}$ in the first inequality and $-\alpha_1\lambda_{12}$ in the second one. Adding negative terms only strengthens strict inequalities. Hence, for $\lambda_{ij} > 0$ and $\alpha_i > 0$, any positive solutions of the system (6.14) are also positive for (6.12). Then the quadratic form $f(u)$ will be negative definite with respect to the Nn-dimensional vector $u = (u_1, \dots, u_N)$ if the system (6.12) (or the system (6.14)) has the positive solution $\alpha = (1, \alpha_1, \dots, \alpha_N)$, $\alpha_\gamma > 0 (\gamma = 2, \dots, N)$ that is, all numbers. Let us establish this result for the system (6.14). To this end, we find α_2 from the first two strict inequalities of (6.14):

$$\begin{cases} \alpha_1\Lambda_{11} - \alpha_2\lambda_{21} < 0, \\ -\alpha_1\lambda_{12} + \alpha_2\Lambda_{22} < 0. \end{cases}$$

If $\alpha_1 = 1$, then for $\Lambda_{ii} > 0$ and $-\lambda_{ij} > 0$ $(i, j \in \square, i \neq j)$, there exists a positive number α_2 such that

$$\begin{Bmatrix} \Lambda_{11} - \alpha_2 \lambda_{21} < 0 \\ -\lambda_{12} + \alpha_2 \Lambda_{22} < 0 \end{Bmatrix} \Leftrightarrow \begin{Bmatrix} \dfrac{\Lambda_{11}}{\lambda_{21}} < \alpha_2 \\ \dfrac{\lambda_{12}}{\Lambda_{22}} > \alpha_2 \end{Bmatrix} \Leftrightarrow \left\{ \frac{\Lambda_{11}}{\lambda_{21}} < \alpha_2 \frac{\lambda_{12}}{\Lambda_{22}} \right\}.$$

This inequality holds under $\Lambda_{11}\Lambda_{22} < \lambda_{12}\lambda_{21}$, e.g., for

$$\alpha_2 = \frac{1}{2}\left[\frac{\Lambda_{11}}{\lambda_{21}} + \frac{\lambda_{12}}{\Lambda_{22}}\right]. \tag{6.15}$$

From the third inequality of (6.14), for $\alpha_1 = 1$ and α_2 (6.15), we obtain

$$0 < \alpha_3 < \frac{1}{\Lambda_{33}}\left[\lambda_{13} + \frac{\lambda_{23}}{2}\left(\frac{\Lambda_{11}}{\lambda_{21}} + \frac{\lambda_{12}}{\Lambda_{22}}\right)\right],$$

e.g., by letting $\alpha_3 = \dfrac{1}{2\Lambda_{33}}\left[\lambda_{13} + \dfrac{\lambda_{23}}{2}\left(\dfrac{\Lambda_{11}}{\lambda_{31}} + \dfrac{\lambda_{32}}{\Lambda_{22}}\right)\right]$. Continuing the considerations above, using the subsequent inequalities of (6.14) and the calculated values $\alpha_1 = 1, \alpha_2, \alpha_3, \ldots,$ we finally arrive at the recurrent formula

$$\alpha_N = \frac{1}{2\Lambda_{NN}}[\lambda_{1N} + \alpha_2\lambda_{2N} + \ldots + \alpha_{N-1}\lambda_{N-1N}]. \qquad \square$$

Remark 6.1. By analogy with Lemma 6.3, we have the following result. Assume that in the problem Γ_N, the symmetric matrices D_{ij} of dimensions $n \times n$ and positive numbers Λ_{ii} and λ_{ij} are such that $D_{ii} > 0, D_{ij} < 0$ for $i \neq j$ and $\Lambda_{11}\Lambda_{33} < \Lambda_{13}\Lambda_{31}$.

Then for

$$\alpha_2 = \frac{1}{2}\left(\frac{\lambda_{13}}{\Lambda_{33}} + \frac{\Lambda_{11}}{\lambda_{31}}\right),$$

$$\alpha_3 = \frac{1}{2}\left[\frac{\lambda_{12}}{\Lambda_{22}} + \frac{1}{2}\left(\frac{\lambda_{13}}{\Lambda_{33}} + \frac{\Lambda_{11}}{\lambda_{31}}\right)\frac{\lambda_{32}}{\Lambda_{22}}\right], \ldots$$

and $\alpha_\gamma (\gamma = 4, \ldots, N)$ given by Lemma 6.3, the quadratic form

$$f(u) = f_1(u) + \alpha_2 f_2(u) + \alpha_3 f_3(u) + \ldots + \alpha_N f_N(u) =$$
$$u_1' d_1 u_1 + u_2' d_2 u_2 + u_3' d_3 u_3 + \ldots + u_N' d_N u_N$$

becomes negative definite; the constants $d_i < 0$ are given by (6.13).

Really, α_2 and α_3 in this expression satisfy the strict inequalities (6.12).

Note that in addition to the solutions α_γ (Lemma 6.3 and Remark 6.1), the system of strict inequalities (6.12) have a continuum of other solutions. As demonstrated below, each of them induces a specific equilibrium in sanctions and countersanctions of the differential game Γ under the conditions $D_{ii} > 0, D_{ij} < 0 (i, j \in \mathbb{N}, i \neq j)$.

Remark 6.2. Positive solutions of (6.12) can be found using S.N. Chernikov's approach [37]. To avoid cumbersome transformations and notations dictated by this approach, we propose an original method for proving Lemma 6.3.

Lemma 6.4. The solutions $x(t)$ of the system $\dot{x} = K(t)x,\ x(t_0) = x_0$, where $K(\cdot) \in C_{n\times n}[0, \vartheta]$, satisfy the nontrivial property

$$x_0 \neq 0_n \Rightarrow x(t) \neq 0_n \ \forall t \in [t_0, \vartheta];$$

here 0_n denotes a zero vector from the space $\mathbb{R}^n$.

Proof. Assume on the contrary that $\exists t_1 (t_0, \vartheta]$ such that $x(t) = 0_n$. In other words, at the time instant t_1, two different solutions of the system $\dot{x} = K(t)x$ are passing through the position $(t_1, 0_n)$: the trivial one $x^{(1)}(t) = 0_n \ \forall t \in [0, \vartheta]$ and the nontrivial one $x^{(2)}(t)$ induced by the nonzero initial condition $x_0 \neq 0_n$. This obviously contradicts the existence and uniqueness theorem for the solution of a matrix linear differential equation with continuous coefficients. $\square$

Proposition 6.3. Assume that in the differential game Γ,

$$D_{ii} > 0, D_{ij} < 0, C_i < 0 (i, j \in \square, i \neq j), \text{ and } \Lambda_{11}\Lambda_{22} < \Lambda_{12}\Lambda_{21}. \quad (6.16)$$

Then a Pareto-maximal alternative U^P in the *N*-criteria choice problem Γ_v has the form

$$\begin{aligned} &U^P = (U_1^P, U_2^P, \dots, U_N^P) \div (u_1^P(t,x), u_2^P(t,x), \dots, u_N^P(t,x)) = \\ &u^P(t,x) = (Q_1^P(t)x, Q_2^P(t)x, \dots, Q_N^P(t)x) = \\ &(-d_1^{-1}\Theta^P(t)x, -d_2^{-1}\Theta^P(t)x, \dots, -d_N^{-1}\Theta^P(t)x), \end{aligned} \quad (6.17)$$

where

$$\begin{aligned} &\Theta^P(t) = [X^{-1}(t)]'\{C^{-1} + \int_t^{\vartheta} X^{-1}(\tau)[d_1^{-1} + d_2^{-1} + \dots \\ &\dots + d_N^{-1}][X^{-1}(\tau)]' d\tau\}^{-1} X^{-1}(t) \end{aligned} \quad (6.18)$$

is a continuous symmetric matrix of dimensions $n \times n$ on the time interval $[0, \vartheta]$;

the negative constants d_i are given by (6.13);

$$\alpha_2 = \frac{1}{2}\left[\frac{\Lambda_{11}}{\lambda_{21}} + \frac{\lambda_{12}}{\Lambda_{22}}\right], \alpha_3 = \frac{1}{2}\left[\frac{\lambda_{13}}{\Lambda_{33}} + \frac{1}{2}\left(\frac{\Lambda_{12}}{\lambda_{21}} + \frac{\lambda_{12}}{\Lambda_{22}}\right)\frac{\lambda_{23}}{\Lambda_{33}}\right], \quad (6.19)$$

and the other numbers $\alpha_\gamma (\gamma = 4,...,N)$ are calculated by the recurrent formulas

$$\alpha_m = \frac{1}{2\Lambda_{mm}}[\lambda_{1m} + \alpha_2\lambda_{2m} + ... + \alpha_{m-1}\lambda_{m-1m}](m = 4,...,N), \quad (6.20)$$

where Λ_{ii} is the greatest root of the characteristic equation $\det[D_{ii} - \Lambda E_n] = 0 \ (i \in \square)$, and $-\lambda_{ij}$ is the greatest root of the characteristic equation $\det[D_{ij} - \lambda E_n] = 0 \ (i, j \in \square, i \neq j)$; E_n denotes an identity matrix of dimensions $n \times n$; finally, $X(t)$ means the fundamental matrix of the system $\dot{x} = A(t)x, X(\vartheta) = E_n$.

Proof. We construct a Pareto-maximal alternative U^P using Lemma 6.3 (formula (6.4)) and dynamic programming [263]. Due to Property 6.2, the application of dynamic programming reduces to two stages as follows.

First stage. For the problem Γ, find $(N-1)$ positive numbers $\alpha_m (m = 2,...,N-1)$, a continuously differentiable scalar function $V(t,x) = x'\Theta(t)x, \ \Theta(t) = \Theta'(t) \ \forall t \in [0,\vartheta]$, and *Nn*-dimensional vector functions $u_i(t,x,V)(i \in \square)$ such that

$$V(\vartheta, x) = x'Cx, C = C_1 + \alpha_2 C_2 + ... + \alpha_N C_N \forall x \in \square^n \quad (6.21)$$

Then, using the scalar function

$$W(t,x,u_1,u_2,...,u_N,V)=\frac{\partial V}{\partial x}+\left[\frac{\partial V}{\partial t}\right]'(A(t)x+u_1+u_2+...+u_N)+$$
$$u_1'd_1u_1+u_2'd_2u_2+...+u_N'd_Nu_N,$$

find Nn-dimensional vector functions $u_i(t,x,V)(i\in\square)$ from

$$\max_{u_1,u_2,...,u_N} W(t,x,u_1,u_2,...,u_N,V)=Idem\{u_i\to u_i(t,x,V)\}(i\in\square) \quad (6.22)$$

for any $t\in[0,\vartheta], x\in\square^n$ and $V\in\square$ $\left(\frac{\partial V}{\partial x}=grad_x V\right)$. The functions $u_i(t,x,V)$ in (6.22) exist under the following sufficient conditions: for all $(t,x)\in[0,\vartheta)\times\square^n$,

$$\begin{gathered}\left.\frac{\partial V}{\partial x}\right|_{u(t,x,V)}=\frac{\partial V}{\partial x}+2d_iu_u(t,x,V)=0_n(i\in\square)\\ \frac{\partial^2 W}{\partial u_i^2}=2d_iE_n<0,(i\in\square),\end{gathered} \quad (6.23)$$

where (as before) 0_n denotes an n-dimensional zero vector from the space $\square^n$, and $d_i<0$ by Lemma 6.3.

From (6.23) it follows that

$$u_i(t,x,V)=-\frac{1}{2}d_1^{-1}\frac{\partial V}{\partial x}(i\in\square). \quad (6.24)$$

Then

$$W(t,x,u(t,x,V),V)=W[t,x,V]=$$
$$\frac{\partial V}{\partial t}+\left[\frac{\partial V}{\partial x}\right]'A(t)x-\frac{1}{4}\left(\frac{\partial V}{\partial x}\right)'[d_1^{-1}+d_2^{-1}+...+d_N^{-1}]\frac{\partial V}{\partial x}.$$

The second stage. Find the solution $V = V^P(t,x) = x'\Theta^P x, \Theta^P = [\Theta^P(t)]$, of the partial differential equation

$$W[t,x,V] = 0$$

with the boundary condition

$$V(\vartheta, x) = x'Cx \ \forall x \in \mathbb{R}^n,$$

where $C = C_1 + \alpha_2 C_2 + ... + \alpha_N C_N$. In other words, for all $t \in [0, \vartheta]$ and all $x \in \mathbb{R}^n$,

$$W[t,x,V(t,x)] = x'\Theta^P x = 0, V(\vartheta, x) = x'Cx \ \forall x \in \mathbb{R}^n.$$

Consequently, the symmetric matrix $\Theta^P(t)$ of dimensions $n \times n$ satisfies the Riccati matrix differential equation

$$\dot{\Theta}^P(t) + \Theta^P(t)A(t) + A'(t)\Theta^P(t) - \Theta^P(t)[d_1^{-1} + d_2^{-1} + ...$$
$$... + d_N^{-1}]\Theta^P(t) = 0_{n\times n},$$
$$\Theta^P(\vartheta) = C = C_1 + \alpha_2 C_2 + ... + \alpha_N C_N,$$

where $0_{n\times n}$ denotes a zero matrix of dimensions $n \times n$.

As is well known [263], the solution $\Theta^P(t)$ of the Riccati matrix differential equation has the form (6.18). (Here, the implication

$$C_i < 0 (i \in \mathbb{N}) \Rightarrow C_1 + \alpha_2 C_2 + ... + \alpha_N C_N < 0$$

has been taken into account). Formula (6.18), in combination with another implication

$$[V(t,x) = x'\Theta^P(t)x] = \left[\frac{\partial V(t,x)}{\partial x} = 2\Theta^P(t)x\right],$$

finally yields (6.17). Thus, a Pareto-maximal alternative U^P in the multicriteria choice problem Γ_v is given by (6.17) and (6.18).

Now we construct the Pareto-maximal payoffs

$$J^P = (J_1(U^P, t_0, x_0), J_2(U^P, t_0, x_0), \dots, J_N(U^P, t_0, x_0)) = (J_1^P, J_2^P, \dots, J_N^P)$$

using dynamic programming and [272].

Proposition 6.4. Let conditions (6.16) of Proposition 6.3 be valid. Assume that for the differential game Γ, there are N scalar continuously differentiable functions $V_i(t,x) = x'\Theta_i(t)x (i \in \mathbb{N})$ such that:

1. $V_i(\vartheta, x) = x'C_i x \ \forall x \in \mathbb{R}^n$,
2. The system of N partial differential equations

$$\frac{\partial V_i}{\partial t} + \left(\frac{\partial V_i}{\partial x}\right)' (N(t)x + x'\Theta^P(t)M_i(t)\Theta^P(t)x) = 0, \qquad (6.25)$$
$$V_i(\vartheta, x) = x'C_i x, \forall x \in \mathbb{R}^n (i \in \mathbb{N})$$

has the solution $V_i(t,x) = x'\Theta_i(t)x,\ [\Theta_i(t)]' = \Theta_i(t)(i \in \mathbb{N})$.

Then for any initial position $(t_0, x_0) \in [0, \vartheta) \times \mathbb{R}^n, x_0 \neq 0_n$,

$$J_i^P = J_i(U^P, t_0, x_0) = x_0'\Theta_i^P(t_0)x_0 (i \in \mathbb{N}).$$

In (6.25),

$$N(t) = A(t) - (d_1^{-1} + d_2^{-1} + \dots + d_N^{-1})E_n,$$
$$M_i(t) = \Theta^P(t)\left([d_1^{-1}]^2 D_{i1} + [d_2^{-1}]^2 D_{i2} + \dots + [d_N^{-1}]^2 D_{iN}\right)\Theta^P(t)$$
$$(i \in \mathbb{N})$$

are continuous matrices of dimensions $n \times n$; the matrix $\Theta^P(t)$ is given by (6.17) and (6.18); the numbers d_i are given by (6.13);

$$\Theta_i(t) = \left[Y^{-1}(t)\right]' \left\{C_i - \int_t^{\vartheta} Y'(\tau)\Theta(\tau)M_i(\tau)Y(\tau)d\tau\right\} Y^{-1}(t)(i \in \square) \quad (6.26)$$

are symmetric matrices of dimensions $n \times n$; finally, $Y(t)$ denotes the fundamental matrix of the homogeneous system $\dot{y} = N(t)y, Y(\vartheta) = E_n$.

Proof. We construct the *N* scalar functions

$$W[t,x,V_i] = \frac{\partial V}{\partial t} + \left[\frac{\partial V}{\partial x}\right]' (N(t)x + [u_1^P(t,x)]'D_{i1}u_1^P(t,x) + \\ [u_2^P(t,x)]'D_{i2}u_2^P(t,x) + \ldots + [u_N^P(t,x)]'D_{iN}u_N^P(t,x)(i \in \square), \quad (6.27)$$

where $u_i^P(t,x)$ are the *n*-dimensional vector functions given by (6.17) and (6.18).

Let us find the solution $V_i(t,x)(i \in \square)$ of the system of *N* partial differential equations

$$W_i[t,x,V_i] = 0, V_i(\vartheta,x) = x'C_i x \ \forall x \in \square^n (i \in \square) \quad (6.28)$$

as the quadratic form $V_i(t,x) = x'\Theta_i(t)x, [\Theta_i(t)]' = \Theta_i(t)(i \in \square)$.

We will establish two facts as follows.

First, the solution of the system (6.27), (6.28) has the property

$$V_i(t_0,x_0) = J_i(U^P,t_0,x_0)(i \in \square), \quad (6.29)$$

where the strategy profile $U^P = (U_1^P, U_2^P, \ldots, U_N^P)$ has the form (6.17) and (6.18). Really, if U^P is a strategy profile from (6.12)–(6.14), then by (6.27) and (6.28), the solution $x^P(t)$ of the system $\dot{x} = N(t)x, x(t_0) = x_0 \neq 0_n$, for $x = x^P(t)$ will be

$$0 = W_i[t, x^P(t), V_i(t, x^P(t))] =$$

$$\frac{\partial V_i(t, x^P(t))}{\partial t} + \left[\frac{\partial V_i(t, x^P(t))}{\partial x}\right]' N(t)x^P(t) +$$

$$\sum_{j=1}^{N}[u_j^P(t, x^P(t))]' D_{ij} u_j^P(t, x^P(t)) = \bar{W}_i[t]$$

$$\forall t \in [t_0 \vartheta](i \in \square).$$

Integrating both sides of this identity from t_0 to ϑ subject to the boundary conditions (6.28) yields

$$0 = \int_{t_0}^{\vartheta} \bar{W}_i[t]dt = \int_{t_0}^{\vartheta} \frac{dV_i(t, x^P(t))}{dt} dt + \int_{t_0}^{\vartheta} \sum_{j=1}^{N} [u_j^P(t, x^P(t))]' D_{ij} u_j^P(t, x^P(t)) dt =$$

$$V_i^P(\vartheta, x^P(\vartheta)) - V_i^P(t_0, x^P(t_0)) + \int_{t_0}^{\vartheta} \sum_{j=1}^{N} [u_j^P(t, x^P(t))]' D_{ij} u_j^P(t, x^P(t)) dt =$$

$$x'(\vartheta) C_i x(\vartheta) + \int_{t_0}^{\vartheta} \sum_{j=1}^{N} [u_j^P(t, x^P(t))]' D_{ij} u_j^P(t, x^P(t)) dt - V_i^P(t_0, x^P(t_0)) =$$

$$J_i(U^P, t_0, x_0) - V_i^P(t_0, x^P(t_0))(i \in \square).$$

Hence, the property (6.29) is proved.

Second, the solution of the system (6.29) has the form $V_i(t,x) = x'\Theta_i(t)x$, where a symmetric matrix $\Theta_i(t)$ of dimensions $n \times n$ is given by (6.26). Really, substituting $V_i(t,x) = x'\Theta_i(t)x$ into (6.28) leads to (6.29) if $\Theta_i(t)$ is the solution of the matrix linear inhomogeneous differential equation

$$\Theta_i + \Theta_i N + N\Theta_i + \Theta^P(t)M_i\Theta^P(t) = 0_{n\times n}, \Theta^P(\vartheta) = C_i (i \in \square).$$

A direct substitution of (6.26) into equation (6.29) shows that this symmetric matrix $\Theta_i(t)$ of dimensions $n \times n$ is the desired solution. The proof of Proposition 6.4 is complete.

Note that

$$\frac{dY^{-1}(t)}{dt} = -Y^{-1}(t)A(t), \frac{d[Y^{-1}(t)]'}{dt} = -A(t)[Y^{-1}(t)]'. \qquad \square$$

Remark 6.3. Propositions 6.3 and 6.4 considered together finally yield the following explicit form of the Pareto-maximal solution $(U^P, J^P) \in U \times \square^n$ of the game Γ.

Assume that in the differential game Γ:

1. The symmetric constant matrices D_{ij} and C_i of dimensions $n \times n$ are such that

$$D_{ii} > 0, D_{ij} < 0, C_i < 0 (i, j \in \square, i \neq j).$$

2. $\Lambda_{11}\Lambda_{22} < \lambda_{12}\lambda_{21}$.

Then for all $(t_0, x_0) \in [0, \vartheta) \times \square^n, x_0 \neq 0_n$,

$$U^P \div u^P(t,x) = (-d_1^{-1}\Theta^P(t)x, -d_2^{-1}\Theta^P(t)x, \ldots, -d_N^{-1}\Theta^P(t)x),$$
$$J^P = (J_1^P, J_2^P, \ldots, J_N^P), (J_i^P = x_0'\Theta_i(t_0)x_0 (i \in \square),$$

where

$$\Theta^P(t) = [X^{-1}(t)]'\{C^{-1} + \int_t^{\vartheta} X^{-1}(\tau)[d_1^{-1} + d_2^{-1} + ... + d_N^{-1}][X^{-1}(\tau)]'X^{-1}(t),$$

$$\Theta_i(t) = [Y^{-1}(t)]'\left\{C_i - \int_t^{\vartheta} Y'(\tau)\Theta^P M_i(\tau)\Theta^P Y(\tau)d\tau\right\}Y^{-1}(t),$$

are symmetric matrices of dimensions $n \times n$; the matrices $X(t)$ and $Y(t)$ of dimensions $n \times n$ are the fundamental matrices of the systems $\dot{x} = A(t)x, X(\vartheta) = E_n$, and $\dot{y} = N(t)x, Y(\vartheta) = E_n$, respectively;

$$C = C_1 + \alpha_2 C_2 + ... + \alpha_N C_N,$$
$$N(t) = A(t) - (d_1^{-1} + d_2^{-1} + ... + d_N^{-1})\Theta^P(t),$$
$$M_i(t) = \Theta^P(t)\left([d_1^{-1}]^2 D_{i1} + [d_2^{-1}]^2 D_{i2} + ... + [d_N^{-1}]^2 D_{iN}\right)\Theta^P(t),$$

the numbers $\alpha_2 = \frac{1}{2}\left(\frac{\lambda_{13}}{\Lambda_{33}} + \frac{\Lambda_{11}}{\lambda_{31}}\right)$,

$\alpha_3 = \frac{1}{2}\left[\frac{\lambda_{12}}{\Lambda_{22}} + \frac{1}{2}\left(\frac{\lambda_{13}}{\Lambda_{33}} + \frac{\Lambda_{11}}{\lambda_{31}}\right)\frac{\lambda_{32}}{\Lambda_{22}}\right], \ldots,$ and $\alpha_\gamma (\gamma = 4, ...N)$ are given by (6.20); the negative numbers d_i are given by (6.13); Λ_{ij} and $-\lambda_{ij}$ are the greatest roots of the characteristic equations $\det[D_{ii} - \Lambda E_n] = 0$ and $\det[D_{ij} - \lambda E_n] = 0$, respectively $(i, j \in \square, i \neq j)$.

6.4. Lemmas of Majorants

Now, consider some results that:

1. can be used to establish the absence of Nash equilibria in the differential game Γ under conditions (6.11);
2. implement the concept of equilibrium in sanctions and countersactions for the differential game Γ.

What is important? These results involve the denifiteness of quadratic forms figuring in the integral terms of the payoff functions (6.3). From this point onwards, assume that conditions (6.11) are satisfied. Hence, there exists a Pareto-maximal alternative

$$
\begin{aligned}
&U^P=(U_1^P,U_2^P,\ldots,U_N^P)\div(u_1^P(t,x),u_2^P(t,x),\ldots,u_N^P(t,x))=\\
&u^P(t,x)=(Q_1^P(t)x,Q_2^P(t)x,\ldots,Q_N^P(t)x)=\\
&(-d_1^{-1}\Theta^P(t)x,-d_2^{-1}\Theta^P(t)x,\ldots,-d_N^{-1}\Theta^P(t)x).
\end{aligned}
$$

in the N-criteria choice problem Γ_v.

Lemma 6.5. Let the payoff function (6.3) be such that $D_{11}>0$. Then for a Pareto-maximal strategy profile alternative U^P in the game Γ, there exists a constant $\alpha^{(1)}(U^P,t_0,x_0)>0$ such that, for all $\alpha=\alpha^{(1)}(U^P,t_0,x_0)>0$ and the strategy $U_1^T\div\alpha x$ of player 1, the inequality

$$
J_1(U_1^T,U_2^P,\ldots,U_N^P,t_0,x_0)>J_1(U_1^P,U_2^P,\ldots,U_N^P,t_0,x_0) \tag{6.30}
$$

will hold for any initial positions $(t_0,x_0)\in[0,\vartheta)\times[\mathbb{R}^n\setminus\{0_n\}]$.

Proof. According to Proposition 6.4, there exists a Bellman function $V_1(t,x)=x'\Theta_1(t)x$ such that

$$
J_1(U^P,t_0,x_0)=V_1(t_0,x_0)=x_0'\Theta_1(t_0)x_0,
$$

where the symmetric matrix $\Theta_1(t)$ of dimensions $n\times n$ is continuous on $[0,\vartheta)$ and has the form (6.26) $(i=1)$.

Consider the strategy $U_1^T\div u_1^T(t,x)=\alpha x$ of player 1, in which the numerical parameter $\alpha>0$ will be determined below. Due to the symmetry of the matrix D_{11} and $D_{11}>0$,

$$u_1' D_{11} u_1 \geq \lambda_1 \|u_1\|^2 = \lambda_1 u_1' u_1 \;\; \forall u_1 \in \mathbb{R}^n, \tag{6.31}$$

where $\|\cdot\|$ denotes the Euclidean norm, and $\lambda_1 > 0$ is the smallest root of the characteristic equation $\det[D_{11} - \lambda E_n]$; see [[62]].

We take the symmetric matrix $\Theta^P(t)$ of dimensions $n \times n$ from (6.18) and the strategies $U_2^P \div Q_2^P(t)x, \ldots, U_N^P \div Q_N^P(t)x$ of players $2, \ldots, N$ respectively, from (6.17). We introduce the scalar function

$$\begin{aligned}
&W_1[t,x] = \\
&[W_1(t,x,u_1^T(t,x) = \alpha x, u_2^T(t,x) = Q_2^P x, \ldots\ldots, u_N^T(t,x) = Q_N^P x, \\
&V(t,x)_1 = x'\Theta_1(t)x] = \\
&\frac{\partial V_1(t,x)}{\partial t} + \left[\frac{\partial V_1(t,x)}{\partial x}\right]' (A(t)x + u_1^T(t,x) + u_2^T(t,x) + \ldots + u_N^T(t,x)) + \\
&[u_1^T(t,x)]' d_1 u_1^T(t,x) + [u_2^T(t,x)]' d_2 u_2^T(t,x) + \ldots \\
&\ldots + [u_N^T(t,x)]' d_N u_N^T(t,x) \geq \\
&x' \frac{d\Theta_1(t)}{dt} x + 2x'\Theta_1(t)[A(t) + \alpha E_n + Q_2^P(t) + \ldots Q_N^P(t)]x + \\
&x'(\lambda_1 \alpha^2 E_n)x + x'[Q_2^P(t)]' D_{12} Q_2^P(t)x + \ldots \\
&\ldots + x'[Q_N^P(t)]' D_{1N} Q_N^P(t)x = \\
&x'\{\frac{d\Theta_1(t)}{dt} + \Theta_1(t)[A(t) + \alpha E_n + Q_2^P(t) + \ldots + Q_N^P(t)] + \\
&[A'(t) + \alpha E_n + (Q_2^P(t))' + \ldots + (Q_N^P(t))']\Theta_1(t) + \lambda_1 \alpha^2 E_n + \\
&[Q_2^P(t)]' D_{12} Q_2^P(t) + \ldots + [Q_N^P(t)]' D_{1N} Q_N^P(t)\}x = \\
&x' M_1(t,\alpha)x.
\end{aligned}$$

The matrix $M_1(t,\alpha)$ in curly brackets is symmetric and has the form

$$M_1(t,\alpha) = \lambda_1 \alpha^2 E_n + 2\alpha\Theta_1(t) + K_1(t),$$

where

$$K_1(t) = \dot{\Theta}_1(t) + \Theta_1(t)[A(t) + Q_2^P(t) + ... + Q_N^P(t)] +$$
$$[Q_2^P(t)]' D_{12} Q_2^P(t) + ... + [Q_N^P(t)]' D_{1N} Q_N^P(t) +$$
$$[A'(t) + (Q_2^P(t))' + ... + (Q_N^P(t))']\Theta_1(t)$$

is a symmetric and continuous matrix of dimensions $n \times n$.

The elements of the matrices $\Theta_1(t)$ and $K_1(t)$ are continuous on $[0, \vartheta]$ and hence uniformly bounded on the compact set $[0, \vartheta]$. The factor α^2 enters only the diagonal elements of the matrix $M_1(t, \alpha)$. Recall that $\lambda_1 > 0$ is the *smallest* root of the characteristic equation $\det[D_{11} - \lambda E_n] = 0$, where E_n denotes an identity matrix of dimensions $n \times n$. Therefore, the constant $\alpha = \alpha^{(1)}(U^P, t_0, x_0) > 0$ can be chosen sufficiently great for making all principal minors of the matrix $M_1(t, \alpha)$ positive $\forall t \in [0, \vartheta]$ $\alpha \geq \alpha^{(1)}(U^P, t_0, x_0)$. (This fact will be proved below). According to Lemma 6.2 and [[223]], the quadratic form $x' M_1(t, \alpha) x$ is positive definite for all $t \in [0, \vartheta]$ and all constants $\alpha \geq \alpha^{(1)}(U^P, t_0, x_0)$.

Now we show the existence of a constant $\alpha^{(1)}(U^P, t_0, x_0) > 0$ such that, for all $\alpha \geq \alpha^{(1)}(U^P, t_0, x_0)$, the quadratic form $x' M_1(t, \alpha) x$ is positive definite for all $t \in [0, \vartheta]$ and $x \in \mathbb{R}^n$. Note that the matrix $M_1(t, \alpha)$ of dimensions $n \times n$ is symmetric. By Sylvester's criterion, the quadratic form $x' M_1(t, \alpha) x$ is positive definite if all principal minors $\Delta_r (r = 1, ..., n)$ of the matrix $M_1(t, \alpha)$ are positive. The minors Δ_r are located in the first r rows and first r columns of the matrix $M_1(t, \alpha)$ $(r = 1, ..., n)$:

$$\Delta_r(t, \alpha) = \begin{vmatrix} \lambda_1 \alpha^2 n + \alpha l_{11}(t) + k_{11}(t) & \cdots & \alpha l_{1r}(t) + k_{1r}(t) \\ \vdots & \ddots & \vdots \\ \alpha l_{r1}(t) + k_{r1}(t) & \cdots & \lambda_1 \alpha^2 n + \alpha l_{rr}(t) + k_{rr}(t) \end{vmatrix}.$$

They must be positive $\forall t \in [0, \vartheta]$ and $\forall \alpha \geq \alpha^{(1)}(U^P, t_0, x_0)$. Expanding the determinants $\Delta_r(t, \alpha)$ and rearranging the terms in the descending order of the power of the parameter α , we obtain

$$\Delta_r(t,\alpha) = \alpha_0(t)\alpha^{2r} + \alpha_1(t)\alpha^{2r-1} + \ldots + \alpha_{2r-1}(t)\alpha + \alpha_{2r}(t),$$

where $\alpha_0 = \lambda^r n^r > 0$ (constant), and the other coefficients $\alpha_1(t), \ldots, \alpha_{2r}(t)$ are continuous on the compact set $[0, \vartheta]$, hence being uniformly bounded. This uniform boundedness guarantees the existence of $\Omega_r = const > 0$ such that

$$\max_{0 \leq t \leq \vartheta} \{\alpha_p(t) \,|\, p = 0,1,..,2r\} < \Omega_r.$$

Let us demonstrate that if

$$\alpha > \frac{\Omega_r}{|\alpha_0|} + 1 = \alpha^{(1)}(U^P, t_0, x_0),$$

then

$$|\alpha_1(t)\alpha^{2r-1} + \alpha_2(t)\alpha^{2r-2} + \ldots + \alpha_{2r-1}(t)\alpha + \alpha_{2r}(t)| < |\alpha_0 \alpha^{2r}|.$$

In other words, for a sufficiently great value $|\alpha|$, the sign of the polynomial $\Delta_r(t, \alpha)$ is determined by the sign of its leading term. Really,

$$|\alpha_1(t)\alpha^{2r-1} + \alpha_2(t)\alpha^{2r-2} + \ldots + \alpha_{2r-1}(t)\alpha + \alpha_{2r}(t)| \leq$$
$$|\alpha_1(t)\alpha^{2r-1}| + |\alpha_2(t)\alpha^{2r-2}| + \ldots + |\alpha_{2r-1}(t)\alpha| + |\alpha_{2r}(t)| \leq$$
$$\Omega_r(\alpha^{2r-1} + \alpha^{2r-2} + \ldots + \alpha + 1) = \Omega_r \frac{\alpha^{2r-1}}{\alpha - 1}.$$

In addition,

$$\left[\alpha > \frac{\Omega_r}{|\alpha_0|} + 1\right] \Rightarrow [\Omega_r < \alpha_0(\alpha - 1)].$$

Replacing Ω_r in this inequality by a greater value $\alpha_0(\alpha-1)$ yields

$$|\alpha_1(t)\alpha^{2r-1} + \alpha_2(t)\alpha^{2r-2} + \ldots + \alpha_{2r-1}(t)\alpha + \alpha_{2r}(t)| <$$
$$\alpha_0(\alpha-1)\frac{\alpha^{2r-1}}{\alpha-1} = \alpha_0(\alpha-1) < \alpha_0\alpha^{2r}.$$

Thus $\forall \alpha \geq \Omega_r = \alpha^{(r)}(U, t_0, x_0) > 0$, and $\forall t \in [0, \vartheta]$, we have

$$|\alpha_1(t)\alpha^{2r-1} + \alpha_2(t)\alpha^{2r-2} + \ldots + \alpha_{2r-1}(t)\alpha + \alpha_{2r}(t)| < \alpha_0\alpha^{2r}.$$

Well, for a sufficiently great value α, the sign of the polynomial $\Delta_r(t,\alpha)$ is determined by the sign of its leading term. Finally, for each $r = 1,\ldots,n$, we calculate $\Omega_r > 0$ and let $\alpha^{(1)}(U^P, t_0, x_0) = \max_{r=1,\ldots,n} \Omega_r$

Then, for $\alpha^{(1)}(U^P, t_0, x_0)$, it follows that

$$\tilde{W}_1[t,x] = x'M_1(t,\alpha^{(1)})x > 0 \;\; \forall t \in [0,\vartheta] \;\; \forall x \in \mathbb{R}^n \setminus \{0_n\}. \qquad (6.32)$$

We denote by $\tilde{x}(t)$, $t \in [0,\vartheta]$, the solution of the vector differential equation

$$\dot{x} = A(t)x + \alpha^{(1)}x + Q_2^P(t)x + \ldots + Q_N^P(t)x, \; x(t_0) = x_0 \neq 0_n.$$

Due to Lemma 6.2, the implication $[x_0 \neq 0_n] \Rightarrow (\tilde{x}(t) \neq 0_n \; t \in [0,\vartheta])$ and (6.32),

$$\tilde{W}_1[t, \tilde{x}(t)] > 0, \forall t \in [0,\vartheta].$$

Integrating both sides of (6.32) from t_0 to ϑ subject to the boundary condition $\Theta_1(\vartheta) = C_1$ and $u_1^T[t] = \alpha^{(1)}\tilde{x}(t)$ gives:

$$0 = \int_{t_0}^{\vartheta} \tilde{W}_1[t, \tilde{x}(t)]dt =$$

$$\int_{t_0}^{\vartheta} \left\{ \frac{\partial V_1(t,x)}{\partial t} + \left[\frac{\partial V_1(t,x)}{\partial x} \right]' [A[t]x + \alpha^{(1)} E_n x + Q_2^P(t)x + \ldots \right.$$

$$\left. \ldots + Q_N^P(t)x] \right\}_{x=\tilde{x}(t)} dt =$$

$$\int_{t_0}^{\vartheta} \{(\alpha^{(1)})^2 x' D_{11} x + x'[Q_2^P(t)]' D_{12} Q_2^P(t) + \ldots$$

$$\ldots + x'[Q_N^P(t)]' D_{1N} Q_N^P(t)\}_{x=\tilde{x}(t)} dt =$$

$$\int_{t_0}^{\vartheta} \frac{dV_1(t, \tilde{x}(t))}{dt} + \int_{t_0}^{\vartheta} \sum_{j=1}^{N} [u_j^T[t]]' D_{1j} u_j^T[t] dt =$$

$$[\tilde{x}(\vartheta)]' C_1 \tilde{x}(\vartheta) + \int_{t_0}^{\vartheta} \sum_{j=1}^{N} [u_j^T[t]]' D_{1j} u_j^T[t] dt - V_1(t_0, x_0) =$$

$$J_1(U_1^T, U_2^P, \ldots, U_N^P, t_0, x_0) - V_1(t_0, x_0).$$

This result, in combination with the equality $J_1(U_1^P, U_2^P, \ldots, U_N^P, t_0, x_0) = V_1(t_0, x_0)$, finally proves Lemma 6.5.

Remark 6.4. Consider the inner optimization problem in the game Γ: for fixed strategies $U_2 = U_2^P \in \mathcal{U}_2, \ldots, U_N = U_N^P \in \mathcal{U}_N$ of players $2, \ldots, N$ respectively, and for any $(t_0, x_0) \in [0, \vartheta) \times [\mathbb{R}^n \setminus \{0_n\}]$, find $\max_{U_1 \in \mathcal{U}_1} J_1(U_1, U_2^P, \ldots, U_N^P, t_0, x_0)$ subject to the system (6.1). Lemma 6.5 claims that for $D_{11} > 0$ and $x_0 \neq 0_n$, this problem maximization problem has no solution. Really, whatever strategy $U_1 \in \mathcal{U}_1$ is chosen by player 1, there always exists another strategy U_1^T of this player such that

$$J_1(\tilde{U}_1^T, U_2^P, \ldots, U_N^P, t_0, x_0) > J_1(U_1, U_2^P, \ldots, U_N^P, t_0, x_0)$$
$$\forall (t_0, x_0) \in [0, \vartheta) \times [\mathbb{R}^n \setminus \{0_n\}].$$

When choosing an appropriate solution of the game Γ, this result allows directly eliminating those concepts of equilibrium that involve the maximization of the payoff function of player 1 with respect to U_1. (For example, if $D_{11} > 0$, the concept of Nash equilibrium should not be used as the solution of the game Γ).

Thus, under conditions (6.11), the differential game Γ has no Nash equilibrium. At the same time, the strategy $U_1^T \div \alpha x \; \forall \alpha \geq \alpha^{(1)}(U^P, t_0, x_0)$ implements the sanction of player 1 to the Pareto-maximal (efficient) strategy profile U^P; see (6.5). In the lemmas below, the initial position (t_0, x_0) is fixed and coincides with the one from Lemma 6.5; in addition, the sanction strategy $U_1^T \div \alpha x$ of player 1 has a constant scalar $\alpha = \alpha^{(1)}$. Recall that conditions (6.11) are assumed to hold without special mention. Well, Lemma 6.5 establishes the following result.

Proposition 6.5. Assume that in the game Γ, at least one of the constant symmetric matrices $D_{ii} > 0$ $(i \in \mathbb{N})$ of dimensions $n \times n$ is positive definite. Then this game has no Nash equilibrium, i.e., there does not exist a strategy $U_i^e \in \mathcal{U}_i$ satisfying Definition 6.2.

Note that:

1. The condition $D_{ii} > 0$ with a fixed number $i \in \mathbb{N}$ breaks only the ith equality of Definition 6.2. This is enough for the absence of a Nash equilibrium U^e in the game Γ. If $D_{ii} > 0$ for all $i \in \mathbb{N}$, then the N equalities of Definition 6.2 will be violated.
2. The equivalence
$$D > 0 \Leftrightarrow -D < 0$$

is obvious. (Here, $-D$ means that all elements of the matrix D are multiplied by -1).

Then Lemma 6.5 also implies the following.

Lemma 6.6. Let the payoff function (6.3) be such that $D_{12} > 0$. Then there exists a constant $\alpha^{(2)} = \alpha^{(2)}(U^P, U_1^T, t_0, x_0) > 0$ such that, for all $\forall \alpha \geq \alpha^{(2)}$ and the strategy $U_2^C \div \alpha x$ of player 2,

$$J_1(U_1^T, U_2^C, U_3^P, \ldots, U_N^P, t_0, x_0) < J_1(U^P, t_0, x_0) . \tag{6.33}$$

In other words, the strategy $U_2^C \div \alpha x \; \forall \alpha \geq \alpha^{(2)}$ implements in the game Γ an incomplete countersanction to the sanction U_1^T of player 1.

Proof. With some obvious modifications, the proof is immediate from Lemma 6.5.

Let a Bellman function $\tilde{V}_1(t,x) = x'\tilde{\Theta}(t)x$, $\tilde{\Theta}(t) = \Theta_1(t)$, be constructed, satisfying

$$J_1(U_1^T, U_2^P, \ldots, U_N^P, t_0, x_0) = \tilde{V}_1(t_0, x_0). \tag{6.34}$$

By analogy with Lemmas 6.5 and 6.6, we will establish another important result below. Recall that an initial position (t_0, x_0), a continuous matrix $\Theta^P(t)$ of dimensions $n \times n$, and an incomplete countersanction strategy $U_2^C \div \alpha^{(2)} x$ figuring in Lemmas 6.5 and 6.6 are assumed to be fixed, and conditions (6.11) are assumed to hold.

Lemma 6.7. The condition $D_{22} > 0$ implies the existence of a value $\alpha^{(3)}(U^P, U_1^T, t_0, x_0) = const > 0$ such that, for all $\alpha > \alpha^{(3)}$ and the strategy $U_2^C \div \alpha x$,

$$J_2(U_1^T, U_2^C, U_3^P, t_0, x_0) < J_2(U_1^T, U_2^P, U_3^P, t_0, x_0).$$

In other words, the strategy $U_2^C \div (\max\{\alpha^{(2)}, \alpha^{(3)}\})x$ of player 2 implements a complete countersanction, jointly with $U_2^C \div \alpha^{(2)}x$, to the sanction of player 1 to U^P. □

The sanctions of another player and countersanctions of the other players are constructed similarly.

6.5. Proof of Existence

Theorem 6.1. Assume that the game Γ satisfies conditions (6.16). Then the $(N+1)$-tuple

$$\begin{aligned}&(U^P, J_1^P, J_2^P, \ldots, J_N^P) = ((U_1^P, U_2^P, \ldots, U_N^P), J_1(U^P, t_0, x_0), J_2(U^P, t_0, x_0), \ldots\\&\ldots, J_N(U^P, t_0, x_0) = ((-d_1^{-1}\Theta^P(t)x, -d_2^{-1}\Theta^P(t)x, \ldots\\&\ldots, -d_N^{-1}\Theta^P(t)x), x_0'\Theta_1(t_0)x_0, x_0'\Theta_2(t_0)x_0, \ldots, x_0'\Theta_N(t_0)x_0)\end{aligned}$$

is an equilibrium in sanctions and countersanctions of the differential game

$$\Gamma = \langle □, \Sigma \div (2.2), \{U_i\}_{i\in□}, \{J_i(U, t_0, x_0) \div (2.3)\}_{i\in□} \rangle;$$

where:

$$\begin{aligned}&\Theta^P(t) = [X^{-1}(t)]'\{C^{-1} - \int_t^{\vartheta} X^{-1}(\tau)[d_1^{-1} + d_2^{-1} + \ldots\\&\ldots + d_N^{-1}][X^{-1}(\tau)]'dt\}^{-1} X^{-1}(t);\end{aligned}$$

the constants d_i are given by (6.13); $C = C_1 + \alpha_2 C_2 + \ldots + \alpha_N C_N$, where $\alpha_2 = \frac{1}{2}\left(\frac{\Lambda_{11}}{\lambda_{21}} + \frac{\lambda_{12}}{\Lambda_{22}}\right)$, $\alpha_3 = \frac{1}{2}\left[\frac{\Lambda_{13}}{\lambda_{33}} + \frac{1}{2}\left(\frac{\Lambda_{11}}{\lambda_{21}} + \frac{\lambda_{12}}{\Lambda_{22}}\right)\frac{\lambda_{23}}{\Lambda_{33}}\right]$ and

$\alpha_m = \frac{1}{2\Lambda_{mn}}[\lambda_{1m} + \alpha_2\lambda_{2m} + ... + \alpha_{m-1}\lambda_{m-1m}]$ $(m = 4,..., N)$ and Λ_i and $-\lambda_{ij}$ are the smallest and greatest roots of the equations $\det[D_{ij} - \Lambda E_n] = 0$ and $\det[D_{ij} - \lambda E_n] = 0$, respectively; $X(t)$ denotes the fundamental matrix of the system $\dot{x} = A(t)x,\ X(\vartheta) = E_n$ $(i, j \in \square, i \neq j)$; finally, the symmetric matrices $\Theta_i(t)(i \in \square)$ are given by (6.26).

Proof. The absence of a Nash equilibrium in the game Γ and the presence of a sanction U_1^T imposed by player 1 to a Pareto-maximal alternative U^P in the *N*-criteria choice problem Γ_v immediately follow from $D_{11} > 0$; see Remark 6.4. The existence of a Pareto-maximal alternative and Pareto-maximal outcomes in Γ_v (including their explicit forms in this case) has been established by Propositions 6.3 and 6.4, respectively. The condition $D_{21} > 0$ allows constructing an incomplete countersanction U_2^C of player 2 to the sanctions of player 1 (Lemma 6.6). The condition $D_{22} > 0$ and Lemma 6.7 enable transforming the incomplete countersanction U_2^C of player 2 into the complete one U_2^C. The requirement $D_{22} > 0$ simultaneously implies the absence of a Nash equilibrium ($\max_{U_1} J(U_1, U_2^e, U_3^e, ..., U_N^e, t_0, x_0)$ is not achieved $\bar{U}_1^C \in U_1$) and the ability of player 2 to design analytically a sanction U_2^T to U^P in the game Γ:

$$J_2(U_1^C, U_2^T, U_3^P, ..., U_N^P) \leq J_2(U^P t_0, x_0). \tag{6.35}$$

The condition $D_{22} > 0$ and Lemma 6.7 guarantee the existence of an incomplete countersanction $\bar{U}_1^C \in U_1$ of player 1 to the sanction U_2^T of player 2:

$$J_2(U_1^C, U_2^T, U_3^P, ..., U_N^P) < J_2(U^P t_0, x_0). \tag{6.36}$$

Finally, the Pareto maximality of U^P and Property 6.1 lead to

$$J_1(U_1^P, U_2^T, U_3^P, \ldots, U_N^P) < J_1(U^P t_0, x_0). \tag{6.37}$$

Due to $D_{11} > 0$ and Lemma 6.5, there exists a $\bar{U}_1^C \in U_1$ such that

$$J_1(\bar{U}_1^C, U_2^T, U_3^P, \ldots, U_N^P) > J_1(U_1^P, U_2^T, U_3^P, \ldots, U_N^P, t_0, x_0). \tag{6.38}$$

The countersanction to the sanctions imposed by players $3, .., N$ to U^P is designed by analogy.

Thus, one of the other players in the game Γ always has a complete countersanction to a sanction imposed by any player to the Pareto-maximal strategy profile U^P. The proof of Theorem 6.1 is complete.

Conclusion

As shown above, the linear-quadratic game Γ under conditions (6.11) has no Nash equilibrium and, at the same time, has an equilibrium in sanctions and countersanctions. Hence, the corresponding game-theoretic equilibrium models are economically and legally justified and expand the application domain of the class of problems considered in this chapter. However, we do not claim the universal use of game-theoretic tools in modelling economic processes. It is necessary to investigate further the properties used in the analytical design of various equilibria, including the equilibrium in sanctions and countersanctions, as a mechanism for balancing complex controlled systems.

The next chapter will consider the practical use of the proposed game-theoretic models and decision methods in complex socio-economic macrosystems under uncertainty. An applications-oriented approach to game-theoretic decision-making tools lies in the field of intelligent decision support systems, where formal mathematical models are adopted at the modeling stage.

Chapter 7

Structural Analysis of Intelligent Decision Support Systems under Uncertainty

Introduction

Chapter 7 justifies the need to design and implement intelligent decision support systems based on game-theoretic models and the latest artificial intelligence and intellectualize management processes for complex socio-economic macrosystems under uncertainty.

7.1. Factors Transforming Decision-Making Technologies in Complex Socio-economic Macrosystems

A significant increase and complication of information flows in modern society lead to fundamental changes in management practices. They require automatic data processing and analysis, intellectual management for complex socio-economic systems, and new intelligent technologies-based approaches [213] to the design of decision support systems. On the one hand, the planning, forecasting, and management of complex systems are associated with economic-mathematical modeling; on the other, with the human's intellectual potential. This process is implemented in intelligent decision support systems (IDSSs) based on game-theoretic modeling, modern artificial intelligence (AI) technologies [178], and dynamic adaptive knowledge base models [209]. Such assistance systems are characterized by openness, semiotics, and cognitivity.

AI is generally understood as an information model of natural intelligence and IDSSs as systems that assist decision-makers (DMs) using the following tools:

1. data mining,
2. economic-mathematical modeling,
3. a friendly graphical user interface (GUI).

Such a system should have stable performance and be interactive and flexible in settings.

Note that decision-making, in principle, cannot be strictly formalized without considering its inherent uncertainty. Therefore, IDSSs are intended to help the decision-maker (the control system), as a rule, with non-deterministic strategies for managing complex systems and decision processes under uncertainty over some period. (Uncertainty is understood as incomplete, inaccurate, or inconsistent initial information). Such IDSSs combine rigorous mathematical models (game-theoretic, logical, expert, or linguistic ones) to find solutions using either the principle of fuzzy control (imitation of the DM's actions) or the multicriteria approach to current conflicts.

Since the mid-1990s, IDSSs have been developed based on statistics, game theory, complex modeling, neural networks, and AI. At the moment, several classifications of decision support systems have been proposed [180]. Here are some of them:

- by the field of application of IDSSs: business and management (strategy, labor resources, pricing, products), engineering (e.g., quality control), finance (lending), medicine (diagnosis, directions and types of medical treatment, pharmaceuticals), and environment and social reality;
- by the data–model correlation: File Drawer Systems (FDS, systems for providing access to data), Data Analysis Systems (DAS, systems for fast data handling), Analysis Information Systems (AIS, data access systems by solution type), Accounting & Financial Models (AFM, systems for calculating financial consequences), Representation Models (RM, systems for simulations, e.g., AnyLogic), Optimization Models (OM, systems for solving optimization problems), and Suggestion Models (SM, logical inference systems based on appropriate rules);
- by the type of tools: Model Driven (systems based on linear models, inventory management models, transport models, financial models, etc.), Data Driven (systems based on statistical data), Communication Driven (systems based on group decision-making by experts; systems for facilitation, opinion exchange, and calculation of average expert values), Document Driven (systems representing an indexed or multidimensional repository of documents), and Knowledge Driven (systems based on knowledge).

Note that some factors are being formed that change management practices and, consequently, decision-making technologies at all hierarchy levels in macrosystems:

1. the complexity due to the need for an accurate assessment of various alternatives and predicted functionality and the presence of multiflow input information (decision-making requires inference and conclusions based on certain data, expert assessments, restrictions, etc.);
2. the growing rates and novelty of information flows and the associated need to make decisions in nonstationary conditions. In this case, the human factor also plays a significant role: the DM's information load is adjusted depending on his competence, ability to generate knowledge, and adaptive level of perceiving social and economic reality.

When information flows become more complex and, accordingly, the uncertainty in decision-making increases, the problems can be solved by developing and implementing Knowledge Management (KM) technologies [202] in combination with active visualization models of the decision process by natural (human) intelligence. The components of such a control system are humans, including their knowledge and experience, socio-economic processes, and digital technologies. The evolution of information technology and software tools with KM support (and not only) yields IDSSs with AI, i.e., hybrid or integrated intelligent knowledge management systems [13]. Such systems are developed and adapted using complex interdisciplinary research in the field of engineering, AI, mathematical modeling, and neuroscience.

At the moment, according to McKinsey [193], at least half of managerial decisions turn out to be wrong, and therefore many researchers have faced the need to include the so-called Social Intelligence [76] in decision-making. As expected, it can contribute to finding an optimal decision scheme in complex socio-economic macrosystems under uncertainty. Therefore, when designing hybrid IDSSs for DMs, the following stages should be considered:

1. determining the application domain of the system (domain analysis, data collection, and processing),
2. developing and (or) selecting formal mathematical models, including their expert analysis, interpretation, and validation;

3. assessing and implementing the IDSS, including feedback at each stage.

Despite the variety of approaches, attempts are undertaken to suggest a universal IDSS architecture. In a simplified form, it can be represented as follows: Interface (interactivity and visualization), Modeling (statistical and dynamic control models and (or) machine learning [141], numerical models, and game-theoretic models), Data Mining (data flows, databases, and expert assessment), and Data Collection.

7.2. Game-Theoretic Methods in the Design of Intelligent Decision Support Systems in the Social Sphere

Game-theoretic tools are, of course, not universal from the decision-making viewpoint. Nevertheless, they can be used, e.g., to construct a multilevel model for managing the dynamics of a complex socio-economic macrosystem under uncertainty; see Chapter 3 of the book. The new approaches to decision-making and formal management models presented in Chapters 2-5 create prerequisites for developing and applying IDSSs in the social sphere. Moreover, they have several advantages over machine learning, where statistical data are required for further generalization and forecasting. Within the game-theoretic methodology, an equilibrium of the model is calculated and incorporated into the IDSS.

For example, researchers at the ASU-SFI Center for Biosocial Complex Systems, working at the junction of neuroscience, control theory, theory of collective behavior, and statistical physics, developed a dynamic stochastic distributed decision model and validated it on a large amount of experimental data. Using the model, they identified the organizational scheme of collective decision-making on an example of the brain and its huge network of communicating neurons. The corresponding methodology was called the coding duality [47]. This scheme consists of two stages as follows. The first stage is the accumulation of information under suppressing information noise. The second stage is reaching consensus, when information quickly spreads from "knowledgeable" neurons (accessing the information) to the set of other neurons participating in the scheme, dramatically increasing the system redundancy. The stages of accumulation and consensus differ by time scales, which is crucial for the efficiency of this scheme.

In fact, this model can be adapted to develop IDSSs for managing real socio-economic macrosystems.

Translating the complexity of the model under consideration to the management processes of socio-economic macrosystems under uncertainty, we expect that such a study will fundamentally change the decision models at the macrolevel in socio-economic systems with their varying complexity. In this regard, the proposed scheme explains the process of improving the quality of management, i.e., the share correct and optimal decisions in the total number of decisions made. The model obtained by the ASU-SFI Center for Biosocial Complex Systems researchers answers the following questions:

1. How are decisions made by the brain at the level of individual neurons or by a huge network of communicating neurons?
2. How is the decision-making process organized?

The cited researchers discovered the decision-making scheme of the brain neurons and, using game-theoretic tools, proved that this scheme is optimal for any collective computations performed by a network of intelligent agents. In the course of evolution, nature created mechanics and biophysics of living beings, which are not surpassed by modern science. Consequently, in finding the best decision-making scheme for the neurons of the brain, nature is ahead of modern science, and we should try to reach it when constructing game-theoretic mathematical models.

There already exist IDSSs based on neural networks and AI, e.g., an artificial neural network-based decision support system for solving the buffer allocation problem in reliable production lines [205], a decision support system for water distribution systems based on neural networks and graphs theory for leakage detection [10], and others. Note that such IDSSs best suit decision-making under uncertainty.

According to the international interdisciplinary, integrated studies considered above, the general direction in designing AI-based IDSSs is the development of active visualization models for decision-making by natural intelligence using game-theoretic tools, the latest technologies associated with artificial intelligence, and intellectual management for complex socio-economic macrosystems under uncertainty.

In the course of digitalization, the systems under consideration will transform into increasingly complex, hybrid, flexible, and mobile structures, with knowledge, intelligence, and information as the main objects of control and management. Therefore, it seems promising to develop IDSSs using different approaches of control theory and management, game theory, performance measurement, the theory of state and law, the constitutional law doctrine, and, possibly, the latest AI technologies to overcome administrative regulation and form effective management systems for socio-economic processes.

Conclusion

This chapter has identified the main components of knowledge management technology and discussed new interdisciplinary studies for modelling human thinking. We have proposed the basic principles, general design stages, and a classification of intelligent decision support systems in which formal mathematical models of the game-theoretic approach are applied at the modeling stage. In addition, we have considered their advantages.

The results presented in this chapter may contribute to the formation of effective management systems for socio-economic processes to overcome administrative regulation in the social sphere. The theoretical and practical significance of the study lies in new approaches to artificial intelligence as a strategic tool for administering socio-economic macrosystems in a digital society.

Chapter 8

A Mechanism for Implementing Berge Equilibrium of the Complex Metasystem Based on Modelling Decision Processes

8.1. A Mechanism for Balancing the Economic, Social, and Legal Macrosystems

The development of economic-mathematical modeling of decision processes in complex macrosystems [2-4, 89, 91, 95-98, 100,107, 135, 149, 165, 166, 168, 186, 187, 189, 215-18, 241] gradually changes the requirements to the performance of controlled systems. In the course of modeling, researchers need to consider several main factors: two or even more criteria assessing the controlled system's performance and various types of interval uncertainties with given limits but without statistical characteristics.

Most of the strategic decisions in socio-economic systems are accompanied by the conflict of interests between individual control systems with appropriate power and influence groups defending their own interests and various additional factors inherent in the decision process. As a rule, the conflicting nature of such a process does not imply any open confrontation between the parties but indicates their different interests (mostly economic). In such situations, traditional optimization methods become almost impracticable. According to S.Yu. Glaz'ev [66], the followers of A. Smith, D. Ricardo, J.S. Mill, A. Marshall, and L. Walras constructed a harmonious, but not reflecting real economic processes, mathematized theory of market equilibrium.

For example, in real economic and social macrosystems, the same decisions can be optimal for one party and nonoptimal for the other. The resulting decisions can depend on all parties with different interests (conflicting ones). Game theory is a mathematical framework that studies such situations, representing a branch of the general theory for describing and analyzing optimal decision processes with one or several participants under uncertainty and conflict. Recall that a conflict is understood as a situation in which the parties have different interests and opportunities to choose appropriate actions for their benefit.

Within game theory, any conflicts can be, in principle, described mathematically, including economic, legal, and social ones. Game-theoretic tools mathematically justify important aspects of decision-making in the economic, legal, and social macrosystems. In addition, game theory gives a promising approach to control, planning, and forecasting.

Note that games differ from real conflicts: they are played according to certain rules. Real conflicts are usually difficult to simulate economically and mathematically. Therefore, any game is a simplification of the original real problem that covers only the main (primary) factors reflecting the essence of the process or phenomenon studied.

In modern conditions, the management of complex socio-economic systems at the macrolevel should be treated as multicriteria decision-making under uncertainty, considering the interconnections and mutual influence of economic, legal, and social processes.

Many researchers—economists, legal scholars, and sociologists—understand the social state as the welfare state. (In the book, these terms are synonyms). According to Article 2 of the Constitution of the Russian Federation, the highest value is a person, his rights and freedoms, and their recognition, observance, and protection is the state's duty. Article 7 of the Constitution of the Russian Federation directly claims that Russia is "a social state, the policy of which is aimed at creating conditions for a decent life and free human development." Such constitutional norms are declarative, although they represent the foundations of legal regulation of the economic and social spheres.

Nevertheless, the doctrinal claims on the social state declared by the Constitution of the Russian Federation came into conflict with the neoliberal economic doctrine, with led to negative consequences of the transformation processes, especially in the socio-economic sphere: increased poverty for the bulk of the population, income polarization, degradation of the society, and decreased quality of life. These mutually influencing tendencies even multiplied the negative effects, and the consequences of the adopted strategic decisions still directly impact the current state of the national economic, legal, and social macrosystems.

To replace the existing neoliberal economic doctrine, we have proposed a philosophical and moral concept—the Golden Rule of ethics—expressed mathematically via the construction of a formal equilibrium model for the economic, legal, and social macrosystems of the complex public metasystem.

A new mechanism for balancing the economic, social, and legal macrosystems put forward in this book involves an original equilibrium model with *the social state idea underlying their mutual influence and interaction.* The new mechanism is based on the concept of Berge equilibrium, which reveals the Golden Rule of ethics.

As the author believes, the new models of decision-making and the "altruistic" Berge equilibrium in modern management practice are a good alternative to the vain policy of "band-aid," fast response, and manual control. They may become a mathematical justification for designing national social and economic policy within a new economic paradigm based on philosophical and moral principles.

The introduction of new game-theoretic approaches to model decision processes in managing complex macrosystems under incomplete information, conflicts, and uncertainty will yield the least risky and most guaranteed decisions. As a result, the operation of the three complex macrosystems and, consequently, the operation of the complex metasystem will be stabilized. Thus, adopting new game-theoretic models of decision-making in the macrosystems under uncertainty, incomplete information, and conflict into economic theory and practice will contribute to the socio-economic development of the country [190, 191].

8.2. The Social State Concept and Modelling Strategic Decisions in the Social Sphere

What is a social state from the standpoint of systems analysis? This term can refer to a complex, large-scale, multilevel mesosystem aimed at improving the population's well-being. In the axiological aspect, the social state (or welfare state) [8] is an ideal theoretical construct and the concept of ethics and morality that reflects the systemic complex of population's social rights filled with economic content. At the same time, note the following. On the one hand, the complex metasystem under consideration is an integral part of the mesosystem; on the other, it constitutes the latter's structural foundation designed to ensure social and legal security and a decent quality of life for the population.

The new concept of a balanced equilibrium of the economic, legal, and social macrosystems described above can be used to develop a macromodel and perform economic-mathematical modeling of decision processes in a welfare state based on the philosophical and moral doctrine of the Golden Rule of ethics [249].

The social state's macromodel involves the mechanism proposed in Chapter 2 for constructing a balanced equilibrium of the economic, legal, and social macrosystems. It includes:

- a formal interaction model of the three macrosystems;
- a formalized equilibrium model that combines the concepts of Berge equilibrium (the Golden Rule of ethics) and Nash equilibrium (individual rationality) in the macrostructure of the three macrosystems.

The proposed approach has been validated by studying the dynamics of family structures and relations that affect the population's life system, the state, prospects, and possibilities of public administration of sociodemographic processes in Russia. In addition, mathematical models of relations in three-person families have been constructed using the concepts of Berge equilibrium and Nash equilibrium.

Thus, the significance of this research lies in the development of theoretical and methodological provisions for game-theoretic modeling of complex macrosystems and decision processes under uncertainty. In particular, the system (balanced) equilibrium of the economic, social, and legal macrosystems is valuable for implementing the social state doctrine in Russia and improving decision processes in the social sphere at the macrolevel. These results enlarge the application domain of game theory in economics and develop the mathematical apparatus of economic studies by combining scientific approaches of game theory, management, economics, law, and sociology.

Note that the regulation of the social sphere is one of the main elements in implementing the essential content of the social state. The constitutional and legal development of mechanisms for exercising the right to receive social services and products by the population, the development and implementation of new legal institutions should be focused on achieving consistent dynamic growth in the population's quality of life and well-being. The effectiveness and reality of constitutional rights for social services are directly related to their mechanism, the development and implementation of new legal institutions guaranteeing high-quality prerequisites for a decent human life and personal development as the foundation of a social state.

Given all these factors and the features of strategic decision-making in stationary and nonstationary macrosystems (Chapter 1), this book introduces a new scientific approach to improving decision processes in the social sphere at the macrolevel (Chapter 3). More specifically:

- We have constructed a new multilevel mathematical model for managing the dynamics of complex socio-economic systems under uncertainty and have suggested a scientifically grounded approach to posing and solving this management problem.
- We have proposed a method for formalizing guaranteed solutions in multicriteria problems of managing complex socio-economic systems under interval uncertainty with given limits.
- We have formalized a guaranteed solution by modifying Savage's principle of minimax regret. To this end, we have considered the following pair: the set of social state guarantees for the population and socio-economic life risks in case of which definite categories of the population exercise their constitutional right to obtain appropriate social guarantees. Also, we have proved an existence theorem for this solution under standard assumptions of multicriteria choice problems and have developed a method to find it.

In the social state, strategic decision-making at the macrolevel secures the population against guaranteed (life) risks, such as old age, illness, unemployment, accidents, etc. Chapter 4 has presented in detail the mathematical apparatus used in Chapter 3. We have suggested new game-theoretic approaches to modelling decision processes, increasing the outcomes and simultaneously reducing the associated Savage risk. We have constructed the guaranteed solutions and risks and have explored the features of Nash equilibrium. The results described in Chapters 3 and 4 mathematically justify the development of new state programs in the social sphere to improve the population's well-being.

The new methodology, proposed in Chapter 5 and proved in Chapter 4, involves the GR to design the guaranteed solutions considering the associated risks and study the features of Berge equilibrium. To identify the features (stability and unimprovability), we have formalized the Pareto-guaranteed Berge equilibrium, have established its existence in mixed strategies, and have examined its properties. The mathematical framework of Chapter 5 justifies the studies carried out in Chapter 2, that is, the model of balanced equilibrium of the complex national metasystem. Chapter 6 has presented a methodology for modelling decision processes in complex controlled dynamic systems. The idea of balancing such systems (driving them to an equilibrium) has been implemented, and a new mechanism for the stability of equilibria has been proposed. As shown therein, the linear-quadratic game under appropriate constraints has no Nash equilibrium and, at the same time, has an equilibrium in sanctions and countersanctions. Hence, the corresponding game-theoretic equilibrium models are economically and legally justified and expand the application domain of the class of problems under consideration. It is necessary to investigate further the properties used in the analytical design of various equilibria, including the equilibrium in sanctions and countersanctions, as a mechanism for balancing complex controlled systems. To increase the groundedness of decision-making and develop decision support for the social sphere, Chapter 6 has considered new approaches to modelling decision processes in complex socio-economic systems under uncertainty, particularly their advantages. They can be used to design intelligent decision support systems, where formal game-theoretic models are applied at the modeling stage (Chapter 7).

The new methodology for balancing the economic, legal, and social macrosystems of the public metasystem based on Berge equilibrium (as a mechanism for implementing the social state idea) and the new scientific approach to improving decision processes in the social sphere at the macrolevel are aimed at solving the current integral problems: imbalance of the economic, social, and legal macrosystems and denationalization of social sectors due to changes in economic and legal institutions. In other words, they are aimed to eliminate poverty in all forms.

The new economic paradigm based on the Golden Rule of ethics will reorient "the weak state in the economy" to "the strong state in the economy" [115], directing strategic decision-making in the social sphere "towards satisfying the wide interests of most Russian citizens and the country in general, reducing the unacceptably high and socially dangerous level of income differentiation of various population groups, decreasing poverty and unemployment through developing production potential and significantly raising wages of employees and, consequently, diminishing the number of Russian citizens with incomes below the living wage adequate to the real conditions, and lowering the high fees for education, health care..." [118].

Thus, it is necessary to transform the current constitutional, legal, and economic mechanisms for exercising the population's rights. The new mechanisms should involve the social state macromodel with the philosophical and moral doctrine of the Golden Rule of ethics for ensuring the consistent dynamic growth in the population's quality of life and well-being.

Conclusion

This book has developed a new concept of balancing the economic, legal and social macrosystems based on the mathematical model of Berge equilibrium and a novel scientific approach to improving decision processes in the social sphere at the macrolevel. The concept proposed in the book has the following advantages:

- First, the balancedness of the economic, legal, and social macrosystems has not been previously examined within a game-theoretic approach based on Berge and Nash equilibria.
- This concept models strategic decision-making with adequate consideration of uncertainty (incomplete information), conflict, and risks in the social sphere as a complex controlled macrosystem.

The following tasks have been solved:

1. A methodology for designing a metasystem equilibrium of the economic, legal, and social macrosystems has been developed using the concepts of Berge and Nash equilibrium.
   - The interaction and mutual influence of the economic, legal, and social macrosystems as stationary and (or) non-stationary objects have been structurally analyzed within the social state idea declared in Russia.
   - The interaction of these systems has been modeled at the macrolevel. In addition, their Berge and Nash equilibria (expressing the Golden Rule of ethics and individual rationality, respectively) have been formalized and justified.
   - The dynamics of family structures and relations affecting the current state, prospects and possibilities of public administration of sociodemographic processes in Russia have been examined. In addition, mathematical models of relations in three-person

families have been constructed using the concepts of Berge and Nash equilibrium and compared with one another.
- As an example of the mutual influence of the economic, legal, and social macrosystems, the national social legislation has been analyzed through the prism of strategic decisions transforming the social sphere (in particular, the transition from a universal social security system to the targeted one).

2. For improving decision processes in the social sphere at the macrolevel, a new hierarchical model for managing the dynamics of the social sphere and decision-making at each level of the hierarchy has been developed and justified.
    - A multilevel mathematical model for managing the dynamics of the population's social security and support system has been constructed.
    - Guaranteed solutions have been formalized for multicriteria management problems in complex socio-economic systems under interval uncertainty with given limits. the concept of a guaranteed solution has been formalized by modifying Savage's principle of minimax regret. To this end, the following pair has been considered: the set of state social guarantees for the population and life risks in case of which definite categories of the population exercise their constitutional right to obtain appropriate social guarantees. An existence theorem for the guaranteed solution has been proved under standard assumptions of multicriteria choice problems, and a method to find this solution has been proposed.
3. The theory and methodology of economic-mathematical modeling have been further developed: new game-theoretic approaches have been introduced to model decision-making, increasing the outcomes and simultaneously reducing the associated Savage risk.
4. The theoretical approach to improving decision processes at the macrolevel has been justified: a methodology has been proposed to design guaranteed solutions and risks and study the corresponding Berge equilibrium. Important properties of this equilibrium (particularly stability and unimprovability) have been revealed by formalizing an original solution—the so-called guaranteed solution in payoffs and risks (guarantee)—in a noncooperative N-player game. The guaranteed solution is efficient (represents a Pareto-maximal

Berge equilibrium). Its existence in mixed strategies has been proved, and some properties have been established.

5. For making this research practice-oriented, intelligent decision support systems under uncertainty have been studied, and the need for developing and adopting intelligent decision support systems based on the latest technologies in the social sphere has been justified. Basic principles, general design stages, and a classification have been considered for intelligent decision support systems where formal game-theoretic models are applied at the modeling stage. In addition, their advantages have been emphasized.

The research presented above yields the following **conclusions**.

1. The new concept of a balanced equilibrium of the complex public metasystem has been developed, and the new Berge equilibrium-based models of the economic, legal, and social macrosystems have been constructed. The proposed approaches are advantageous since the corresponding models of strategic decision-making consider uncertainties and involve the philosophical and moral concept of the Golden Rule as the basic economic doctrine.
2. In practice, this concept will properly adapt the game-theoretic tools decision problems in nonstationary systems, mainly at the micro- and mesolevel. The new concept is theoretically oriented towards solving the current integral problems: the imbalance of the economic, legal, and social macrosystems and the denationalization of the social sphere. Consequently, it will reduce the population's poverty in all forms.
3. A new mechanism for balancing the economic, social, and legal macrosystems put forward in this book involves an original equilibrium model with *the social state idea underlying their mutual influence and interaction*. The new mechanism is based on the concept of Berge equilibrium, which reveals the Golden Rule of ethics.
4. The new models of decision-making and the "altruistic" Berge equilibrium in modern management practice may become a mathematical justification for designing national social and economic policy within a new economic paradigm based on philosophical and moral principles.

5. The introduction of new game-theoretic approaches to model decision processes in managing complex macrosystems under incomplete information, conflicts, and uncertainty will yield the efficient (Pareto-maximal), least risky and most guaranteed decisions. As a result, the operation of the three complex macrosystems and, consequently, the operation of the complex metasystem will be stabilized. These results enlarge the application domain of game theory in economics and develop the mathematical apparatus of economic studies by combining scientific approaches of game theory, management, economics, law, and sociology.
6. As established, the regulation of the social sphere is one of the main elements in implementing the essential content of the social state. The constitutional and legal development of mechanisms for exercising the right to receive social services and products by the population, the development and implementation of new legal institutions should be focused on achieving consistent dynamic growth in the population's quality of life and well-being. The effectiveness and reality of constitutional rights for social services are directly related to their mechanism, the development and implementation of new legal institutions guaranteeing highquality prerequisites for a decent human life and personal development as the foundation of a social state.
7. Given all these factors and the features of strategic decision-making in stationary and nonstationary macrosystems (Chapter 1), this book introduces a new scientific approach to improving decision processes in the social sphere at the macrolevel (Chapter 3). More specifically:
   - We have constructed a new multilevel mathematical model for managing the dynamics of complex socio-economic systems under uncertainty and have suggested a scientifically grounded approach to posing and solving this management problem.
   - We have proposed a method for formalizing guaranteed solutions in multicriteria problems of managing complex socio-economic systems under interval uncertainty with given limits.
   - We have formalized a guaranteed solution by modifying Savage's principle of minimax regret. To this end, we have considered the following pair: the set of state social guarantees for the population and socio-economic life risks in case of which definite categories of the population exercise their constitutional right to obtain appropriate social guarantees. Also, we have proved an existence theorem for this solution under standard

assumptions of multicriteria choice problems and have developed a method to find it.

8. In the social state, strategic decision-making at the macrolevel secures the population against guaranteed (life) risks, such as old age, illness, unemployment, accidents, etc. Chapter 4 has presented in detail the mathematical apparatus used in Chapter 3. We have suggested new game-theoretic approaches to modelling decision processes, increasing the outcomes and simultaneously reducing the associated Savage risk. We have constructed the guaranteed solutions and risks and have explored the features of Nash equilibrium.
9. The new methodology, proposed in Chapter 5 and proved in Chapter 4, involves the GR to design the guaranteed solutions considering the associated risks and study the features of Berge equilibrium. To identify the features (stability and unimprovability), we have formalized the Pareto-guaranteed Berge equilibrium, have established its existence in mixed strategies, and have examined its properties. The mathematical framework of Chapter 5 justifies the studies carried out in Chapter 2, that is, the model of balanced equilibrium of the complex national metasystem.
10. To increase the groundedness of decision-making and develop decision support for the social sphere, Chapter 6 has considered new approaches to modelling decision processes in complex socio-economic systems under uncertainty, particularly their advantages. They can be used to design intelligent decision support systems, where formal game-theoretic models are applied at the modeling stage (Chapter 7).
11. The new economic paradigm based on the Golden Rule of ethics will reorient Russia's economic doctrine, directing strategic decision-making in the social sphere towards the wide interests of most Russian citizens. Thus, it is necessary to transform the current constitutional, legal, and economic mechanisms for exercising the population's rights. The new mechanisms should involve the social state macromodel with the philosophical and moral doctrine of the Golden Rule of ethics for ensuring the consistent dynamic growth in the population's quality of life and well-being.

The design and justification of the approaches and models mentioned above contributes to:

- the development of mathematical apparatus for analyzing complex controlled socio-economic systems: mathematical economics, game theory, optimal decision-making, and other methods used in economic-mathematical modeling;
- the development of economic-mathematical modeling as well as its capabilities and ranges of application to theoretical and practical issues of describing socio-economic processes and systems in the form of mathematical models;
- the development of mathematical methods and models for studying and forecasting the dynamics of socio-economic processes of public life (demographic processes, the labor market and employment of the population, the population's quality of life, etc.);
- the development and investigation of economic dynamics macromodels in equilibrium conditions;
- the development of decision support systems to justify national programs in the social sphere.

References

[1] Ackoff, R. L. 1963. "General System Theory and Systems Research: Contrasting Conceptions of Systems Science." *General Systems* 8:117-121.

[2] Aivazyan, S. A. 2012. *Analysis of the Quality and Lifestyle of the Population*. Moscow: Nauka.

[3] Aivazyan, S. A. 2000. *Integral Indicators for the Population's Quality of Life: Their Construction and Use in Socioeconomic Management and Interregional Comparisons*. Moscow: Central Economics and Mathematics Institute, Russian Academy of Sciences.

[4] Aivazyan, S. A. 2016. *Quality of Life and Living Standards Analysis. An Econometric Approach.* Berlin: de Gruyter.

[5] Alexander, C. 1998. *Risk Management and Analysis: New Markets and Products.* New York: John Wiley & Sons.

[6] Alexander, C. 1998. *Risk Management and Analysis: Measuring and Modelling Financial Risk.* New York: John Wiley & Sons.

[7] Andreeva, T. V. 2016. *Family Psychology.* St. Petersburg: Rech'.

[8] Aristov, E. V. 2016. *A Legal Paradigm of the Social State*. Moscow: Yuniti-Dana.

[9] Arnol'd, V. I. 1992. *Catastrophe Theory.* Berlin-Heidelberg: Springer-Verlag.

[10] Arsene, C. T. C., Gabrys, B., and Al-Dabass, D. 2012. "Decision Support System for Water Distribution Systems Based on Neural Networks and Graphs Theory for Leakage Detection." *Expert Systems with Applications* 39(18):13214-13224.

[11] Aumann, R. J. and Maschler, M. 1985. "Game Theoretic Analysis of a Bankruptcy Problem from the Talmud." *Journal of Economic Theory* 36:195-213.

[12] Aumann, R. J. and Maschler, M. 1995. *Repeated Games with Incomplete Information.* Cambridge: MIT Press.

[13] Bartyshin, I. Z., Nedosekin, A. A., Stetsko, A. A., Tarasov, B. V., Yazenin, A. V., and Yarushkina, Ya. G. 2007. *Fuzzy Hybrid Systems. Theory and Practice*. Moscow: Fizmatlit.

[14] Bellman, R. E. 1961. *Adaptive Control Processes: A Guided Tour.* Princeton: Princeton University Press.

[15] Berge, C. 1957. *Théorie générale des jeux de plusieurs personnes* [*General theory of many-person games.*] Paris: Gauthier Villars, 1957.

[16] Berge, C. 1954. "Sur une Convexite Reguliere et ses Applications a la Theorie des Jeux" [On a Regular Convexity and its Applications to Game Theory.] *Bull. Soc. Math. France* 81: 301-315.

[17] Bernstein, P. L. 1998. *Against the Gods: The Remarkable Story of Risk*. New York: Wiley & Sons, inc.

[18] Bertrand, J. 1883. "Theorie Mathematique de la Richesse Sociale." *Journal des Savants* 67:499-508.

[19] Biltchev, S. V. 1984. "ε − Z-Equilibrium in a Differential Game Described by a Parabolic System." In *Many Players Differential Game,* 47-52. Bulgaria, Rousse: Technical Univ.

[20] Biryukova, L. V. (Zhukovskaya, L. V.) and Zhukovskiy, V. I. "Competition of Two Homogeneous Economies," in *3rd Intern. Conf. on Global Optimization*. Irkutsk, 1993.

[21] Biryukova, L. V. (Zhukovskaya, L. V.) and Zhukovskiy, V. I., "Guaranteeing Equilibria in Threats and Counterthreats in a Differential Game," in Voronezh Spring Math. School *"Pontryagin Readings 6"* Voronezh: Voronezh State University, April 20-26, 1995, p. 13.

[22] Biryukova, L. V. (Zhukovskaya, L. V.) and Zhukovskiy, V. I., "On a Property of Quadratic Functionals," in Voronezh Winter Math. School *"The Contemporary Metric Theory of Functions and Related Problems of Applied Mathematics and Mechanics,"* Voronezh: Voronezh State University, 1995.

[23] Biryukova, L. V. (Zhukovskaya, L. V.), 1995. "An Unimprovable Equilibrium in a Differential Game." *Cybernetics and Computer Science (Complex Control Systems)* 107:25-33. Kiev: National Academy of Sciences of Ukraine.

[24] Biryukova, L. V. (Zhukovskaya, L. V.) "Equilibrium in Threats and Counterthreats under Uncertainty." *Problems of Management and Informatics* 2:21-26.

[25] Biryukova, L. V. (Zhukovskaya, L. V.) 1996. "Equilibrium in Threats and Counterthreats under Uncertainty" Cand. Sci. Phys.-Math. Diss., St. Petersburg State University.

[26] Biryukova, L. V. (Zhukovskaya, L. V.) "Vector Guarantees in Games," in *3rd Int. Seminar on Nonsmooth and Discontinuous Control and Optimization Problems and Their Applications*, St. Petersburg, June 26-July 2, 1995.

[27] Blackwell, D. and Girshick, M. A. 1954. *Theory of Games and Statistical* Decisions. New York: John Wiley & Sons.

[28] Borel, E., 1921. "La théorie du jeu et les equations intégrales à noyau symétrique gauche." *Comptes Rendus de l'Académie des Sciences* 173:1304-1308. Translated by L. J. Savage under the title "The Theory of Play and Integral Equations with Skew—Symmetric Kernels," *Econometrica,* 1953, vol. 21, pp. 97-100.

[29] Borel, E. 1927. "Sur les systèmes de formes linéaires a determinant symétrique gauche et la théorie generale du jeu," *Comptes Rendus de l' Académie des Sciences* 184:52-53. Translated by L. J. Savage under the title "On Systems of Linear Forms of Skew Symmetric Determinant and the General Theory of Play," *Econometrica,* 1953, vol. 21, pp. 116-117.

[30] Borel, E. 1924. "Sur les jeux ou le hasard se combine avec l'Habilite joueurs," [On games where chance is combined with the ability of the players.] *Comptes Rendus de l'Académie des Sciences* 178:24-25.

[31] Borel, E. 1938. "Traite du calcul des probabilites et ses applications" [Treatise on the calculus of probabilities and its applications.] In T.4. *Applications aux jeux de hasard* [*Applications to games of chance.*] Paris: Gauthier Villars.

[32] Born, P., Tijs, S., and van der Aarsen, J. 1988. "Pareto-equilibrium in Multi-objective Games." *Methods of Operation Research* 60:302-312.

[33] Bouton, C. L., 1905. "Nim, a Game with a Complete Mathematical Theory." *Ann. Math.* 3:35-39.

[34] Caldwell, J. C. 1976. "Toward a Restatement of Demographic Transition Theory." *Population and Development Review* 2(3/4):321-366.

[35] Case, J. H. 1974. "A Class of Games Having Pareto Optimal Nash Equilibrium." *Optimiz. Theory Appl.* 13(3):378-385.

[36] Caudwell, C. 1976. "Toward a Restatement of Demographic Transition Theory." *Population and Development Review* 2(3/4):321-366.

[37] Chernikov, S. N. 1968. *Linear Inequalities*. Moscow: Nauka.

[38] Chernogor, N. N., Pulyaeva, E. V., Chesnokova, M. D., Glazkova, M. E. 2010. "Monitoring of Efficiency of Legal Mechanism of Rendering Social Services." *Journal of Russian Law* 8:66-76.

[39] Chikrii, A. A. 1992. *Conflict-Controlled Processes*. Kiev: Naukova Dumka.

[40] Colman, A. M., Korner, T. W., Musy, O., and Tazdait, T. 2001. "Mutual Support in Games: Some Properties of Berge Equilibria." *Journal of Mathematical Psychology* 55(2):166-175.

[41] *Contributions to the Theory of Games.* 1950. Vol. I. Kuhn, H. W. and Tucker, A. W., eds., *Ann. of Math. Studies*, vol. 24. Princeton: Princeton Univ. Press.

[42] *Contributions to the Theory of Games*, Vol. II. 1953. Kuhn, H. W. and Tucker, A. W., eds. *Ann. of Math. Studies*, vol. 28. Princeton: Princeton Univ. Press.

[43] *Contributions to the Theory of Games*, Vol. III. 1957. Dresher, M., Tucker, A. W., and Wolfe, P., eds. *Ann. of Math. Studies,* vol. 39, Princeton: Princeton Univ. Press.

[44] *Contributions to the Theory of Games*, Vol. IV. 1959. Tucker, A. W. and Luce, R. D., eds. *Ann. of Math. Studies*, vol. 40, Princeton: Princeton Univ. Press.

[45] Cournot, A. A. 1838. *Recherches sur les principes mathématiques de la théorie des richesses [Research on the mathematical principles of the theory of wealth.]* Paris: L. Hachette.

[46] Damodaran, A. 2007. *Strategic Risk Taking: A Framework for Risk Management.* FT Press.

[47] Daniels, B., Flack, J., David, C., and Krakauer, D., 2017. "Dual Coding Theory Explains Biphasic Collective Computation in Neural Decision-Making." *Front. Neurosci.*, June 6, 2017. https://doi.org/10.3389/fnins.2017.00313.

[48] DeGroot, M. 1970. *Optimal Statistical Decisions.* New York: John Wiley & Sons.

[49] Dement'ev, V. E., Kleiner, G. B., Polterovich, V. M., et al. 2015. *On Measures to Overcome the Crisis Situation in Russia's Economy.* Moscow: The State Duma.

[50] Dochev, D. T. and Stojanov, N. V. 1984. "Existence of *Z*-Equilibrium in a Differential Game with Delay." In *Many Players Differential Game,* 64-72. Bulgaria, Rousse: Technical Univ.

[51] Dubins, L. and Savage, L. 1965. *How to Gamble if You Must. Inequalities for Stochastic Processes.* New York: McGraw-Hill.

[52] Elizarov, V. V. 2011. "Stimulating Reproduction and Supporting Families with Children in Modern Russia." In *Reproduction and Family Planning in Russia: History and Prospects.* Troitskaya, I. A. and Avdeedv, A. A., eds. Moscow: Demographic Studies. 18:123-152.

[53] Engels, F. 1909. *The Origin of the Family, Private Property and the State.* Translated by E. Untermann. Chicago: C. H. Kerr & Company.

[54] Engels, F. 1877. *Anti-Dühring* [*Anti-Duhring.*] Abteilung III. Ch. V. Der Staat, Familie, Bildung.

[55] Engels, F. 1884. *Der Ursprung der Familie, des Privateigenthums und des Staats [The Origin of the Family, Private Property, and the State].* https://marxwirklich studieren.files.wordpress.com/2012/11/engels-ursprung-der-familie-usw.pdf.

[56] Fiedler, M., Nedoma, J., Ramik, J., Rohn, J., and Zimmermann, K. 2006. *Linear Optimization Problems with Inexact Data.* Springer US.

[57] Fishburn, P. C. 1971. *Utility Theory for Decision-Making.* New York: Wiley.

[58] Fisher, R. A. 1934. "Randomisation, and an Old Enigma of Card Play." *Math. Gazette* 18:294-297.

[59] Flood, M. M. 1952. *Some Experimental Games.* Research Memorandum RM-789-1. Santa Monica, CA: RAND Corporation.

[60] Fudenberg, D. and Tirole, J. 1991. *Game Theory.* Cambridge, MA: MIT Press.

[61] Gaidov, S. D. 1984. "Z-Equilibrium in Stochastic Differential Game" *Many Players Differential Game.* Bulgaria, Rousse: Technical Univ.

[62] Gantmacher, F. R. 1959. *The Theory of Matrices.* Vols. 1 and 2. New York: Chelsea Publishing.

[63] Germeier, Yu. B. 1989. *Non-antagonistic Games.* Reidel.

[64] Germeier, Yu. B. 1971. *Introduction to Operations Research.* Moscow: Nauka.

[65] Gibbons, R. 1992. *Game Theory for Applied Economists.* Princeton: Princeton Univ. Press.

[66] Glaz'ev, S. Yu. 2010. *A Strategy for Russia's Priority Development under the Global Crisis.* Moscow: Ekonomika.

[67] Glicksberg, I. L. 1952. "A Further Generalization of Kakutani's Fixed Point Theorem with Application to Nash Equilibrium Point." *Proceedings of the American Mathematical Society* 3(1): 170-174.

[68] Guseinov, A. A. 1988. *The Golden Rule of Ethics.* Moscow: Molodaya Gvardiya.

[69] *Handbook of Game Theory with Economic Applications.* Vol 1. 1992. Aumann, R. J. and Hart, S., eds., Amsterdam: Elsevier.

[70] *Handbook of Game Theory with Economic Applications.* Vol 2. 1994. Aumann, R. J. and Hart, S., eds., Amsterdam: Elsevier.

[71] *Handbook of Game Theory with Economic Applications.* Vol. 3. 2002. Aumann, R. J. and Hart, S., eds., Amsterdam: Elsevier.

[72] Harsanyi J. C. and Selten R. 1988. *A General Theory of Equilibrium Selection in Games.* Cambridge: MIT Press.

[73] Harsanyi, J. C. and Selten, R., 1972. "A Generalised Nash Solution for Two-Person Bargaining Games with Incomplete Information." *Management Science* 18(5): 80-106.

[74] Harsanyi, J. C. 1995. "A New Theory of Equilibrium Selection for Games with Incomplete Information." *Games and Economic Behavior* 10(2): 318-332.

[75] Harsanyi, J. C. 1967-1968. "Games with Incomplete Information Played by 'Bayesian' Players." *Management Science* 14(I-III): 159-182., 14(I-III): 320-334., 14(I-III): 486-502.

[76] Harysson, M., Métayer, E., and Sarrazin, H. 2012. "How 'Social Intelligence' Can Guide Decision." *McKinsey Quarterly*, November 1. https://www.mckinsey.com/industries/high-tech/our-insights/how-social-intelligence-can-guide-decisions.

[77] Heath, C. and Sibony, O. 2013. "Making Great Decisions." *McKinsey Quarterly*, April 1. https://www.mckinsey.com/business-functions/strategy-and-corporate-finance/our-insights/making-great-decisions#0.

[78] Hegel, G. 1991. "Only the Family as a Whole Represents Personality." In *Family*. Moscow: Izd. Polit. Lit.

[79] Howard, N. 1971. *Paradoxes of Rationality: Games, Metagames, and Political Behavior*. Cambridge, Mass.: MIT Press.

[80] Howard, N. 1966. "The Theory of Metagames." *General Systems*, *Yearbook of the Society for General Systems Research* 11:167-186.

[81] Hua, J. 2009. "Optimal Investment in Information System Security: A Game Theoretical Approach." PhD diss. in Inf. Sci. and Syst., Baltimore.

[82] Hurwicz, L. 1945. "The Theory of Economic Behavior." *American Economic Review* 35(5): 909-925.

[83] Huygens, C. 1714. *Libellus De Ratiosiniis in Ludo Aleae. Oeuvres Completes.* eds. 1657. Translated under the title "*The Value of All Chances in Games of Fortune*," in Cards, Dice, Wagers, Lotteries&c. Mathematically Demonstrated. London: printed by S. Keimer for T. Woodward, Near the Inner-Temple-Gate in Fleetstreet. https://math.dartmouth.edu/~doyle/docs/huygens/huygens.pdf.

[84] Intriligator, M. 1971. *Mathematical Optimization and Economic Theory.* New York: Prentice Hall.

[85] Isaacs, R. 1965. *Differential Games*. New York: John Wiley & Sons.

[86] Jain, S. 2010. "Incentives in Social Computing." PhD diss. in Comp. Sci., Cambridge, Mass.

[87] Kachalov, R. M. 2012. *Economic Risk Management: Theoretical Grounds and Applications*. St. Petersburg: Nestor-Istoriya.

[88] Kakutani, S. 1941. A Generalization of Brouwer's Fixed Point Theorem. *Duke Math. Journal* 8:457-458.

[89] Kantorovich, L. V. 2011. *Mathematical-Economic Articles* (*Selected Works*). Novosibirsk: Nauka.

[90] Karlin, A. B. 2004. "Social State and Legal Problems of Freedom of Economic Activity." *Proc. All-Russ. Sci.-Pract. Conf. Topical Problems of Improving Russian Legislation at the Present Stage,* pp. 8-11. Moscow: The All-Russian State University of Justice.

[91] Karlin, S. 1959. *Mathematical Methods and Theory in Games, Programming and Economics*. London–Paris: Pergamon Press.

[92] Keeney, R. L. and Raiffa, H. 1991. *Decisions with Multiple Objectives: Preferences and Value Tradeoffs*. Cambridge: Cambridge University Press.

[93] Kelly, A. 2003. *Decision Making Using Game Theory. An Introduction for Managers.* Cambridge: Cambridge Univ. Press, 2003.

[94] Kilgour, D. M. 1977. "Equilibrium Points of Infinite Sequential Truels." *Intern. J. Game Theory* 6(3):167-180.

[95] Kleiner, G. B. and Rybachuk, M. A. 2017. *The Systemic Balancedness of Economy.* Moscow: Central Mathematics and Economics Institute, Russian Academy of Sciences.

[96] Kleiner, G. B. 2016. *Economics. Modeling. Mathematics. Selected Works.* Moscow: Central Mathematics and Economics Institute, Russian Academy of Sciences.

[97] Kleiner, G. B. 2004. *Evolution of Institutional Systems.* Moscow: Nauka.

[98] Kleiner, G. B. 2006. *Developing the Concept of Russia's Economic Policy: Problem Statement.* Moscow: Nauchnyi Ekspert.

[99] Knight, F. H. 1921. *Risk, Uncertainty and Profit.* Boston–New York: Houghton Mifflin Company.

[100] Kolemaev, V. A. 2005. *Mathematical Economics.* Moscow: Yuniti Dana.

[101] Kornai, J. 2000. "The System Paradigm." In *Paradigms of Social Change* by Schekle, W., Krauth, W., Kohli, M., and Elwert, G., Eds., 111-133. Frankfurt and New York: Campus Verlag – St. Martin's.

[102] Kostyuk, V. N. 1979. "Systems Theory as Relations Theory." In *Systems Research,* 344-357. Moscow: Nauka.

[103] Kostyuk, V. N. 2013. *Nonstationary Economy: The Effect of Growing Complexity on Economic Development.* Moscow: Lenand.

[104] Krasovskii, N. N. and Subbotin, A. I. 1985. *Positional Differential Games.* Moscow: Nauka.

[105] Kuhn, H. W. 1950. "Extensive Games." *Proc. Nat. Acad. Sci. USA* 36:570-576.

[106] Kullback, S. and Leibler, R. A. 1951. "On Information and Sufficiency." *Annals of Mathematical Statistics* 22(1):79-86.

[107] Lancaster, K. 1968. *Mathematical Economics.* New York: Macmillan.

[108] Laplas, P. S. 1816. *Essai philosophique sur les probabilités* [*Philosophical essay on probability.*] Paris: V. Courcier.

[109] Lasker, E. 1918. *Die Philosophie des Unvollendbaren* [*The philosophy of the incomplete*]. Leipzig: Veit & Co.

[110] Lasker, E. 1907. *Kampf* [*Struggle*]. New York: Lasker's Publishing Co.

[111] Lazarev, V. V. and Lipen', S. V. 2000. *Theory of State and Law.* Moscow.

[112] Lefevbre, V. A. 2003. "Conflicting Structures." In *Reflexion*, 95-107. Moscow: Kogito-Tsentr.

[113] Lefevbre, V. A. 1962. "On Ways to Represent Objects as Systems." Symposium *Research Logic.* Kiev.

[114] Leist, O. E. 1962. *Sanctions in the Soviet Law.* Moscow: Gos. Izd. Yurid. Lit.

[115] Livshits, V. N. and Livshits, S. V. 2008. *Macroeconomic Theories, Real Investments, and Russian State Economic Policy.* Moscow: LKI.

[116] Livshits, V. N. and Livshits, S. V. 2010. *Systems Analysis of Russia's Nonstationary Economy (1992-2009): Market Reforms, Crisis, Investment Policy.* Moscow: PoliPrintServis.

[117] Livshits, V. N. and Livshits, S. V. 2011. *Systems Analysis of Russia's Nonstationary Economy (1992-2010): Market Reforms, Crisis, Investment Policy.* Moscow: Maroseika.

[118] Livshits, V. N. 2018. *Poverty and Income Inequality of the Population in Russia and Abroad: Systems Analysis of Some Important Fragments of the Problem.* Moscow: Institute of Economics, Russian Academy of Sciences.

[119] Livshits, V. N. 2007. "Riddles of the Modern Russian Economy and Its State Regulation Policy." *Economics and Mathematical Methods* 43(1):113-128.

[120] Livshits, V. N. 2015. "Russian State Economic Policy as an Inefficient Large-Scale Measure." *In Management of Large-Scale Systems Development.* Moscow: Fizmatgiz, pp. 116-137.

[121] Livshits, V. N. 2015. *Systems Analysis of Markets Reforms of Russia's Nonstationary Economy, 1992-2013.* Moscow: Lenand.

[122] Livshits, V. N. 2013. *Systems Analysis of Markets Reforms of Russia's Nonstationary Economy, 1992-2013.* Moscow: URSS.

[123] Livshits, V. N. 2007. "What State Is Needed for Our Economy and What Economy Is Needed for Our State?" *Proc. Seminar on Economic Problems of the Energy Complex.* Moscow: Institute of Economic Forecasting, Russian Academy of Sciences.

[124] Lokosov, V. V. and Yarasheva, A. V. 2014. *Russia's Social Code: Pro et Contra.* Moscow: Institute of Socio-Economic Studies of Population, Russian Academy of Sciences.

[125] Lovallo, D. and Sibony, O. 2013. "Early-Stage Research on Decision-Making Styles." *McKinsey Quarterly,* April 1. https://www.mckinsey.com/business-functions/strategy-and-corporate-finance/our-insights/early-stage-research-on-decision-making-styles

[126] Luce, R. D. and Raiffa, H. 1957. *Games and Decisions: Introduction and Critical Survey,* New York: Dover Publications.

[127] Lvov, D. S., 2003. *The Future of Russia: Civil Manifesto.* Volgograd: Volgograd State University.

[128] Lvov, D. S., 2004. *Economic Growth and Quality of the Economy.* Moscow: Gudok, Russkaya Kniga.

[129] Lvov, D. S. 2006. *The Mission of Russia: Civil Manifesto.* Moscow: Institute for Economic Strategies, Russian Academy of Sciences.

[130] Lvov, D. S. 2004. *Ethical Economics.* Moscow: Institute for Economic Strategies, Russian Academy of Sciences.

[131] Lvov, D. S., Porshnev, A. G., Grebennikov, V. G., Dement'ev, V. E., Zotov, V. V., Kleiner, G. B., Makarov, V. L., et al. 2002. *Management of Russia's Socio-economic Development: Concepts, Goals, Mechanisms.* Moscow: Ekonomika.

[132] Lvov, D. S. 2003. *Problems of Russia's Long-Term Socio-Economic Development.* Volgograd: Volgograd State University.

[133] Lvov, D. S. 2004. *Return the Rent to the People. Reserve for the Poor.* Moscow: Eksmo.

[134] Makarov, V. L., Khristolyubova, N. E., and Yakovenko, E. G. 2003. *Handbook of Economic Tools.* Moscow: Ekonomika.

[135] Makarov, V. L. 2010. *Social Clustering. Russian Challenge*. Moscow: Biznes Atlas.

[136] Mamedov, M. B. 1983. "On a Pareto-Optimal Nash Equilibrium." *Izv. Akad. Nauk Azerb.* Ser. *Fiz. Tekh.* 4(2): 11-17.

[137] Markowitz, H. M. 1952. "Portfolio Selection." *Journal of Finance*. 7(1):77-91.

[138] Markowitz, H. M. 1959. *Portfolio Selection: Efficient Diversification of Investments.* New York: John Wiley & Sons.

[139] Marschak, J. 1946. "Neumann's and Morgenstern's New Approach to Static Economics." *Journal of Political Economy.* 54:97-115.

[140] Mas-Collel, A., Whinston, M. D., and Green, J. R. 1995. *Microeconomic Theory.* Oxford: Oxford Univ. Press.

[141] Merkert, J., Mueller, M., and Hubl, M. 2015. "A Survey of the Application of Machine Learning in Decision Support Systems." *The 23rd European Conference on Information Systems (ECIS).* Münster, Germany.

[142] Mesarovic, M. D. and Takahara, Y. 1975. *General Systems Theory: Mathematical Foundations.* New York: Academic Press.

[143] Meziriac, B. 1874. *Problèmes plaisants & délectables qui se font par les nombres* [*Pleasant and delectable problems that are done by numbers*]. Paris : Gauthier-Villars.

[144] Moiseev, N. N. 1975. *Elements of Optimal Systems Theory.* Moscow: Nauka.

[145] Montmort, R. 1713. *Essay d'analyse sur les jeux de hazard* [*Analytical essay on games of chance*]. Paris.

[146] Moore, E. H. 1909. "A Generalization of the Game Called Nim." *Ann. Math.* 11(3):93-94.

[147] Moore, P. G. 1983. *The Business of Risk.* Cambridge: Cambridge University Press.

[148] Morozov, V. V., Sukharev, A. G., Fedorov, V. V. 1989. *Operations Research in Tasks and Exercises*. Moscow: Nauka.

[149] Moulin, H. 1981. *Théorie des jeux pour l'économie et la politique* [*Game theory for economics and politics*]. Hermann: Paris.

[150] Myerson, R. B. 1984. "Cooperative Games with Incomplete Information." *International Journal of Game Theory* 13(2):69-96.

[151] Myerson, R. B. 1991. *Game Theory: Analysis of Conflict.* London: Harvard Univ. Press.

[152] Myerson, R. B. 1978. "Refinements of the Nash Equilibrium Concept." *International Journal of Game Theory* 15:133-154.

[153] Nash, J. F. 1950. "Equilibrium Points in N-Person Games." *Proc. Nat. Acad. Sci. USA* 36:48-49.

[154] Nash, J. F. 1951. "Non-Cooperative Games." *Ann. of Math.* 54:286-295.

[155] Nash, J. F. 1950. "The Bargaining Problem." *Econometrica* 18:155-162.

[156] Nash, J. F. 1953. "Two Person Cooperative Games." *Econometrica* 21:128-140.

[157] Nelson, R. R. and Winter, S. G. 1985. *An Evolutionary Theory of Economic Change.* Belknap Press.

[158] Nureev, R. M., et al. 2018. *Economic Sanctions against Russia and Russian Anti-sanctions: Costs and Benefits of Confrontation.* Moscow: Knorus.

[159] Nureev, R. M., et al. 2017. *Economic Sanctions against Russia: Expectations and Reality.* Moscow: Knorus.

[160] Owen. 1968. *Game Theory.* Saunders.

[161] Pareto, V. 1909. *Manuel d`economie* [*Economics textbook*]. Paris: Geard.

[162] Petrakov, N. Ya. and Rotar', V. I. 1985. *The Uncertainty Factor and Management of Economic Systems*. Moscow: Nauka.

[163] Petrosyan, L. A. and Zenkevich, N. A. 2016. *Game Theory*, 2nd ed. World Scientific.

[164] Podinovskii, V. V. and Noghin, V. D. 2007. *Pareto-Optimal Solutions of Multicriteria Problems.* Moscow: Fizmatlit.

[165] Polterovich, V. M. 2007. *Elements of Reform Theory.* Moscow: Ekonomika.

[166] Polterovich, V. M., Popov, V. V., and Tonis, A. S. 2007. *Economic Policy, Quality of Institutions and Mechanisms of the "Resource Curse."* Moscow: Higher School of Economics.

[167] Popkov, Yu. S. 2008. *Macrosystem Models of Spatial Economics*. Moscow: KomKniga.

[168] Popkov, Yu. S. 2014. *Mathematical Demoeconomy: Integrating Demographic and Economic Approaches.* De Gruyter.

[169] Pozamantir, E. I. 2014. *Computable General Equilibrium of the Economy and Transport. Transport in a Dynamic Intersectoral Balance*. Moscow: PoliPrintServis.

[170] Prangishvili, I. V., Pashchenko, F. F., and Busygin, B. P. 2001. *System Laws and Patterns in Electrodynamics, Nature and Society*. Moscow: Nauka.

[171] Raiffa, H. 1968. *Decision Analysis. Introductory Lectures on Choices under Uncertaint.* Longman Higher Education Division.

[172] Rapoport, A. 1986. *General System Theory. Essential Concepts and Applications.* Cambridge, Mass.: Abacus Press.

[173] Rashkov, P. I. 1984. "Sufficient Conditions for Z-Equilibrium in a Differential Game in Banach Space." In *Many Players Differential Game.* Bulgaria, Rousse: Technical Univ., pp. 91-99.

[174] Report at the meeting of the Presidium of the State Council of the Russian Federation "*On State Policy in the Field of Family, Motherhood, and Childhood*" Moscow, February 17, 2014.

[175] Rimashevskaya, N. M., et al. 2015. *The Present and Future of the Family in a Changing World*. Moscow: Ekon-Inform.

[176] Rimashevskaya, N. M. and Ivanishenko, N. N. 2013. *A Participatory Approach to Improving the Population's Quality of Life*. Nizhny Novgorod: Lobachevsky State University.

[177] Ross, C. T., Borgerhoff Mulder, M., Oh, S.-Y., Bowles, S., Beheim, B., Bunce, J., Caudell, M., Clark, G., Colleran, H., Cortez, C., Draper, P., Greaves, R. D., Gurven, M., Headland, T., Headland, J., Hill, K., Hewlett, B., Kaplan, H. S., Koster, J., Ziker, J.. 2018. "Greater Wealth Inequality, Less Polygyny: Rethinking the Polygyny Threshold Model." *J. R. Soc. Interface.* 15:20180035. http://doi.org/10.1098/rsif.2018.0035.

[178] Russell, S. and Norvig, P. 2020. *Artificial Intelligence: A Modern Approach*, 4th ed. Pearson.

[179] Saaty, T. L. 2005. *Creative Thinking, Problem Solving and Decision Making.* Pittsburgh: RWS Publ.

[180] *Sànchez-Marrè*, M. and Gibert, K. 2012. *Evolution of Decision Support Systems.* University of Catalunya.

[181] Savage, L. J. 1954. *The Foundation of Statistics.* New York: Wiley.

[182] Savage, L. J. 1951. "The Theory of Statistical Decisions." *Journal of the American Statistical Association.* 46:55-67.

[183] Schelling, T. 1960. *The Strategy of Conflict.* Cambridge, MA: Harward University Press.

[184] Seung-Yun, Oh, Ross, C. T., Borgerhoff Mulder, M., and Bowles, S. 2017. *The Decline of Polygyny: An Interpretation*. Santa Fe Institute, Paper no. 2017-12-037.

[185] Shannon, C. E. 1948. "A Mathematical Theory of Communication." *Bell System Technical Journal.* 27(3):379-423, 27(4):623-656.

[186] Shapley, L. S. and Shubik, M. 2010. "Pure Competition, Coalitional Power and Fair Division." *International Economic Review* 10(3):337-362.

[187] Shevyakov, A. Yu. 2011. *Myths and Realities of Social Policy*. Moscow: Institute of Socio-Economic Studies of Population. Russian Academy of Sciences.

[188] Sholomitskii, A. G. 2005. *Risk Theory. Choice under Uncertainty and Risk Modeling*. Moscow: Higher School of Economics.

[189] Shubik, M. 1982. *Game Theory in the Social Sciences: Concepts and Solutions*, Cambridge. Mass.: MIT Press.

[190] Sigal, A. V. 2012. "Game-Theoretic Models of Decision-Making Considering Risk." *Issues of Risk Analysis* 9(4):54-64.

[191] Sigal, A. V. 2016. *Game Theory and Its Economic Applications*. Moscow: Infra-M.

[192] Sinyukov, V. N., 2016. *Russian Legal System. Introduction to General Theory.* Moscow: Infra-M.

[193] Smet, A., Lackey, G., and Weis, L. 2017. Untangling Your Organization's Making, *McKinsey Quarterly.* June 21. https://www.mckinsey.com/business-functions/organization/our-insights/untangling-your-organizations-decision-making

[194] Smol'yakov, E. R. 2005. *Theory of Conflict Equilibria*. Moscow: URSS.

[195] Solozhentsev, E. D. 2011. *I^3-Technologies for the Economy*. St. Petersburg: Nauka.

[196] Sorokin, P. A. 1956. *The American Sex Revolution.* Boston: Sargent.

[197] Stackelberg, H. 1934. *Marktform und Gleichgewicht.* Wien & Berlin: Springer.

[198] Stiglitz, J. 2010. *Freefall: America, Free Markets, and the Sinking of the World Economy.* New York: W. W. Norton & Company.

[199] Stiglitz, J. E., Sen, A., and Fitoussi, J. P. 2010. *Mismeasuring Our Lives: Why GDP Doesn't Add Up.* The New Press.

[200] Sudhir, K. S. 2008. "Information, Incentives, and the Internet" PhD diss. in Electrical Engineering, Los Angeles.

[201] Suslova, Z. M., Pokrovskaya, A. P., and Fokin, I. A. 2013. *Russia with Many Children: The Family as a Foundation of Russian Statehood. Legislative Support of the Modern Demographic Policy of the State.* Moscow: Committee on the Family, Women and Children, the State Duma of the Russian Federation.

[202] Tariq, A. and Rafi, K. 2012. "Intelligent Decision Support Systems — A Framework." *Information and Knowledge Management* 2(6):12-20.

[203] Tersian, St. A. 1984. "On the Z-Equilibrium Points in a Differential Game." In *Many Players Differential Game.* Bulgaria, Rousse: Technical Univ., pp. 106-111.

[204] Todhunter, I. 1865. *A History of the Mathematical Theory of Probability from the Time of Pascal to that of Laplace.* Cambridge: Cambridge Univ. Press.

[205] Tsadiras, A. K., Papadopoulos, C. T., and O'Kelly, M. E. J. 2013. "An Artificial Neural Network Based Decision Support System for Solving the Buffer Allocation Problem in Reliable Production Lines." *Computers and Industrial Engineering* 66(4):1150-1162.

[206] Tucker, A. W. 1950. "On Jargon: The Prisoner's Dilemma." *UMAP Journal.* 1:101.

[207] Vaisbord, E. M. and Zhukovskiy, V. I. 1988. *Introduction to Multi Player Differential Games and Their Applications.* New York: Gordon and Breach.

[208] Vaisbord, E. M. 1974. "On Cooperative Differential Games." *Diff. Uravn.* 10(4):613-623.

[209] Val'kman, Yu. R., Val'kman, R. Yu., and Ismagilova, L. R. 2009. "Business Intelligence and Knowledge Management: Concepts, Technologies, Intellectuality," in *Proc. Int. IEEE Conf. on Artificial Intelligence Systems.* Moscow: Fizmatlit.

[210] Vasil'ev, F. P. 2002. *Optimization Methods*. Moscow: Faktorial Press.

[211] Vega-Redondo, F. 2003. *Economics and the Theory of Games.* Cambridge: Cambridge University Press.

[212] Vega-Redondo, F. 1996. *Evolution, Games, and Economic Behaviour.* Oxford: Oxford University Press.

[213] Velikhov, E. P. 1987. *Intelligent Processes and Their Modeling*. Moscow: Nauka.

[214] Vilenskii, P. L. and Livshits, V. N. 2013. *Investment Analysis*, 2nd ed. Moscow: Higher School of Economics.

[215] Vilenskii, P. L. and Livshits, V. N. 2010. *Investment Analysis.* Moscow: Biznes-Elainmen.

[216] Vilenskii, P. L., Kosov, V. V., Livshits, V. N., Smolyak, S. A., and Shakhnazarov, A. G. 2010. *Systematic Performance Measurement for Investment (Innovation) Projects*. Moscow: Research Institute of the Audit Chamber of the Russian Federation.

[217] Vilenskii, P. L., Livshits, V. N., and Smolyak, S. A. 2008. *Measuring the Performance of Investment Projects*, 4th ed. Moscow.

[218] Vilenskii, P. L., Livshits, V. N., and Smolyak, S. A. 2015. *Measuring the Performance of Investment Projects: Theory and Practice*, 5th ed. Moscow: PoliPrintServis.

[219] Vilkas, E. I. and Maiminas, E. Z. 1981. *Decision: Theory, Information, Modeling.* Moscow: Radio i Svyaz'.

[220] Vilkas, E. I. 1972. "Formalizing the Problem of Choosing a Game-Theoretic Criterion of Optimality." *Mathematical Methods in Social Sciences* 2:9-55. Vilnius: Institute of Mathematics and Cybernetics, Lit. SSR Academy of Sciences.

[221] Vilkas, E. I. 1990. *Optimality in Games and Decisions*. Moscow: Nauka.

[222] Vilkas, E. I. 1968. "The Axiomatic Definition of Equilibrium Points and the Value of a Non-Coalitional *n*-Person Game." *Theory Probab. Appl.* 13(3):523-527.

[223] Voevodin, V. V. and Kuznetsov, Yu. A. 1984. *Matrices and Calculations*. Moscow: Nauka.

[224] Volkonskii, V. A. 2005. *The Drama of the Spiritual Life: A Non-economic Foundation of the Economic Crisis*. Moscow: Master-Lain.

[225] von Bertalanffy, L. 1968. *General System Theory: Foundations, Development, Applications*. New York: George Braziller.

[226] von Bertalanffy, L. 1972. "The History and Status of General Systems Theory." *The Academy of Management Journal* 15(4):407-426.

[227] von Neumann, J. and Morgenstern, O. 1944. *Theory of Games and Economic Behavior*. Princeton: Princeton Univ. Press.

[228] von Neumann, J. and Morgenstern, O. 1947. *Theory of Games and Economic Behavior*, 2nd ed. Princeton: Princeton Univ. Press.

[229] von Neumann, J. 1928. "Zur Theorie der Gesellschaftsspiele." *Math. Ann.* 100:295-320.

[230] Vorob'ev, N. N. 1982. *Game Theory for Economists-cyberneticians*. Moscow: Nauka.

[231] Vorob'ev, N. N. 1984. *Fundamentals of Game Theory. Noncooperative Games*. Moscow: Nauka.

[232] Wagman, L. 2009. "Essays on Privacy, Information, and Anonymous Transactions." PhD Diss. in Economics, Durham.

[233] Wald, A. 1947. *Sequential Analysis*. New York: John Wiley & Sons.

[234] Wald, A. 1945. "Generalization of a Theorem by von Neumann Concerning Zero-Sum Two-Person Games." *Ann. of Math.* 46:281-286.

[235] Wald, A. 1945. "Statistical Decision Functions Which Minimize the Maximum Risk." *Ann. of Math.* 46:265-280.

[236] Wald, A. 1949. "Statistical Decision Functions." *Ann. Math. Statist.* 20(2):165-205.

[237] Williams, J. D. 1954. *The Compleat Strategyst. Being a Primer on the Theory of Games of Strategy*. New York–London: McGraw-Hill.

[238] Yeung, D. W. K. and Petrosyan, L. A. 2012. *Subgame Consistent Economic Optimization*. New York: Springer Science.

[239] Zadeh, L. A. 1975. "The Concept of a Linguistic Variable and Its Application to Approximate Reasoning." *Information Sciences* 8(4):301-357.

[240] Zadeh, L. A. 1965. "Fuzzy Sets." *Information and Control* 8:338-353.

[241] Zakharov, A. V. 2011. *Game Theory in Social Sciences*. Moscow: Higher School of Economics.

[242] Zermelo, E., 1913. "Über eine Anwendung der Mengenlehre auf die Theorie des Schachspiels" ["On an application of set theory to the theory of chess."] In *Proceedings of the 5th International Congress of Mathematicians*. Cambridge: Cambridge Univ. Press., pp. 501-504.

[243] Zhukovskaya, L. V. and Mikrin, E. A. 2004. "A New Approach to Estimation of the Effectiveness of Control Decisions under Conditions of Risk in ACS's." *Autom. Remote Control* 65(4):654-659.

[244] Zhukovskaya, L. V. (Mitrofanova, L. V.). 2001. *Mathematical Foundations of Risk in Multicriteria Problems.* Moscow: Russian Correspondence Institute of Textile and Light Industry.

[245] Zhukovskaya, L. V. and Mirkin, E. A. 2003. "An Approach to Formalization of a Risk in Making Decision in ACS." *Automation and Remote Control* 64(8):1346-1353.

[246] Zhukovskaya, L. V. and Mirkin, E. A. 2005. "A New Approach to Risk Estimation in Many-Criteria Automatic Control System. II." *Automation and Remote Control* 66(4):503-510.

[247] Zhukovskaya, L. V. and Zhukovskiy, V. I. 2009. "A Feature of Savage–Niehans Risks in a Noncooperative Game under Uncertainty." *Vestn. North-Caucasus Fed. Univ.* 74(5):39-44.

[248] Zhukovskaya, L. V. and Zhukovskiy, V. I. 2019. "Sanctions and Countersanctions in a Differential Game." In *Proc. Sci. Conf. "Tikhonov Readings."* Moscow: MAKS Press.

[249] Zhukovskaya, L. V. 2019. "Economic-mathematical Modeling as an Instrument of Transition to the New Economic Doctrine." Central Mathematics and Economics Institute, Russian Academy of Sciences. doi: 10.33276/S0000158-6-1.

[250] Zhukovskaya, L. V. 2019. "Formal and Systemic Mechanisms for Implementing the Idea of Balancing Economic, Social and Legal Macro-systems." *Trudy Inst. Sist. Analiz. Ross. Akad. Nauk* 69(3):28-42. doi: 10.14357 / 20790279190303.

[251] Zhukovskaya, L. V. 2019. "Formalization of Social Guarantees in Complex Socio-economic Macrosystems." In *Proc. 19th Int. Sci.-Pract. Conf. "From Economics to Business Behavior."* Grabov, O. N. and Palash, S. V., Eds. Kostroma: Kostroma State University, May 21-22.

[252] Zhukovskaya, L. V. 2018. "Game-Theoretic Approach to Modeling of Family Relations in Conditions of Transformation of Social and Economic System." *Trudy Inst. Sist. Analiz. Ross. Akad. Nauk* 68(3):12-27. doi: 10.14357/ 20790279180302.

[253] Zhukovskaya, L. V. 2003. "Internally Risk-Stable Solutions of Multicriteria Choice Problems." *Tambov Univ. Reports. Ser. Nat. and Tech. Sci.* 8(3):380.

[254] Zhukovskaya, L. V. 2004. "Methodological Foundations of Studying Conflict Systems under Uncertainty." *Control Sciences* 3:54-58.

[255] Zhukovskaya, L. V. 2018. "Om Some Modern Methods for Assessing the Public Efficiency of Social State Programs." In *Proceedings of the 5th International Conference "Systems Analysis in Economics" (SEinE-2018).* Moscow: Prometei, pp. 411-414.

[256] Zhukovskaya, L. V. 2005. "On Models and Methods for Managing Complex Socio-economic Dynamic Systems." *Control Sciences* 1:38-44.

[257] Zhukovskaya, L. V. 2019. "On the Balancedness of the Economic, Legal, and Social Macrosystems," in *Proc. Int. Sci.-School "Youth and Business: Experience, Problems, Interaction Horizons,"* Ushvitskii, L. I., ed. Stavropol: Sekvoiya, pp. 125-128.

[258] Zhukovskaya, L. V. 2018. "Public Administration of the Difficult Socio-economic Systems on the Different Levels of Hierarchy in Conditions of Uncertainty." *Trudy Inst. Sist. Analiz. Ross. Akad. Nauk* 68(4):17-25. doi: 10.14357/20790279180402.

[259] Zhukovskaya, L. V. 2014. "Risk in a Noncooperative Game under Uncertainty." *Proc. of the Inst. of Math. and Inf. of the Udmurt State University* 2:79-84.

[260] Zhukovskaya, L. V. 2019. "Systemic Analysis and Theoretical-Game Tools of Interaction between Economic, Legal and Social National Macrosystems." *Actual Problems of Economics and Law* 3(3):1287-1300. doi: 10.21202/1993-047X.13.2019.3.1287-1300.

[261] Zhukovskaya, L. V. 2017. "The Issues of Managing Social Support Programs for Elderly and Older People." *The Challenge of Management* 3:15-24.

[262] Zhukovskaya, L. V., Zhukovskiy, V. I., and Molostvov, V. S. 2003. "The Guaranteed Solution in Risk of a Multicriterion Choice Problem." *Tambov Univ. Reports. Ser. Nat. and Tech. Sci.* 8(3):382.

[263] Zhukovskiy, V. I. and Chikrii, A. A. 2017. *Differential Equations. Linear-Quadratic Differential Games*. Moscow: Yurait.

[264] Zhukovskiy, V. I. and Chikrii, A. A. 1994. *Linear-Quadratic Differential Games*. Kiev: Naukova Dumka.

[265] Zhukovskiy, V. I. and Kudryavtsev, K. N. 2017. "Coalition Equilibrium in a Three-Person Game," in *Constructive Nonsmooth Analysis and Related Topics (dedicated to the memory of V. F. Demyanov), CNSA*. St. Petersburg, May 22-27, pp. 1-4.

[266] Zhukovskiy, V. I. and Kudryavtsev, K. N. 2016. 'Pareto-Optimal Nash Equilibrium: Sufficient Conditions and Existence in Mixed Strategies." *Autom. Remote Control* 77(8):1500-1510.

[267] Zhukovskiy, V. I. and Salukvadze, M. E. 2014. *Guarantees and Risks in Conflicts and Applications.* Tbilisi: National Academy of Sciences of Georgia.

[268] Zhukovskiy, V. I. and Salukvadze, M. E. 1998. *Some Game-Theoretic Problems of Control and Their Applications.* Tbilisi: Metsniereba.

[269] Zhukovskiy, V. I. and Salukvadze, M. E. 2020. *The Berge Equilibrium: A Game-Theoretic Framework for the Golden Rule of Ethics*. Springer.

[270] Zhukovskiy, V. I. and Salukvadze, M. E. 2021. *The Golden Rule of Ethics. A Dynamic Game-Theoretic Framework Based on Berge Equilibrium.* CRC Press.

[271] Zhukovskiy, V. I. and Salukvadze, M. E. 1994. *The Vector-Valued Maximin.* New York: Academic Press.

[272] Zhukovskiy, V. I. and Tynyanskiy, N. T. 2010. *Equilibrium Controls of Multicriteria Dynamic Problems.* Moscow: Krasand.

[273] Zhukovskiy, V. I. and Zhukovskaya, L. V. 2017. *Risk in Multicriteria Choice and Conflict Systems under Uncertainty*, 3rd ed. Moscow: URSS.

[274] Zhukovskiy, V. I. and Zhukovskaya, L. V. 2007. *Risk in Multicriteria Choice and Conflict Systems under Uncertainty*, 2nd ed. Moscow: URSS.

[275] Zhukovskiy, V. I. and Zhukovskaya, L. V. 2003. *Risk in Multicriteria Choice and Conflict Systems under Uncertainty*. Moscow: URSS.

[276] Zhukovskiy, V. I., Gorbatov, A. S., and Kudryavtsev, K. N. 2017. "Nash and Berge Equilibria in a Linear-Quadratic Game." *Mat. Teor. Igr Prilozh.* 9(1): 62-94.

[277] Zhukovskiy, V. I. 2007. *Conflicts and Risks.* Moscow: Russian Correspondence Institute of Textile and Light Industry.

[278] Zhukovskiy, V. I., Kudryavtsev, K. N., and Smirnova, L. V. 2013. *Guaranteed Solutions of Conflicts and Applications*. Moscow: URSS.

[279] Zhukovskiy, V. I., Kudryavtsev, K. N., Samsonov, S. P., Vysokov, M. I., and Bel'skikh, Yu. A. 2018. "A Class of Differential Games in Which Nash Equilibrium is Absent but There Exists a Berge Equilibrium." *Vestn. South Ural State Univ. Ser. Math. Mech. Phys.* 10(2): 5-21.

[280] Zhukovskiy, V. I. 1985. "Some Problems of Non-Antagonistic Differential Games," in *Mathematical Methods in Operations Research.* Sofia: Bulgarian Academy of Sciences.

[281] Zhukovskiy, V. I. 2010. *An Introduction to Differential Games under Uncertainty. The Equilibrium in Threats and Counterthreats*, 2nd ed. Moscow: Krasand.

[282] Zimmermann, H. J. 2006. *Fuzzy Set Theory and Its Applications.* Boston: Springer US.

[283] Zolotarev, V. V. 2002. "Hybrid Equilibria in Games under Uncertainty." Cand. Sci. Phys.-Math. Diss., Moscow.

About the Author

Lidiya V. Zhukovskaya
Dr. Sci. (Econ.), Cand. Sci. (Phys.–Math.)
Senior Researcher, CEMI RAS
IstinaResearcherID (IRID): 152420159;
https://istina.msu.ru/profile/ZhukovskayaLV/
ResearcherID: B-1319-2017
ORCID: 0000-0002-4152-3161

Since 1994, Lidiya has been working in science and education; since 2012, in the Russian Academy of Sciences; from 2018 to present, in Central Economics and Mathematics Institute, the Russian Academy of Sciences (CEMI RAS).

In 1996 she defended candidate's dissertation in physics and mathematics at St. Petersburg State University (The equilibrium in Threats and Counterthreats under Uncertainty). The solutions of a noncooperative game based on the concept of active equilibrium in threats and counterthreats were classified and compared with Nash equilibrium. An existence theorem of these solutions was proved under standard assumptions in the theory of noncooperative games. For differential positional linear-quadratic games under uncertainty, solutions were formalized, and their classification was presented. Sufficient conditions of existence were obtained using dynamic programming; an explicit form of the solutions was found; a method for constructing the payoffs of the players was proposed.

In 2020 Lidiya defended the doctoral dissertation in economics in the Federal Research Center "Computer Science and Control," the Russian Academy of Sciences (Balancing the Economic, Legal, and Social Macrosystems Based on Modelling Decision Processes). Her most significant scientific results are the theoretical substantiation and development of an original concept of equilibrium for the complex public metasystem (the economic, legal, and social macrosystems) based on Berge equilibrium (the Golden Rule of ethics) as well as an original methodology for improving strategic decision processes in the social and economic sphere under uncertainty.

Lidiya has 83 publications, including 12 papers indexed by the Web of Science and the monograph "Risk in Multi-criteria and Conflict Systems under Uncertainty" (co-authored). She developed 2 university courses: "Mathematical Foundations of Risk in Multi-criteria Problems" and "Mathematical Foundations of Risk in Conflict Systems."

Index

#

20th century, 17

A

access, 8, 11, 168
accessibility, 70
AFM, 168
age, 29, 41, 42, 45, 49, 50, 73
algorithm, 12, 133
altruism, 47
anxiety, 11
artificial intelligence, 167, 171, 172
aspiration, 30
assessment, 74, 169, 170
assets, 59, 60, 65, 66
attitudes, 11
authorities, 8, 17, 19, 27, 29, 58, 59, 66, 71, 72
authority, 72
awareness, 6, 13, 50, 66

B

balanced equilibrium, xxiv, 2, 21, 22, 38, 40, 175, 176, 177, 183, 185
balancedness, ix, xx, xxiii, xxiv, 18, 132, 181, 192, 200
base, 15, 48, 167, 183
benefits, 8, 17, 49, 50, 70, 72, 76, 81
Berge equilibrium, ix, xvii, xviii, xix, xx, xxi, xxii, xxiii, xxiv, xxv, 19, 20, 21, 22, 26, 30, 31, 32, 35, 36, 37, 40, 45, 47, 48, 51, 108, 113, 115, 117, 119, 120, 121, 122, 124, 126, 127, 128, 129, 173, 175, 176, 177, 178, 181, 182, 183, 185, 200, 201, 204
birth rate, 42
births, 41
bounds, 98, 112, 127
brain, 170, 171
Buddhism, ix
budget allocation, 72
budget deficit, 16, 29
budgetary resources, 55
Bulgaria, 188, 189, 190, 195, 197

C

calculus, 12, 189
cash, 49
catalyst, 6
category a, 47
Caucasus, 199
Census, 41
checks and balances, 89
Chicago, 190
childhood, 49
children, 41, 42, 44, 45, 46, 49, 50, 57, 58
Christianity, ix
citizens, 3, 8, 25, 49, 50, 55, 57, 58, 85, 178, 185
civil law, 16
civil service, 57
civilization, 43, 45
classes, 4
classification, 13, 172, 183, 204

coding, 170
coercion, 132, 137
collisions, 8
commercial, 55, 59
communication, 11
communities, 43
compensation, 49
competition, 134
competitors, 26
complex interactions, 2
complex metasystem, xvii, xx, xxi, xxiii, xxv, 1, 2, 6, 7, 15, 16, 18, 19, 20, 21, 30, 31, 36, 38, 173, 175, 184
complexity, 50, 70, 169, 171
compliance, 75
complications, 75
conceptualization, 28
conflict, xx, 2, 4, 5, 7, 8, 11, 14, 17, 19, 22, 23, 26, 28, 29, 54, 55, 89, 90, 103, 113, 173, 174, 175, 181, 189, 194, 196, 199, 200, 201, 204
conflict of interest, 4, 8, 22, 89, 173
confrontation, 22, 89, 173
Confucianism, ix
Congress, 198
consciousness, 10
consensus, 170
Constitution, 3, 25, 27, 174
constitutional law, 27, 172
construction, 38, 174
consumption, xviii, 23, 76
continuous random variable, 6
control systems, 11, 12, 13, 22, 27, 28, 29, 89, 91, 115, 173, 188
controlled systems, 2, 7, 11, 13, 22, 28, 56, 115, 131, 132, 166, 173, 178
coordination, 70
corporate sector, 55
correlation, xix, 18, 24, 168
corruption, 57
cost, 54, 65
covering, 3, 12, 19, 25
culture, xvi, xviii, 21, 22, 70, 72, 115

D

danger, 5
data collection, 169
data mining, 167
data processing, 167
data set, 12
deaths, 10
decision-making process, 171
decomposition, 57
deficit, 31
deformation, 15
degradation, 4, 42, 174
demography, 41, 42, 57
destruction, xvii
detection, 171
deviation, xviii, 5, 30, 44, 80, 93, 95, 101, 131, 132
differential equations, 68, 134
digital technologies, 169
disability, 17, 80
disaster, 49
discomfort, 11
discrimination, 32, 102
diseases, 10
dissatisfaction, 7
distribution, xviii, 6, 8, 9, 15, 17, 23, 171
domestic violence, 43
dominance, 43
draft, 72, 73
drugs, 17
duality, 170
Duma, 189, 197
dynamic control, 13, 170
dynamic systems, 13, 131, 178
dynamics of marriage structures, xxi
dynamism, 56, 57

E

earnings, 80
economic activity, 18, 27, 31
economic change, 8
economic consequences, 17
economic development, xix, 3, 16, 18, 24, 25, 27, 31, 43, 91, 132, 175

economic doctrine, ix, xv, xxii, 14, 27, 109, 183, 185, 199
economic efficiency, 3, 25, 76
economic growth, 54
economic incentives, 3, 25
economic institutions, 56
economic losses, 80
economic macrosystem, xv, xvi, xviii, xix, 1, 3, 7, 8, 16, 18, 23, 24, 25, 29, 31, 38, 39, 53, 54, 55, 56, 57, 59, 69, 89, 166, 167, 169, 170, 171, 172
economic policy, xix, 54, 175, 183
economic problem, 51
economic reform, 42
economic reforms, 42
economic relations, xv, xviii, 2, 8, 18, 23, 24, 54, 66
economic resources, 23
economic status, 2, 24
economic systems, xvii, xxi, xxiv, 4, 20, 22, 23, 25, 53, 54, 55, 56, 70, 85, 87, 89, 90, 167, 171, 173, 174, 177, 178, 182, 184, 185, 186
economic theory, 175
economic transformation, 70
economics, ix, xvii, xviii, xix, xxii, 45, 90, 131, 176, 184, 186, 194, 204
education, xv, xvi, xviii, 45, 70, 71, 72, 73, 178, 203
elaboration, xxiii, 11
electricity, 13
emotion, 45
employees, 178
employment, 45, 46, 56, 57, 186
engineering, 54, 168, 169
environment, 42, 54, 168
equality, 17, 39, 98, 161, 162
equilibrium, ix, xiii, xvi, xvii, xviii, xix, xx, xxi, xxii, xxiii, xxiv, xxv, 1, 2, 19, 20, 21, 22, 23, 26, 28, 29, 30, 31, 32, 35, 36, 37, 38, 39, 40, 44, 45, 47, 48, 51, 89, 100, 101, 108, 109, 110, 111, 112, 113, 115, 117, 118, 119, 120, 121, 122, 123, 124, 126, 127, 128, 129, 131, 132, 133, 135, 136, 137, 138, 139, 140, 146, 155, 162, 164, 165, 166, 170, 173, 174, 175, 176, 177, 178, 181, 182, 183, 185, 186, 189, 203, 204
equilibrium in sanctions and countersanctions, xxii, 128, 131, 132, 133, 135, 137, 139, 140, 146, 164, 166, 178
ethics, ix, xvii, 19, 20, 22, 45, 47, 48, 109, 115, 128, 174, 175, 176, 178, 179, 181, 183, 185, 204
ethnographers, 43
Euclidean space, xiii, 14
Europe, 5
evidence, 86
evolution, 2, 4, 13, 24, 43, 44, 169, 171
executive power, 26
exercise, xxii, 17, 53, 69, 87, 177, 182, 184
exercises, 27
expenditures, 15, 73
expertise, 57

F

families, xxi, 40, 41, 42, 43, 49, 50, 57, 58, 176, 182
family members, 46, 47, 48
federal authorities, 63
federal law, 27
fertility, 41, 42
fertility rate, 41, 42
financial, xviii, 16, 27, 63, 64, 90, 168
financial resources, 27, 63, 64
force, 133
forecasting, 5, 11, 90, 167, 170, 174, 186
formation, xv, 43, 172
formula, 59, 116, 123, 124, 145, 148
foundations, xv, xix, 15, 17, 30, 45, 174
France, 187
freedom, 27
funding, 15, 16, 55, 60, 64, 65, 66, 70, 72, 73, 74
funds, 29, 55, 59, 64, 65, 71

G

game theory, ix, xvii, xix, xxiii, 1, 2, 6, 11, 19, 22, 27, 28, 30, 38, 48, 54, 56, 57, 75, 87, 90, 119, 131, 132, 133, 137, 139, 168, 172, 174, 176, 184, 186
game-theoretic modeling of decision processes under uncertainty and risk, xx
GDP, xv, 59, 196
gene pool, 44
Georgia, 200
Germany, 194
goal-setting, 17
goods and services, 8, 16
grants, 55
growth, 10, 24, 46, 63, 176, 179, 184, 185
guaranteed equilibrium in payoffs and risks, 111, 113
guaranteed solutions, xx, xxi, xxii, xxiv, 6, 53, 69, 71, 75, 89, 102, 112, 113, 115, 128, 129, 177, 182, 184, 185, 201
guarantees, xxii, 3, 16, 25, 26, 31, 38, 49, 53, 69, 71, 72, 79, 80, 86, 87, 91, 93, 94, 95, 96, 99, 100, 104, 107, 108, 111, 112, 116, 127, 128, 159, 177, 182, 184, 188, 200
guardian, 49
guidelines, 16

H

harmonization, 56, 57
health, xv, xvi, 5, 16, 45, 50, 70, 71, 72, 80, 178
health care, xv, xvi, 45, 70, 178
higher education, 49
history, 5, 43
housing, 13, 17, 70, 72
human, 3, 25, 43, 44, 54, 167, 169, 172, 174, 176, 184
human capital, 54
human development, 3, 25, 43, 44, 174
husband, 45
hybrid, xix, 169, 171
hypothesis, 67

I

ideal, 3, 25, 175
identity, 141, 148, 153, 158
image, 3, 25
imbalances, 91
imitation, 168
income, xv, xvi, xviii, 55, 56, 61, 66, 174, 178
individuals, 26, 55, 80
industrialization, 46
industries, 3, 191
inequality, 17, 32, 36, 42, 54, 58, 71, 72, 86, 99, 104, 105, 106, 110, 118, 121, 125, 126, 136, 138, 141, 144, 145, 156, 160
inevitability, 132, 133
information exchange, 11
information technology, 169
infrastructure, xix, 3, 4, 17, 25, 26
injury, 5
institutions, 3, 15, 23, 24, 45, 55, 58, 67, 85, 176, 178, 184
integration, 70
intelligence, 167, 169, 171, 191
interaction process, 70
interface, 167
internal mechanisms, 43
interrelations, 23
investment, 27, 65, 66
investments, 59
Islam, ix
issues, xix, xx, 12, 30, 55, 90, 186
Italy, 5

J

jumping, 2
justification, xix, 2, 70, 132, 175, 183, 185

K

Kenya, 44

L

labor market, 186
labor relations, 57
law enforcement, 24
laws, xix, 8, 17, 18, 19, 24, 55, 132
lead, 8, 28, 43, 103, 166, 167
leakage, 171
legal macrosystem, xvi, xvii, xviii, 7, 18, 23, 29, 38, 173, 175, 176, 178, 183
legal relations, xv, xviii, 18, 23, 67
legislation, xv, xix, xxi, 1, 8, 17, 18, 19, 23, 29, 49, 50, 71, 133, 182
lending, 168
level of education, 46, 73
life cycle, 42
linear model, 168
living conditions, 71, 76
loans, 61, 62, 63, 64
love, 45

M

machine learning, 170
macroeconomics, 43
macrosystem, xv, xvi, xvii, xviii, xx, 1, 3, 4, 5, 7, 9, 15, 18, 19, 23, 24, 26, 28, 31, 54, 56, 65, 66, 181, 195
magnitude, 141
majority, 16, 45
management, ix, xvii, xix, xx, xxi, xxiii, xxiv, 2, 11, 12, 13, 16, 20, 23, 27, 53, 54, 57, 58, 63, 70, 73, 85, 87, 90, 131, 167, 168, 169, 170, 171, 172, 174, 175, 176, 177, 182, 183, 184
mapping, 68, 76
market economy, 69
marriage, xxi, 42, 43, 44
married couples, 41, 42
mass, 55
mass media, 55
mathematical achievement, 87
mathematical methods, 186
mathematics, 203
matrimonial relations, 40
matrix, 134, 141, 142, 147, 148, 150, 152, 153, 154, 156, 157, 158, 163, 165
matter, 132
measurement, 10
measurements, xv, 11
medical, 57, 168
medicine, 168
memory, 200
messages, 12
metasystem, ix, xv, xvi, xvii, xix, xx, xxi, xxiii, xxiv, 1, 2, 7, 30, 177, 181, 185
metasystem equilibrium, ix, xvi, xx, xxi, 30, 181
methodology, xvii, xviii, xix, xx, xxi, xxii, xxiv, 6, 20, 69, 74, 86, 113, 117, 119, 131, 140, 170, 177, 178, 181, 182, 185, 204
migrants, 70
migration, 57
minors, 158
modelling, xvi, xvii, xx, xxiv, xxv, 19, 89, 113, 131, 166, 172, 177, 178, 185
models, xvi, xvii, xviii, xix, xx, xxi, xxii, xxiii, xxiv, 4, 6, 14, 19, 20, 21, 30, 42, 43, 51, 54, 56, 57, 85, 86, 91, 115, 129, 132, 166, 167, 168, 169, 170, 171, 172, 175, 176, 178, 181, 183, 185, 186
modern science, 171
modern society, 42, 167
modifications, xxi, xxv, 86, 163
moral behavior, 115
moral standards, 45
morality, ix, 22, 115, 175
morbidity, 12
mortality, 12, 72
Moscow, xi, xxv, 187, 189, 190, 191, 192, 193, 194, 195, 196, 197, 198, 199, 200, 201
multicriteria, xiii, xxi, xxii, xxiv, 14, 23, 32, 33, 34, 38, 53, 54, 69, 70, 71, 72, 73, 75, 80, 81, 82, 86, 87, 89, 90,

91, 92, 96, 97, 98, 99, 113, 122, 151, 168, 174, 177, 182, 184, 185, 195, 199, 200, 201
multidimensional, 168

N

Nash equilibrium, ix, xiii, xvi, xvii, xix, xxii, xxiii, xxiv, 19, 20, 21, 28, 29, 30, 32, 34, 35, 36, 39, 44, 45, 47, 51, 89, 100, 101, 107, 108, 109, 110, 111, 113, 117, 123, 124, 128, 131, 133, 135, 136, 139, 140, 162, 165, 166, 176, 177, 178, 181, 182, 185, 189, 190, 194, 200, 201, 203
National Academy of Sciences, 188, 200
natural science, 41
natural sciences, 41
natural selection, 44
negative consequences, 29, 57, 133, 174
negative effects, 3, 25, 174
negative emotions, 10
neoliberal economic doctrine, ix, xvi, xxiii, 2, 15, 19, 24, 26, 51, 109, 131, 132, 135, 174
neural network, 168, 171
neural networks, 168, 171
neurons, 170, 171
neuroscience, 169, 170
Nobel Prize, 30, 132
nonstationary macrosystems, 1, 2, 177, 184

O

obstacles, 10, 70
old age, xxiv, 74, 177, 185
oligopolies, 31
openness, 57, 167
operations, 32
operations research, 32
opinion polls, 76
opportunities, xvi, 17, 22, 90, 174
optimal solutions, 91, 113, 195
optimization, 22, 96, 161, 168, 173
optimization method, 22, 173
organize, 11
ownership, 16, 55

P

parallel, 55
parental care, 49, 58
parents, 42, 44, 48
Pareto, xiii, xiv, xxii, xxiv, 31, 32, 33, 34, 36, 38, 39, 48, 51, 97, 99, 105, 106, 109, 110, 111, 112, 113, 115, 117, 118, 119, 121, 122, 126, 127, 128, 129, 132, 133, 135, 136, 138, 139, 140, 143, 147, 148, 151, 154, 156, 162, 165, 166, 177, 182, 184, 185, 189, 194, 195, 200
Pareto optimal, xiv, 112, 113, 117, 127
Pareto-guaranteed Berge equilibrium, xxiv, 115, 128, 129, 177, 185
Pareto-maximal Berge equilibrium, xiii, xxii, 31, 32, 39, 48, 51, 117, 118, 119, 121, 122, 126, 128, 183
Pareto-maximal Nash equilibrium, xiii, 109, 110, 111
partial differential equations, 151, 152
participants, xvi, 4, 9, 23, 26, 30, 75, 89, 90, 91, 128, 133, 173
penalties, 66
pensioners, 31, 76
performance indicator, 2
performance measurement, xvii, xx, 131, 172
personal development, 176, 184
pessimism, 90
pharmaceuticals, 168
physics, 170, 203
polarization, 174
policy, 3, 16, 25, 26, 49, 50, 57, 60, 63, 71, 174, 175
politics, 22, 194
polygamy, 43, 44, 45
population, xv, xvi, xvii, xviii, xxi, xxii, xxiii, xxiv, 3, 4, 5, 7, 8, 9, 10, 11, 15, 16, 17, 18, 19, 21, 22, 24, 25, 29, 31, 41, 42, 43, 44, 45, 46, 49, 50, 51, 53,

54, 55, 56, 57, 58, 59, 61, 62, 64, 66, 67, 69, 70, 71, 72, 73, 75, 76, 79, 80, 85, 86, 87, 174, 175, 176, 177, 178, 182, 183, 184, 185, 186, 187, 189, 193, 195, 196
population group, 3, 25, 31, 76, 178
population size, 50
poverty, xvii, xxiii, 3, 8, 16, 25, 45, 51, 54, 58, 72, 74, 75, 79, 174, 178, 183
predictability, 71
pregnancy, 50, 81
prejudice, 29
preparation, iv, 70
preschool, 45, 46
preservation, 41
President, 27
principles, xviii, xxiii, 15, 26, 51, 55, 67, 91, 109, 172, 175, 183, 189
privatization, xix, 3, 25
probability, 6, 7, 14, 78, 119, 192
probability distribution, 6, 14
professional educators, 45
profit, xvi, 55, 63
programming, 148, 151, 204
project, 72, 75
protection, 174
public administration, xv, xxiii, 4, 15, 16, 21, 23, 25, 40, 43, 48, 51, 58, 63, 86, 176, 181
public expenditures, 15
public goods, 9
public life, 41, 186
public metasystem, ix, xv, xvi, xix, xxi, xxv, 174, 178, 183, 204
public service, 58
punishment, 64, 132, 133

Q

quality control, 168
quality of life, 3, 7, 9, 16, 17, 24, 31, 54, 55, 69, 70, 72, 76, 86, 174, 175, 176, 179, 184, 185, 186

R

radiation, 49
RAS, 203
rationality, xvii, xxii, xxiii, 19, 26, 30, 31, 35, 51, 55, 139, 176, 181
real numbers, 12
reality, 4, 28, 70, 74, 86, 169, 176, 184
recognition, 174
recovery, 70
recreation, 50
redistribution, 13, 17, 31
redundancy, 170
reform, 26, 31, 73
Reform, 195
reforms, 11, 55
regulations, 25, 132
rehabilitation, 57
relevance, xix, xxiii
rent, 31, 66
repetitions, 115
reproduction, 41, 43, 45
requirement, 31, 40, 73, 91, 132, 140, 165
requirements, 9, 22, 23, 28, 56, 71, 76, 173
researchers, xix, 22, 42, 43, 44, 45, 46, 131, 169, 170, 171, 173, 174
resolution, 30
resource allocation, 67
resources, 9, 26, 54, 64, 65, 67, 70, 74, 94, 168
response, 137, 175
restrictions, 3, 11, 25, 63, 169
retirement, 29, 81
retirement age, 29, 81
rewards, 66
rights, 2, 3, 17, 24, 25, 50, 174, 175, 176, 178, 184, 185
risk, xiii, xvii, xx, xxii, xxiv, 2, 4, 5, 12, 17, 19, 74, 75, 78, 79, 80, 86, 89, 91, 92, 93, 94, 95, 96, 98, 99, 100, 101, 102, 104, 105, 106, 107, 111, 112, 113, 115, 116, 127, 129, 177, 182, 185, 187, 188, 189, 191, 192, 194, 196, 198, 199, 200, 201, 204
risk management, xx, 17, 91, 113
risk society, 5

risks, xx, xxii, xxiv, 3, 17, 19, 25, 53, 54, 56, 69, 70, 74, 75, 79, 80, 86, 87, 89, 92, 93, 96, 98, 99, 100, 103, 104, 111, 112, 113, 115, 126, 127, 129, 177, 181, 182, 184, 185
root, 5, 141, 148, 157, 158
roots, 141, 142, 155, 165
rules, 4, 6, 9, 15, 23, 27, 29, 54, 66, 90, 115, 132, 137, 168, 174
Russia, xi, xvi, xxi, xxiii, xxv, 2, 3, 18, 21, 25, 26, 41, 42, 50, 51, 174, 176, 181, 185, 189, 190, 192, 193, 194, 195, 197

S

safety, 57
sanctions, xxii, xxiv, 7, 128, 131, 132, 133, 135, 137, 139, 140, 146, 155, 164, 165, 166, 178, 194
savings, 56
scatter, 13
scholarship, 49
school, 5, 45
science, xv, xviii, 73, 171, 203
scientific knowledge, 11
scope, 109
security, 3, 4, 8, 15, 17, 18, 19, 25, 55, 57, 70, 175
semiotics, 167
services, xviii, xix, 13, 16, 17, 18, 19, 27, 49, 58, 59, 67, 70, 72, 176, 184
set theory, 198
SFI, 170, 171
shape, 3, 25
shortage, 74, 75
signs, 42, 70
simulation, 90
simulations, 168
slaves, 43
social activities, 60, 62
social benefits, 17, 23
social conflicts, 8
social group, 8, 42
social guarantees, xx, xxii, 4, 17, 19, 26, 49, 53, 69, 70, 71, 72, 73, 75, 80, 81, 86, 87, 177, 182, 184, 199
social indicator, 16
social infrastructure, 17
social insecurity, 3, 25
social institutions, 40, 45, 70
social interaction, 8
social macrosystem, iii, xv, xvi, xix, xx, xxi, xxiii, xxv, 1, 2, 3, 4, 7, 9, 15, 16, 17, 18, 19, 20, 21, 22, 23, 24, 25, 27, 28, 29, 30, 31, 39, 51, 89, 90, 173, 174, 175, 176, 178, 181, 182, 183, 200, 204
social obligations, 60, 61, 62, 63
social policy, 48, 55, 60
social problems, 73
social programs, 3, 25, 50
social reality, 10, 70, 168
social relations, xvi, xix, 1, 15, 18, 22, 26, 43, 54, 73
social sciences, 87
social security, xviii, xxi, xxiv, 3, 4, 8, 15, 17, 18, 19, 25, 26, 53, 55, 56, 57, 58, 59, 61, 66, 69, 71, 73, 75, 85, 86, 87, 182
Social Security, 53, 57, 58
social security and support system, xxi, xxiv, 17, 53, 55, 56, 57, 58, 69, 85, 87, 182
social services, xvi, 8, 16, 17, 18, 19, 45, 55, 57, 58, 59, 60, 62, 65, 67, 176, 184
social sphere, ix, xv, xvi, xvii, xviii, xix, xx, xxi, xxiii, xxiv, 3, 8, 15, 16, 17, 18, 19, 20, 23, 24, 25, 29, 31, 40, 43, 49, 50, 53, 55, 57, 58, 59, 60, 61, 62, 63, 66, 69, 70, 71, 72, 73, 74, 75, 76, 77, 80, 85, 86, 87, 170, 172, 174, 175, 176, 177, 178, 181, 182, 183, 184, 185, 186
social state, ix, xvii, xviii, xix, xxi, xxii, xxiii, xxiv, xxv, 2, 3, 4, 8, 17, 18, 19, 20, 22, 25, 29, 31, 49, 53, 69, 71, 72, 76, 79, 80, 86, 87, 174, 175, 176,

177, 178, 181, 183, 184, 185, 187, 191, 199
social support, 17, 19, 50, 54, 55, 58, 75
social workers, 59, 62, 75
society, 1, 2, 3, 5, 6, 7, 8, 9, 13, 18, 19, 22, 23, 24, 25, 28, 31, 43, 44, 45, 51, 54, 70, 75, 80, 172, 174
sociology, ix, xvii, xix, xxii, 90, 131, 176, 184
software, 169
solution, xvii, xxii, xxiv, 12, 20, 27, 36, 37, 40, 44, 53, 56, 67, 69, 71, 74, 75, 76, 77, 79, 80, 81, 82, 83, 84, 85, 86, 87, 98, 99, 100, 109, 112, 127, 131, 132, 134, 142, 144, 147, 150, 151, 152, 153, 154, 160, 162, 168, 177, 182, 184
sovereignty, 43
Spain, 5
Spring, 188
St. Petersburg, 187, 188, 191, 196, 200, 203
stability, xxii, xxiv, 46, 56, 115, 129, 131, 132, 177, 182, 185
stabilization, 11, 50
staffing, 75
standard of living, 56, 70, 71
state, ix, xv, xvi, xvii, xviii, xix, xxi, xxii, xxiii, xxiv, xxv, 2, 3, 4, 5, 8, 9, 15, 18, 19, 20, 21, 22, 23, 24, 25, 27, 28, 29, 31, 40, 43, 45, 49, 50, 51, 53, 54, 55, 57, 58, 59, 60, 61, 63, 68, 69, 70, 71, 72, 73, 76, 79, 80, 85, 86, 87, 91, 134, 172, 174, 175, 176, 177, 178, 181, 182, 183, 184, 185
statistics, 41, 42, 46, 168
strategic decisions, ix, 9, 15, 16, 17, 19, 22, 23, 55, 63, 71, 89, 173, 174, 175, 182
strategic planning, 91
stratification, 42
structure, xv, xviii, 1, 2, 3, 4, 16, 18, 23, 24, 25, 27, 38, 39, 41, 44, 46, 53, 54, 56, 59, 69
styles, 193
Styles, 193
subsistence, 49
substitutes, 10
substitution, 154
symmetry, 156
synthesis, xix
system balancedness, 132

T

target, 27, 49, 50, 58, 70, 71, 72, 73, 76
targeted social security, 15
tax rates, xv, 23
tax system, 60
taxes, 31
Tbilisi, 200
techniques, 32
technological progress, 5, 11
technologies, 3, 54, 85, 91, 167, 169, 171, 172, 183
technology, 172
tension, 3, 8, 25, 54, 73, 75, 86
textbook, 195
the Golden Rule of ethics, ix, xvii, 19, 20, 45, 47, 48, 109, 115, 128, 174, 175, 176, 178, 179, 181, 183, 185, 204
the principle of minimax regret, 92, 101
theoretical approach, xvi, xvii, xx, xxi, xxii, xxiii, 69, 86, 182
threats, 109, 128, 132, 133, 139, 203
total product, 61
training, 13
transformation, xix, xxi, 2, 3, 7, 15, 16, 24, 39, 40, 42, 43, 45, 55, 61, 174
transformation processes, xix, 2, 7, 16, 24, 39, 61, 174
transformations, 15, 16, 18, 40, 53, 146
translation, xi, xxv
transmission, 11, 13
transport, 17, 168
treatment, 168

U

Ukraine, 188

uncertainty, ix, xvi, xvii, xx, xxi, xxii, xxiii, xxiv, 2, 4, 5, 6, 7, 8, 9, 10, 11, 12, 13, 14, 18, 19, 20, 22, 23, 30, 32, 33, 34, 35, 36, 37, 38, 40, 51, 53, 54, 55, 56, 66, 69, 70, 71, 73, 74, 75, 77, 78, 79, 80, 81, 82, 83, 85, 87, 89, 90, 91, 92, 93, 94, 96, 97, 98, 100, 101, 102, 103, 104, 107, 111, 113, 116, 166, 167, 168, 169, 170, 171, 173, 174, 175, 176, 177, 178, 181, 182, 183, 184, 185, 204
uniform, 159
unions, 44
universal social security, xxi, 4, 15, 26, 55, 182
urbanization, 46
USA, 192, 194

V

validation, 169
value added tax, 60
variables, 6, 56, 59, 70
VAT, 60, 65
vector, xiii, 10, 14, 32, 33, 37, 38, 40, 68, 72, 73, 74, 75, 76, 77, 78, 79, 80, 84, 92, 93, 96, 99, 102, 105, 112, 121, 128, 134, 135, 136, 137, 140, 141, 143, 144, 146, 148, 149, 152, 160
victims, 16
visualization, 169, 170, 171
vocational education, 49

W

wages, 8, 57, 59, 62, 64, 65, 178
water, 13, 171
wealth, 44, 189
welfare, xviii, 22, 31, 64, 174, 175, 176
welfare state, 174, 175, 176
well-being, 10, 45, 70, 175, 176, 177, 179, 184, 185
Western countries, xxi, xxv
workers, 3, 16

Y

yield, 6, 41, 57, 133, 154, 175, 184